Supervision and Training:
Models, Dilemmas,
and Challenges

FREDERICK LEONG, PH.D.
THE OHIO STATE UNIVERSITY
DEPARTMENT OF PSYCHOLOGY
142 TOWNSHEND HALL
1885 NEIL AVENUE MALL
COLUMBUS OHIO 43210-1222

Supervision and Training: Models, Dilemmas, and Challenges

Florence W. Kaslow

Editor

The Haworth Press
New York • London

Supervision and Training: Models, Dilemmas, and Challenges has also been published as *The Clinical Supervisor*, Volume 4, Numbers 1/2, Spring/Summer 1986.

The Haworth Press, Inc. 10 Alice Street, Binghamton, NY 13904-1580
EUROSPAN/Haworth, 3 Henrietta Street, London WC2E 8LU England

Library of Congress Cataloging-in-Publication Data
Main entry under title:

Supervision and training.

Includes bibliographies.
1. Psychotherapy—Study and teaching—Supervision. 2. Psychotherapists—Supervision of. I. Kaslow, Florence Whiteman. [DNLM: 1. Clinical Competence. 2. Organization and Administration. 3. Psychotherapy. 4. Psychotherapy—education. WM 420 S959]
RC336.S87   1986   616.89'14'07   85-27037
ISBN 0-86656-528-0
ISBN 0-86656-529-9 (pbk.)

Supervision and Training: Models, Dilemmas, and Challenges

The Clinical Supervisor
Volume 4, Numbers 1/2

CONTENTS

EDITOR'S COMMENTS

It is with pleasure that we present this special, double issue of *The Clinical Supervisor* on supervision and training. Florence Kaslow has done an excellent job of organizing this volume. The contributors are highly respected theoreticians and practitioners who present a comprehensive view of the subject. It is my belief this special issue makes a lasting and significant contribution to the literature on supervision and training.

Historically, the specifics of supervision have been neglected in the literature. Good, effective training is a complex undertaking, and this special issue addresses the subject of mastering the complexity. This set of articles will greatly assist the supervisor in approaching the demands of practice.

Carlton E. Munson, DSW

Foreword

As professionals in the caring arts fields well know, there has been an increasing emphasis on accountability in recent years. The public and its social, legislative, and economic bodies are demanding that practitioners deliver services which are effective and of high quality. To many observers of the scene, it is evident that before long only those providers with demonstrated competence will be considered as acceptable by third-party payers and others.

Traditionally, the pathway to competence has been through training and supervision. Innate sensitivity to others, self-understanding, and practical experience are indeed also important, but it is training and supervision above all which have been the crucial shaping factors. That is why this book is so timely, useful, and direction setting: it points to a number of ways in which innovative and tested models of theory and practice can enhance the functional operations—the day to day work—of the psychotherapist, counselor, and related professionals in the caring arts fields.

The editor of this stimulating and challenging work, Florence W. Kaslow, is known internationally as a leader in the development and teaching of new methods of training, consultation, and supervision. Her prior publications in these areas have brought her a well deserved reputation which has been enhanced by the fact that for many years she has been a distinguished educator and noted program director in many of the areas covered by the contents of this volume. One would expect then that this latest book would reflect more than the state of the art and that it would present new concepts and new approaches. And the reader will not be disappointed, for Dr. Kaslow has selected co-contributors and topics, the combination of which can only serve to add to our understanding of and more effective utilization of the process whereby good professionals become better professionals.

Both direct and indirect training methodologies are discussed with clarity and imagination. A variety of dynamic, behavioral, and eclectic approaches to the supervision of individual, group, and family therapies are described. Close attention is paid to the supervisor-supervisee interaction, while the institutional setting in which the professional works is also noted as crucial.

Solo practice, group practice, agency practice, private practice, and co-practice are all considered and examined in the chapters which follow. There is truly something here for everyone who is interested in the process and methods of supervision and training, and the multiplicity of models and alternatives is nothing short of exciting for anyone who is interested in the topics covered by this book.

While each and every chapter can be read and digested profitably, it is the final summing up that I found most useful. In fact, it is recommended that this chapter be read first *and* last. It not only sets the stage but it points the way to the future by highlighting, contrasting, comparing, and synthesizing the many different approaches which the various contributors present. I am confident that you the reader will find this book not only informative and useful but as challenging and exciting as I did. *Bon appetit!*

Melvin A. Gravitz, Ph.D.
Past President,
American Board of Professional Psychology
Clinical Professor of Psychiatry & Behavioral Sciences,
George Washington University School of Medicine
Adjunct Professor of Medical Psychology,
Uniformed Services University of the Health Sciences
Washington, D.C.

Dr. Fred Leong

Psychology

ECK LIST

SOC SEC NUM

000008651

292780533
000012643
295706681
300608435
288866146
284749576
272706490
315805368
181543284
291767797
197389514
295646267
95646267
373584813
282746504
284843620
290549741

Preface

In the past three decades we have witnessed a radical shift in the form, content and structure of supervision. Clinicians trained in the 1940s and 1950s brought process or summary records to their supervisor. These contained selective accounts of what had transpired— generally focused on what the patient did and said and perhaps inclusive of what the therapist asked. Supervisory sessions occurred "after the fact"—usually by several days and were therefore indirect in the sense of being removed from the scene of the action. Since "confidentiality" was considered an overriding principle of all therapy, any other approach would have been heresy.

By the late 1950s and more fully in the 1960s and since, the advent of modern technology has had a tremendous impact on the field. One way mirrors, audiotape and videotape equipment, and television monitors have made their debut in most training sites throughout the country. The confluence of their availability and a changing ethos brought about by the greater openness essential in family and group therapies and the human potential movement has truly revolutionized part of the practice of supervision. Certainly indirect, one on one, process supervision based on process or summary records is still viable and often is the modality of choice. However, other indirect methods have joined it as additions or alternatives. These include group supervision and analysis of the therapy through listening to audiotapes or watching videotapes and using the data derived from such hearing and seeing observations as the material to be discussed. Also in the armamentarium of supervisory approaches are the direct intervention paths—cotherapy, rotations of team members, observation behind the one way screen and calling in messages or entering and participating in the therapy, the therapists exiting from the treatment room to meet with team members and then returning to convey their input—sometimes in the form of a split message.

In searching for material to teach a graduate course on supervision and consultation in the early 1970s, I found a dearth of contemporary literature. This led to my first book on this topic *Issues in*

xv

Human Services: A Sourcebook for Supervision and Staff Development in 1972. It covered such issues as educational models and their influence on supervision, training indigenous paraprofessional staff, race, class and ethnic factors as they influence supervision, and group supervision. Supervision as it occurred in such diverse practice settings as a geriatric center, a large federal agency psychiatric setting and a public welfare agency was considered.

In the next five years the methodology of supervision broadened and as the direct approaches moved more into the foreground and evoked controversy, they demanded greater attention. Out of a continuing interest in the study and practice of supervision came a second book on this broad topic, *Supervision, Consultation and Staff Training in the Helping Professions* (1977). Part I deals with the history and philosophy of supervision and consultation, Part II focuses on supervisory and training techniques and processes—highlighting psychoanalytically oriented supervision of individual therapy, group supervision, training of marital and family therapists and of group therapists. Part III considers supervision and consultation in such special settings as the criminal justice system and mental health centers.

In 1980 Hess edited a fine volume entitled *Psychotherapy Supervision* which serves as an excellent companion to my two earlier books. Because of his acknowledged expertise I have asked him to be a contributing author to this current endeavor.

The field continues to evolve, exploding with new and challenging experiments and models predicated on different ideas about how people learn most effectively. Thus it seemed time for another volume on this subject—again conceiving the topic broadly. Part I—the initial chapter focuses on the ecological context in which supervision/consultation and training occur—considering attitudes formed in graduate school and beyond and then moving into the myriad environs in which these activities occur. The next chapter provocatively illuminates the inner world of what therapists worry about. In perusing it, the reader can easily identify with many of the apprehensions delineated. Part II offers a smorgasbord of models and paradigms—several of which encompass a stage theory of what is appropriate contingent upon the trainees' professional development level. Chapters contained herein describe individual supervision, rotational supervision, peer supervision working in teams, supervision of co-therapists and supervision in private practice. As with any attractive smorgasbord, we trust every reader will find something that appeals to his/her needs, interests, and personality.

Since supervision is a training approach, the line between these is somewhat arbitrary and there is some overlapping. Part III on training has several chapters that encompass both and one that is clearly based on a "training" format. The closing chapter seeks to identify themes and patterns—perhaps the most important of which is the dynamic, everchanging and expanding panorama.

Appreciation is expressed to all of the contributing authors, to Bill Cohen at Haworth Press for the continual encouragement and willingness to publish my books, to Carlton Munson for utilizing this volume as a special issue of *The Clinical Supervisor*, to my secretary, Priscilla Smyth—without whose support and assistance this book would not have reached fruition, and to all of the clinicians I have supervised who taught me so much about the process.

Florence W. Kaslow, Ph.D., Editor
West Palm Beach, Florida

Supervision and Training: Models, Dilemmas, and Challenges

PART I:
THE ECOLOGICAL CONTEXT

1

Supervision, Consultation and Staff Training— Creative Teaching/Learning Processes in the Mental Health Profession

Florence W. Kaslow

ABSTRACT. This chapter explores the structure and nature of the three processes of supervision, consultation and staff training. It considers the initial orientation to each and how the supervisor/supervisee, consultant/consultee, trainer/trainee form special pairings and interact. Learning each process as a recipient also enables one to incorporate some aspects which they may later offer as a provider. And the cycle begins anew.

THE THREE MAJOR TEACHING PROCESSES

Supervision

When students enter graduate or professional school and begin their first practicum, field placement, internship or residency, they

Florence Kaslow, Ph.D., is Director of the Florida Couples and Family Institute, West Palm Beach, Florida and Adjunct Professor of Medical Psychology in Psychiatry, Duke University, Durham, North Carolina.

1

are immediately assigned a supervisor. This is standard operating procedure in all of the mental health disciplines—throughout the formal graduate school educational experience. Similarly it occurs if and when one enters a post graduate training institute program and again in the clinical practice of therapy within an agency setting. What is the raison d'etre?

In assigning cases to students, the educational institution and the host clinical setting share responsibility for the quality of care. The trainee therapist is there primarily as part of his/her educational process and is not considered fully qualified; therefore someone else carries responsibility for insuring that treatment is ethical and efficacious—this someone is the supervisor. The same accountability concerns apply with the beginning staff member; the question to be answered is for how long is intensive supervision essential and advisable and what are the indicators for a decreased amount or change in focus over time?

Nature of the Process

In any role that inherently entails responsibility, there must be concomitant authority. Thus, the supervisor is usually endowed with the authority to truly oversee the work—and to carry back-up and fill-in responsibility if the trainee is absent or veers off what the supervisor deems to be a sound treatment plan utilizing appropriate methodology. To carry out this function, the supervisor should get to know the supervisee's work well—his/her strengths and weaknesses, areas of and gaps in knowledge, interpersonal relationship skills, personality style, areas of flexibility and rigidity, level of maturity, range of skills, etc. Yet, it is critical to remember that the reason for knowing this is to enhance the trainee's learning experience and the effectiveness of the treatment. As Abroms (1977) indicated so succinctly, supervision is a therapy of the therapy and not of the therapist. If the trainee is having problems which interfere with his/her learning and ability to help patients, such blockages or counter-transference phenomena are surely grist for the supervisory mill. To evade dealing with them is to do a disservice to trainees and patient(s) alike. But, to become the trainee's therapist and attempt to delve beyond difficulties specifically germane to the trainee's caseload is to exceed one's function and to be intrusive into the trainee's personal life. If the person's conflicts are such that they can not be handled and resolved appropriately through a learning and insight oriented supervision as a growth process experience, then the trainee should be referred for therapy—preferably to someone not central to the training program as confidentiality is of critical import in such instances (Kaslow, 1984).

Supervision and therapy are parallel processes (Abroms, 1977). The supervisor's behavior constitutes a much more compelling model of how a session should be conducted than does his/her verbalization about the structure of a therapy hour. Like the therapy setting, the supervisory milieu should be designed as a safe sanctuary—private, uninterrupted by phone calls or visitors, and with an atmosphere conducive to exploration of one's concerns—in this instance about their therapeutic work—and to creativity as part of one's professional growth.

Just as therapy is a shared endeavor in which everyone involved in the session determines content and the flow of the process, so too in supervision. However, quite early in therapy, preferably the first session, the therapist must set out the ground rules and the structure; if these are challenged or contested, the therapist must win the battle for structure (Napier & Whitaker, 1978) or it is unlikely that the therapy will evolve effectively.

In supervision, it is posited here that the supervisor should outline the basic structure he/she adheres to yet try to evolve the relationship as a partnership or joint endeavor geared to improving the quality of the supervisee's practice. The more neophyte the trainee, and the more obligatory the supervisory sessions are, the greater the supervisor's role and responsibility for determining the framework, frequency and emphasis of the supervision. The more advanced the clinician, and the more voluntarily supervision is sought—as in private practice when one personally seeks out and pays for supervision—(see Chapter 9) the more the contractual aspects may be negotiated. Short term and long term learning objectives need to be articulated, discussed and agreed upon. I concur with Cleghorn and Levin (1973) that learning objectives can be subdivided into several categories. They delineate perceptual skills, conceptual skills and executive abilities. I would add to these categories another—intervention skills. For junior trainees progressive mastery in *each area* should be evaluated at periodic, pre-established intervals—coinciding with graduate school or institutional calendars when need be—or jointly determined by supervisor and supervisee if no external schedule exists. For senior clinicians who have purchased supervisory time based on a desire for assistance in certain specific areas only, the evaluation should assess only these aspects of practice. Nonetheless, it might be within the supervisor's purview to tactfully highlight other areas of weakness, as he or she perceives them.

Certainly issues around authority, power and control will surface. The trainee's feelings about senior people who represent ''authority'' figures and who do, in reality, have some ''control'' over their professional future may well be a factor to be dealt with in supervision. Similarly, the supervisor's degree of comfort with his/her necessary authority and whether it is perceived and utilized rationally or irrationally, minimally or maximally, will be elements in the tone that evolves in the relationship. Issues of punctuality of sessions, in submission of records and tapes, of making and returning calls, of doing assigned readings, and in working collaboratively with other staff and collateral professionals may need to be addressed. Confronting these issues should be done diplomatically, sensitively and honestly—but only when they exist.

Some supervisees respect and relate to authority well, are self directing and can still respond to what another has to teach and do not have a problem with promptness. The content and focus of supervisory sessions should be tailored to the needs, personality, style and clientele of the trainee therapist and to realization of the learning objectives or goals of the particular supervision. The process does not exist in a vacuum nor can each supervision of different trainees by the same supervisor be a carbon copy of all his/her other supervisions.

One or Multiple Supervisors?

One question that frequently arises amongst the faculty in graduate and professional school programs as well as in post graduate training institutes is: should the trainee be assigned to only one supervisor to whom they will be accountable on all cases or can the trainee have multiple supervisors to be consulted on different cases and even participate in the selection of the supervisors? Traditionally, schools of social work have followed the first procedure (Kutzik, 1977) using the rationale that the student's growth and learning would be maximized if it were coordinated through one person; that assignment to two or more supervisors would dilute the intensity of the relationship and the pressure to work through perplexing clinical dilemmas, interpersonal conflicts, and personal blocks or counter-transference problems. By working with the student on many cases over time, the supervisor can become familiar with the repetitive patterns and have more data to work with regarding his or her knowledge base and characteristic mode of functioning. This preference also centers around the fact that this model prevents: splitting of supervisory staff, showing favoritism, and difficulties in making certain all cases have supervisory backup. When social work students are assigned to more than one supervisor—the division usually is that one handles clinical matters and the other deals with administrative concerns (Hanlan, 1972).

Arguments against the trainee having only one supervisor for an academic or clinical year, and against their having no voice in the selection of that person include: (1) that if there is a personality clash—the trainee is locked in to the relationship with little recourse and no one to take his/her part—if he/she goes over the supervisor's head to the next higher ranking person in the administrative hierarchy he/she is accused of being rebellious, aggressive, "difficult", and unable to "fit"; (2) that few supervisors are "expert" in all kinds of cases and that training is enriched by the opportunity to work with several people—each in their area of greatest competency; (3) that this narrows the students chance to be exposed to different styles and theoretical perspectives during their formative, flexible years in training.

Many psychology and psychiatry training programs and post graduate institutes, including those in group and family therapy, provide greater latitude. An intern, extern or resident may be assigned (or can request) a primary supervisor who carries major responsibility for his/her clinical practice. In addition, the trainee is free to, and encouraged to, seek supervision from others in cases which fall outside of the scope of the main supervisor's expertise. In one program in which I taught, some of the psychology and psychiatry trainees had as many as five supervisors. One might be for psychological testing, another for a child play therapy case, a third for a family therapy case, a fourth for behavioral therapy in a case of phobic anxiety and a fifth for group therapy. Interestingly, during the seven years I taught at this medical school and graduate school in the northeast I saw little splitting, dilution of relationships, unnecessary duplication, or jealousy. At faculty meetings, those supervising a particular student pooled their observations and concerns and the director of the program channeled these back to the student when the need to do so arose. In this program the vast majority of trainees felt privileged to be able to seek supervision from many talented clinicians, across professional disciplines and theoretical persuasions, and rarely were there battles for control or problems of supervisee/supervisor match. Every effort was made to keep these deliberations as confidential as possible.

In all likelihood the flexibility or rigidity of the supervisory selection or assignment and the supervisory processes that the student is exposed to early in his/her training will color his/her idea of what constitutes good and bad supervision. Hopefully, trainees will become familiar with different viable patterns and processes, such as those described in the chapters contained in this volume. Subsequently, when they graduate and are supervising, out of this broad assortment of possibilities they should be stimulated to choose those that are most applicable to their trainees' and agencies' needs and to add to these creatively—continuing to refine, experiment and expand that which exists.

The Ideal Supervisor—Becoming and Being

The portrait of an ideal supervisor that has evolved from my trainees struggling to define such an entity and from my readings and observations is a multifaceted and complex one. He/she should be ethical, well informed, knowledgeable in his/her theoretical orientation, clinically skilled, articulate, empathic, a good listener, gentle, confrontative, accepting, challenging, stimulating, provocative, reassuring, encouraging, possess a good sense of humor, a good sense of timing, be innovative, solid, exciting, laid back—but not all at the same time—the supervisory mode and mood should be appropriate to the trainee's stage of professional development and level of personal maturity (see Friedman & N. Kaslow, Chapter 3).

Unfortunately, too often it is assumed that once a person finishes his/her formal training and receives the requisite graduate or medical degree for practice, he/she is ready to supervise graduate students and residents. It is posited here that no matter how talented and intuitive one might be, they need to acquire a knowledge base and sound clinical training to become a skilled and professional therapist. Similarly, appropriate and stimulating training is essential before one undertakes to serve in a supervisory capacity. Having had experiences with several supervisors during one's training does not, ipso facto, make them qualified. It is important also to acquire: some knowledge of the history of and literature on supervision in the various mental health professions, some conceptual framework for viewing the supervisory process and relationship, some in-depth exposure to the gamut of extant supervisory techniques, and a practicum experience in supervising under supervision. One can either take a course in supervision during their graduate/professional training (the final year is recommended), or at the post graduate level in a training institute. Sometimes graduate schools wisely offer such courses for would be and beginning supervisors. A group milieu in which questions can be raised and ideas and experiences shared is a fine beginning point. "Perks for supervisors in the form of adjunct faculty rank, library privileges, and/or free parking on busy campuses express the department's appreciation for their contribution and underscore the importance of their task. Attendance at a "mandatory" course might be increased through such "perks".

In-agency supervision of supervision is another method for providing a supervised experience. Again, audio and videotapes might be used, as might viewing over a one way screen. It is important to remember that the primary supervisor, and his/her patient(s) comprise a new and special system; this is perhaps clearest in family therapy. Mechanisms for joining with and exiting from as well as process interaction need to be addressed.

Workshops at professional conferences constitute another resource and if they are led by "expert supervisors" and offer an opportunity for neophyte supervisors to receive critique on their work by, for example, viewing a videotape of a supervisory session, this approach would also have much to commend it.

The same holds true for consultation and staff training functions. They are not simply intuited or learned by osmosis. One needs to learn about them from didactic presentations, being a recipient of the approach and gaining some experience in the method of educating under seasoned guidance.

Consultation

Rarely during university or medical school based training is one exposed to the range of possible ways in which consultation is used. Probably the one most frequently utilized is case consultation when a senior clinician listens to a brief presentation about a patient(s), (usually a particularly difficult one), proceeds to conduct an interview with that person(s) whenever possible, and then discusses his/her evaluation, interpretations, and recommendations with the assembled trainees, staff and/or faculty. His/her manner of interviewing also serves as a model of one way that assessment and treatment can be done. Let us take an in-depth view at one kind of case consultation method as an illustration. In the family therapy field visiting consultants from out of town are often asked to see a family that perplexes or stymies the therapist. In a sense, the family and therapist system has gotten stuck. The interview may be conducted with trainees and staff/faculty present as an audience or they may view the interview over a one way mirror or videotape monitor. The ongoing primary therapist should summarize salient data on the family being seen and indicate the reasons for selecting *this* family for presentation at this point in time—what are the focal, critical questions?

Usually the primary therapist introduces the family to the visiting consultant and reiterates the purpose of the visit. Although families may evince some apprehension, by and large almost all of the families I've seen in this kind of consultation throughout the United States and in numerous other countries, and those that I've observed others like Maurizio Andolfi, David Rubinstein, Carlos Sluzki and Carl Whitaker see, feel privileged to be selected and have this special opportunity made available to them. They are flattered that so many people are interested in hearing *their* story and that so much therapeutic talent will be pooled to come up with recommendations, just for them. Most patients have had experience with an internist or family medicine physician who has sought consultation with a specialist like a cardiologist or radiologist and so do not think less of their therapist for not having all the answers and therefore seeking consultative input. Some patients become quite exhibitionistic, especially when they are thanked for their willingness to come and present their situation to the assembled group as part of a teaching seminar. To illustrate:

> Recently, at a Southern Medical School Department of Psychiatry Grand Rounds, I saw a lower middle class minority couple, both of whom were recovering alcoholics. Since they were accustomed to telling their story at Alcoholics Anonymous (AA) meetings, being before an interested group did not seem to cause them much anxiety. They actually were delighted to be there, thoroughly smitten with the idea of having a teaching videotape made of the session, and became quite loquacious. They joined me in "teaching" about alcoholism, detoxification, relationships to their respective children, the role

of AA in maintaining sobriety, and mid life marriage of a couple both in recovery. The session bolstered their self esteem and seemed to give them a fresh perspective on those aspects of their interaction that distressed them, i.e., her sense of deprivation because of his lack of constant attentiveness and therefore her accompanying intrusiveness and his need for space and privacy sometimes so that he could evince his committedness to the relationship the remainder of the time. They sat through the inquiry and feedback session I conducted with the assembled interns, staff and faculty and seemed genuinely attentive to and appreciative of this additional opportunity to receive some reflections about themselves.

Whenever I conduct such open sessions, I decide at the wrap up of the specific therapeutic portion if this is a couple/family who has the intelligence and ego strength to profit from remaining for the feedback period. If I think they will, I invite them to stay, if their schedule permits, but make it clear this is optional. About 90% choose to remain and participate.

Before bringing this part to a close, it is important to reiterate something we discussed in an earlier article, (Nielsen & Kaslow, 1980)—that the visiting consultant should not compete with nor overshadow the primary therapist, nor be destructive to the therapy. He/she should reinforce at least part of what that person has done while still adding in new interpretations and perhaps taking the liberty afforded a consultant of being more confrontative. At the end the consultant should be turned back to the primary therapist and the consultant should exit making it clear he/she is leaving town and can not take over the therapy.

Consultants can be and are also utilized in a variety of other ways, including but not limited to: relationship and team development difficulty, engaging in problem solving approaches to unravel and overcome them, offering guidance on unmet community needs and how the agency, institution or university can develop programs and services to fill the gap, designing and coaching research projects, helping redesign curriculum, public relations and publicity approaches, strengthening community relations. One might also be engaged as a consultant (or part of a consulting team) to conduct an evaluative study of a system's functioning and provide feedback to the agency executive and top level administrators, to a department chairperson, or to a corporate executive and his/her top level personnel. It is not uncommon today for a mental health consultant, in tandem with someone from the insurance industry, to be invited to develop an employee assistance program. The myriad ways in which mental health professionals are currently utilized as consultants is explored in depth in a new volume by Wynne, Weber & McDaniel (in press, 1985)—in which they and their co-authors consider many of the more typical settings and styles as well as more novel endeavors in industry and with the military (Kaslow, 1985).

Internal or External Consultant?

Next, some basic aspects of the consultation function will be explored. Some organizations employ an in-house person to serve as a consultant. Today such a person may be called a human relations specialist, a psychological consultant, or by a variety of other titles. Such an individual is on salary and is a staff or team member of the employer organization. As such, he or she has the best opportunity to become conversant with the interpersonal relationship patterns, the formal and informal network of communications, the specific pressures and conflicts, management style, employee frustrations, etc. In being seen in the agency, university or plant on a regular basis, he becomes familiar to the other personnel and can begin to develop some rapport with them. They may even drop in to his/her office to talk about organizational or personal problems. Conversely, the internal consultant may be the recipient of some suspicion if he/she is perceived as too closely allied with management and other personnel become concerned about violation of confidentiality. After all, he/she is an employee beholden to the boss—or so the thinking goes.

The external consultant is usually hired for a specific task on a fee for service basis. He or she does not become an employee of the corporation or institution. Thus, gaining access to the requisite data necessary for the consultation to proceed may be more difficult than for the internal consultant, but the trust is likely to be greater since an "outsider" is likely to be perceived as more neutral and objective and not as a tool or henchman of the bureaucracy.

Aspects of the Consultation Process

Consultation is a "take it or leave it process" and therein lies its greatest efficacy. Since the consultant has no administrative authority vested in him or her, as the supervisor does, the person in this role—if he or she is not an authoritarian personality, is not likely to engender resistance and hostility. If participation with a consultant is voluntary, if the consultant is well informed and personable, and if involvement is set up as a "privilege" and not as a chore, it is likely to be productive for all.

The consultative process, with variations when it is a case consult like that chronicled earlier, in essence, follows a scientific method for problem solving. First the consultant must determine what is the question or problem that is confronting the organization, i.e., what is the task he/she is being asked to undertake (Bennis, 1969)? Next comes the data gathering phase—soliciting input from a variety of people—each perhaps with a different perspective. During this phase, records and reports may be read, videotapes reviewed, meetings attended to collect whatever information pertinent to the task is deemed necessary. Familiarization with the organizational context and its goals is usually essential. Frequently so too is a thorough reading of the operations or personnel manual.

Next comes formulating some hypothesis and testing out if they fit with the key people involved in the process. Various approaches for arriving at potential solutions or resolutions of problems and conflicts might include brainstorming (Caplan, 1970), mediating, teaching new skills, revising budgets or job descriptions, a weekend retreat with an objective of improving interpersonal relationships or shifting gears toward more participatory management. A wide range of possible routes for improving the situation should be considered, then prioritized and the top ranking one implemented, if it is feasible, as quickly as possible. While the interventions or mechanisms for change are underway, reactions and progress should be noted. If the strategies being utilized do not seem to be bringing about the desired outcomes, a shift may need to be made. Built into all consultative projects should be a written mechanism for evaluation and feedback that can be activated at certain predetermined times during the consultation process and at its conclusion. (This orientation has many similarities to Epstein, et al.'s problem solving approach in family therapy, 1981.)

In light of the above, it becomes evident that a clear consultation contract must be negotiated. Once a person is approached to become the consultant, believes he/she is competent for the specific task, and there is tentative agreement to move ahead—issues such as fees for service and when these are to be paid must be determined. Is the consultant to be compensated for preparation time, travel time, secretarial and support staff time, or only on-site consulting time? What

of telephone time and costs? How many hours of input are esti-
mated? How much time is being allocated for the project? What kind
of final report is expected from the consultant and who will have access to it? The more specifically the answers to these questions are
handled in a written contract, the more clarity all concerned parties
have about the roles, functions and responsibilities of the consultant
and the employing organization—which becomes the consultee(s).
For example:

> For the past several years I have been invited by a Drug and
> Alcohol In-Patient unit to be a consultant in the expansion of
> their family therapy treatment services for substance abusers
> and their families. I met with the Administrative Director, the
> chief psychologist and the clinical director to ascertain (1)
> what they were already doing in this arena; (2) the general
> educational and training level of staff; (3) staff and administra-
> tive receptivity to family therapy and how they saw it in rela-
> tion to confrontational group strategies, AA and NA, and indi-
> vidual psychotherapy. It was learned that the climate was
> receptive and staff were pleased that they were going to have a
> chance to expand their therapeutic repertoire.
> What ensued was a cross between staff training, case consulta-
> tion and consultation to administration about program imple-
> mentation. We ageed on a 30 hour training design—spread out
> over 10 sessions of 3 hours each held monthly. The first 1-1/2
> hours were to take the form of a didactic lecture; the second
> 1-1/2 hours consisted of a case presentation and consult on a
> case preferably pertinent to the subject matter which had been
> discussed earlier that day. Since many staff members were re-
> covering alcoholics and/or addicts, their formal training did
> not include graduate school. Thus lectures covered Theories of
> Personality, Psychopathology, and Theories and Techniques
> of Family Therapy to help their practice become more solidly
> grounded. Case presentations raised issues of deep hurt and
> deprivation, exploitation and manipulation, enmeshment,
> death themes in the addict family and unresolved grief, ethnic
> factors, boundaries, and ethical and legal guidelines in dealing
> with this population. The first year was evaluated quite posi-
> tively so a second year was set up using the same format. The
> lecture topics expanded to encompass addiction and: sexuality,
> marital conflict and divorce, remarriage families.

The contract called for payment for the consultant's services on a per hour basis at the end of each session. Brief phone calls from participants and staff were not set up as billable—nor was travel time since the institution was quite close to my office. Periodic informal meetings were held over lunch with administrative staff for input from them on the direction and effectiveness of the program. At the end of the two years all involved agreed the objectives had been met and so the project was considered completed.

Good consultants usually are accorded high status. Their input has been invited and is usually welcome. Since they are not always accessible, especially if they are external consultants, their visits may become special events which provide time out for reflection, self study, growth and implementation of change processes. But before one becomes a consultant, he or she should be experienced enough to have credibility in the content area of expertise required and be sufficiently conversant with the consultation process to engage in it successfully. If one does not have access to a formal course or workshop in consultation, certainly they can observe skilled consultants working in their agencies, and at professional conferences. In addition, they can immerse themselves in the literature about this process—some of which is alluded to earlier in this section.

Staff Training

In some educational and training programs, students may be exposed to a course that includes some instruction on staff training or they may have an introduction to this phase of the mental health enterprise in their internship setting. It is important for them to have some exposure to conceptualizing, planning and implementing staff training programs before they are thrust into doing it—without any prior preparation. This will help to insure that they have had conveyed to them the fact that high quality staff training is an important avenue for refreshing, updating and expanding one's knowledge and skills, that carefully designed programs are essential if objectives are to be accomplished, that funds should be designated in an agency budget for staff training activities and time allocated for participation as part of the regular work expectation.

When an agency or organization decides it needs to do in-service training, it is incumbent upon them to search for the best possible trainer in the content or skills area they wish to pursue. Here too, as with consultation, it may be through a staff member designated as the trainer or an external person with a reputation for the requisite expertise may be contacted. Once the request for a training service is received and the individual contacted expresses interest in providing it, he/she should draw up and submit a training design. It should include the following components:

1. Host agency and location of session
2. Goals or objectives of training
3. Target audience—how many to participate
4. Number and length of sessions and calendar of proposed dates, times
5. Course outline
6. Evaluation forms
7. Date for delivery of materials to be xeroxed if proposal is accepted, i.e., bibliography, relevant articles
8. Fee for service and how and when payable

The organization's training director or a training committee should determine if the proposal is acceptable. If several have been requested simultaneously from different professionals, the most promising should be selected. Of course the host organization can ask for modifications if they don't get exactly what they want and all involved can refine the proposal until it meets what is being sought.

Once again, let us touch on some "should be obvious basics" which will help ensure a good training event but which all too frequently are overlooked. The physical environment should be attractive, spacious, well lit and heated or cooled, arranged appropriately and conducive to serving as a learning environment. Occasionally I've arrived to fulfill out of town training commitments to find dingy, musty, stuffy and small rooms. This may be particularly true in prison and mental hospital settings. It becomes an initial barrier and should be avoided or be circumvented whenever possible. The trainer should ask in advance about the physical set up.

Next, the training group should be free from distractions—no beepers going off or emergency calls coming through. In settings characterized by emergencies, a skeleton staff should be on duty for adequate coverage so that disruption of the training group session does not occur. If it is important enough to create this activity, and continuity of attendance is warranted, interruptions should be kept to a bare minimum. When it is not possible to do this on site, it may be advisable to hold the training event away from the institution's or organization's premises so all can concentrate and derive maximum benefit.

A third consideration is commitment to the new learning being instituted by top ranking staff. It makes little sense for staff to become proficient in and highly motivated to do neuro-linguistic programming, bio-feedback, hypnotherapy, neuropsychological testing, group therapy, etc. if the setting in which they practice is hostile to the modality. Introduction of new methodologies or expanded usage of some already being utilized does cause reverberations in the larger agency context. Will administration help create a climate receptive to utilization of new approaches? If necessary, will they supply requisite equipment and space as for a biofeedback or neuropsychology laboratory? If not, the training may engender a little knowledge, loads of frustration and not much of immediate practical value.

Gershenfeld's chapter (#13) illustrates how one formulates, implements, refines and evaluates a rather complex training design in a conflicted sociopolitical environment. Her work exemplifies well the process, strategy and potential outcome of staff training.

SUMMARY

In this chapter supervision, consultation and staff training have been handled separately for purposes of description and analysis. At points they intersect; at other times they are quite divergent. Wherever possible, innovative ideas should be used in combination with ones tested out as workable over time. All are methods for teaching and learning utilized to upgrade quality of service and level of practice or productivity.

REFERENCES

Abroms, G.M. (1977). Supervision as metatherapy. In F. W. Kaslow (Ed.), *Supervision, consultation and staff training in the helping professions.* San Francisco: Jossey Bass.

Bennes, W.G. (1969). *Organization development: Its nature, origins and prospects.* Boston: Addison-Wesley.

Caplan, G. (1970). *The theory and practice of mental health consultation.* New York: Basic Books.

Cleghorn, J.M. & Levin, S. (1973). "Training family therapists by setting learning objectives". *American Journal of Orthopsychiatry, 43*, (3), 439-446.

Epstein, N.B. & Bishop, D.S. (1981). Problem centered systems therapy of the family. In A.S. Gurman & D.P. Kniskern (Eds.), *Handbook of Family Therapy.* New York: Brunner/Mazel.

Hanlan, A. (1972). Changing functions and structures. In F.W. Kaslow (Ed.) *Issues in Human Services.* San Francisco: Jossey Bass.

Kaslow, F.W. (Ed.) (1984). *Psychotherapy with psychotherapists.* New York: Haworth.

Kaslow, F.W. (1985). Consultation with the military: A complex role. In L. Wynne, T. Weber & S. McDaniel (Eds.) *The family therapist as consultant.* New York: Guilford.

Napier, A.Y. & Whitaker, C.A. (1978). *The family crucible.* New York: Harper & Row.

Nielsen, E. & Kaslow, F. (1980). "Consultation in family therapy". *American Journal of Family Therapy, 8*, (4), 35-42.

Wynne, L., Weber, T., McDaniel, S. (Eds.) (1985). *The family therapist as consultant.* New York: Guilford.

2

What Do Therapists Worry About:
A Tool for Experiential Supervision

Israel W. Charny

There undoubtedly will be some therapists who will be offended by the very title of this chapter since, according to some sources in the profession, it would appear that therapists do not worry about anything. This is the job of *patients*. The role of therapists is to listen wisely to other peoples' worries and teach them the trick of how to go about life with quiet confidence and good cheer.

It follows from this fairytale that when therapists bring cases to supervision, they are bringing stories of other people who are worried about something or other, and how they—the experts in not being worried—are enabling their patients to solve and resolve their concerns. Perish the thought that supervision might refer to the therapist worrying about anything other than how to more effectively reduce the patient's worrying.

In this kind of supervision, there is a lot of *He (She) Said's* and *I Said's;* and if it is couple or family therapy, then the story expands to *They Said's,* and *I Said's to Them.* The psychotherapist, like the colleague neurologist or ENT specialist, goes looking for the right technology—the wisest strategic intervention that can break up the previously self-perpetuating pattern of neurotic or borderline thinking or dysfunctional behavior.

Such supervision is in the finest Twentieth Century traditions of Science and Technology. Objective Truth and Precision await only our hard work and discovery. There are True Interventions to be discovered by the wise therapist. Granted, from generation to generation, the presumed contents of "Ultimate Therapeutic Wisdom" undergo transformations. Currently, the once-magic of Character

Israel W. Charny, Ph.D., is Associate Professor of Psychology, and Director, Post-Graduate Interdisciplinary Training Program in Family Therapy, School of Social Work, Tel-Aviv University; Past Founding and First President, Israel Family Therapy Association.

Analysis has been transformed into steady *ego-skill work* with a growing population of Borderline Personalities; and once definitive Interpretations of Dreams have yielded to the shattering potency of Strategic Paradoxes so deftly framed that the patient, individual or family group, cannot possibly escape their power to reframe or reorganize even chronic disastrous patterns of being or family interaction. In all of the above, therapists worry about getting to be better and better technical and tactical geniuses, but never about themselves as people-practitioners who also really w-o-r-r-y about:

— Whether they will succeed on a case;
— Will they be admired for their success;
— A case that is going sour and whether the ''bad'' treatment outcome will reflect badly on them;
— Whether they are poor therapists, if not downright immoral, because the truth is they think the patient is a ''pain in the ass'';
— Being bored and restless—in fact, very, very bored;
— What it means that they are absolutely ''turned on'' to a patient—including at night when . . . ;
— Being jealous of a patient's wealth or position;
— Whether they are working at the case because it is financially remunerative or because therapy, in the form being practiced, is really indicated;
— Whether the therapy is keeping therapist and patient busy and off the streets but not leading to any real changes

The worst worry of all for some therapists is that they ruminate over whether they really should be psychotherapists.

A NATURAL EXPERIMENT IN CHOICE OF SUPERVISION

Years ago I had an entirely unplanned opportunity to learn the difference between the *He Said—I Said* type of supervision and the *I Am Worried About* type of disclosure in terms of what was happening to me, the therapist, in my work with a case.

In the years immediately following my doctorate, I worked in several part-time settings, where a number of excellent senior clinicians were available as supervisors. Each proceeded to offer me the type of supervisory instruction that was natural to him/her. I had nothing to do with the choice. At that time I didn't even know how much I wanted supervision; it was nothing more or less than part of the job to continue getting well trained—no doubt in hopes that some day I too could supervise someone else whether or not they asked for it.

I soon discovered that for all the intellectual drama of the case-oriented presentation and responsive supervisory wisdom by top-notch analyst supervisors, what really made a difference *for me* were those supervisory hours where I was taught to build the case presentations around *what was happening inside of me as I worked with the patient (family)*. Before long I realized that at any given point, I could describe a case through the particular subjective truth of how I was feeling working with that case. Some of the subjective reality encompassed:

— I can't stand seeing this kid;
— Its amazing but I can't remember the name of this child from session to session;
— This family makes me crawl in a nameless kind of horror, and I don't know what it is that is causing it because they seem perfectly nice;
— I wish they'd cancel. They're such a drain.

I learned that in the supervision that invited me to speak of my own real feelings, I was more likely afterwards to be released to a new zest and conviction that would spur me to go on more optimistically and powerfully with the therapy. Although in this kind of supervision I spent far less time unraveling the objective diagnosis and dynamics of the case itself, the actual operative gain for the treatment was, often, remarkably greater than what I came away with from content-centered supervision. Further, I recognized that in regard to my own struggles to feel more competent as a young therapist, and as a young adult in general, experiencing a candid dependency on my supervisor was making it possible for me to reach new levels of self-acceptance.

In case presentation types of "supervision," much of the time is filled by a hidden agenda of: (1) the supervisee trying to show off and win the approval of the authoritative supervisor, while (2) the supervisor is being careful to build up the self-esteem of the younger charge because, in truth, the supervision process is intrinsically evaluative, judgmental, and a transfer of information from the more adequate senior to the less adequate junior—who feels it.

In the experiential supervision I was doing the opposite. Given my basic agreement to enter into such supervision, I was telling everything that troubled me in doing therapy and revealing my worst fears, feelings, associations, and behaviors. I remember, as examples, a terrible sense of shame about wanting to take food from one so-hungry autistic patient. On another occasion I was ashamed about having an erection in the presence of, and truth be told, towards my female patient (all of eight years old the wench was). In both these instances, and so many others, my supervisor amazed me by confirming the essential humanity of my experiences, and sharing with me similar experiences he had had. In most cases, the main message was to learn to read my own feelings as signposts for what the patient evoked, and to try to find the best ways to *use* my feelings to advance the therapy. There were many supervisory sessions in which I would be upset, or be deeply ashamed, and sometimes actually cry, over not being genuinely helpful to my patient(s). What was also very reassuring was that many of these supervisory sessions, once finished, were followed by a hail-fellow colleagual and friendly attitude by my supervisor. Often I expected to be drummed out from the profession, and instead here I was treated as a growing young friend. Slowly but surely I began to trust more the possibilities of learning to use my feelings to contribute to my doing better professional work.

I emerged with the conviction that the greatest possibilities of growth in supervision of therapists lay in tapping candidly just what is going on in the heart, mind and body of the therapist in relation to a given case. Yet, it is apparent that not all therapists like to utilize this kind of supervision. The choice is their prerogative. It is true that some very skillful supervisors do address serious personal growth issues in the supervisee through their instructive comments, encouragement and criticism of how a case is being handled and what else should be done. Many supervisors use their insights into the supervisee's personality, seen through his work in therapy, to relate very deeply, even if indirectly, to the supervisee's real emotional needs. Some supervisors are themselves, in their characters, such fine men and women that the didactic instruction they give about how to do better therapy is, at the same time, an inspiring or anxiety-reducing or encouraging experience for the supervisee, as well as an opportunity for a positive identification and the concomitant corrective learning that entails.

Moreover, different types of supervision are more and less appropriate not only for various individuals, supervisors and supervisees, but in relation to the setting in which supervision is done.

There are settings in which it is *impossible* to work in an openly experiential mode because the supervisory process is too deeply embedded in the sequences of evaluation of a student or a worker by the administration. It is not especially fair to get into authentic discussions of the therapist's feelings in these situations, and most supervisees, with good ego boundaries, will not allow themselves to move into too much authentic self-disclosure in these situations. Most often this is true in supervision of students in university-affiliated programs. It is also true in many work situations when supervisors personally decide or report to those who decide on the advancement of workers within an agency. I would acknowledge, though, that occasionally, even these settings can allow for genuine experiential supervision if the supervisor is clear in him/herself that the not-nice and troubled feelings of the supervisee will not be taken to reflect in any way on professional competence, and the supervisee understands from a good discussion of the contract of supervision, that there will be no retaliation for human failings. On the contrary, what is conveyed is that respect will be gained for working with these. Realistically, however, this kind of contract between a supervisor and supervisee is generally possible only when the supervisee is basically a talented professional and has the good fortune to be assigned (or find) a skilled supervisor who accepts his/her once and still current childishness and nastiness, hence also "not-nice parts" in the supervisee.

It is precisely in those situations where supervisees are not outstanding in their talent, or when they have to engage very serious personal limitations, including problems of unethical management of cases, that experiential supervision will not be possible, and probably should not be offered, unless it is entirely separate from administrative or management contexts, i.e., decision making about the supervisee.

In any case, the way I like to work, as supervisee and supervisor, is to focus on the inner life of the psychotherapist in relation to the cases under supervision. Of necessity, this means beginning with a variety of negative concerns and feelings, many in the form of the therapist's worries.

SOME OF THE COMMON WORRIES OF THERAPISTS

Over many years of supervising therapists in this way, I have, of course, identified certain common refrains of worries that eat away at therapists, and these shall be commented on briefly now.

What If They Knew That I Can't Stand My Patient?

Consider the following supervisor-supervisee dialogue:

Trainee: The truth is I don't like her. I am bored by her. I've been at this case for years, and nothing seems to change at all. The woman is lifeless, and I can't help her. I don't know how I dare keep taking her money.

Supervisor: Would you consider discussing with the patient these feelings?

Trainee: How could I? She would be devastated. Maybe I should have told her two years ago. But if I told her now that I am bored, and that I can hardly keep my eyes open sitting with her, she will be deeply offended. She'll never come back. It could be the ultimate crushing experience for her—people have always lost interest in her.

The idea of leveling with patients that they are in some distinct way unattractive, even repulsive, at first sends shudders through therapists who have been taught that to be a really good therapist means to have a big heart and accept the patient essentially unconditionally. Many therapists then act out a role of *as if* acceptance whose ingeniousness and dishonesty trap the patient into making more efforts to bolter their self-esteem in the same failing ways they have been using all along.

"I do have a problem with you," says a therapist to one highly demanding possessive young woman, "and that is that although you keep asking for my affection and love, I feel like you are pounding away at me, trying to eat me up, and I have a sense that if I were really your lover or husband, I would have a hard time feeling able to breathe for myself. I think this may be a very good clue for us as to why you are having difficulties hanging on to a man, and that it is really good that we have this problem experienced between us here in therapy. It will give you a real chance to be able to work at a change, and I can give you the feedback when I feel differently in your presence—more relaxed and free to be myself and want to be with you because I really want to, and not that I have to respond to your demands that I be with you.''

Teaching this kind of therapy in supervision by its very nature means that the supervisor needs to engage the supervisee with a similar frankness. There are times for the supervisor to risk telling the supervisee of being impatient or turned off by the supervisee's overstriving. Just as in therapy, there are narcissistic injuries in these moments; timing, artfulness, and a real respect between supervisor and supervisee are essential, just as in treatment.

"I am Very Frightened That the Patient May Flake Out"

Many therapists are very concerned their patients may collapse— go crazy, commit suicide, and other horrible fates, because, mainly, they are afraid it will reflect badly on them—the therapist. The clear assumption in their upset minds is: "If the case is a failure, then I am a failure. If the case ends in tragedy, I am responsible."

In recent years this point of view has been promoted to a definite professional position especially by some practitioner-proponents of the "structural," "systematic," and "strategic" family therapies who, up to a point, instructively emphasize that the therapist is to be active, and in charge and is to seek to introduce as effective inter- ventions as possible. I cannot agree, however, that the wisdom of active interventions should lead to conclusions such as, "The thera- pist takes credit for all failures and the family takes credit for all success" (Bross, 1982, p. 221). If this philosophy really is seriously embraced, I venture that before long a great many systemic thera- pists will be seeking supervision or therapy (more than likely even with existential-analytic supervisors and therapists).

Therapists who worry that a patient will "die on them" really suffer. Most likely they are really trying to do a good job, with all the thoughtfulness and energy this calls for, but they expend an enormous extra amount of energy worrying that the patient's failure or dread outcome may hurt them—the therapist. This kind of worry can wear a therapist out. It is similar to doing sex with a ruler, a stopwatch, and a record page.

We have learned from the amazingly widespread phenomenon of Survivor Guilt (which seems to haunt virtually everyone who cares about people when something tragic happens to someone else) that feeling responsible for another person's tragedy is an extraordinary painful experience. People who suffer Survivor Guilt not only feel bad as such, but characteristically also feel that they are unable or do not deserve to be effective or enjoy pleasure in their own lives in the face of the other's tragedy. To my knowledge the only know anti-dote for Survivor Guilt is a reaffirmation of the legitimacy and wonder of one's own life and pleasures—notwithstanding the fact that someone else is paying, or has paid, a terrible price.

Therapist Responsibility

When a professional is entrusted with responsibility for stemming a patient's bad fate and fails, there are actually several objective levels of guilt that are triggered. These, I believe, therapists need to live with. They are part of the job. One is—how can I enjoy my life and work when this human being—the patient—no longer can? Sometimes there is also guilt over hostile impulses that were (quite naturally) within the therapist's soul and *might* have contributed to the patient's sad outcome. Another is guilt for not trying really hard enough. But all of these are different from taking on, blindly and slavishly, responsibility for the patient's fate.

Some therapists dread bad outcomes of cases so deeply that they flee difficult cases. Two common outs are to over-hospitalize cases or otherwise refer them prematurely to a "specialist." Some therapists flee the profession and become "supervisors," "adminis-trators," and "teachers."

The situation is the most obvious when it comes to threats of or real dangers of suicide. Sometimes suicidal patients are referred in-appropriately for inpatient treatment or to medical-type psychiatric intervention because the therapist is in a rush to get rid of the responsibility. As a result, the patient may become even more con-firmed in their panic about their inability to control themselves, or even more frightened of their hidden power-mad strategy to punish the world through threats of suicide. (Sometimes the hospitalization itself leads to an increased probability of suicide—patients have been known to kill themselves in hospitals, and in any case there is a frightening risk of suicide following release from psychiatric hos-pitalization.) If the therapist can really try to do the job of treating the person and problem *without being responsible for the outcome*, there are many more creative opportunities for a meaningful con-frontation of the dynamics of the patient.

In supervision, I emphasize to therapists that they *are* responsible for the quality of treatment work they do. Our professional work must be based on the best knowledge available in the field today; it also must be based on the energy of our sincerity and commitment to the treatment. But the outcome of therapy lies, ultimately, in the hands of the patient.

Knowing that the life-and-death decision is the patient's frees a therapist to confront them with their choice. For example: "*You're really going to be dead, and that means really not alive, and that means you're not going to have any pleasure of retaliating against anybody if you take your own life.*" These are tough words, but often they can save a life more than the pseudo-professionalism of a referral to a hospital without the therapist first really trying to battle the suicidal choice.

The Fear of Not Really Helping

Not really trying hard enough is also something that upsets therapists about themselves.

It is a fact that a certain number of cases elicit responses from practitioners that are routine, uninvolved, uninspired, automatic, and exploitative. Often the patients involved are those who have the least to offer therapists; they are not especially admirable; not especially attractive; they themselves don't try that hard to make life better. Sometimes these cases become the guaranteed income base of the private practitioner, and for the institutional practitioner, they are a guaranteed monthly statistic of enough hours on the job.

Characteristically, these patients are not often selected as topics of supervision, except when therapists really discipline themselves to listen to the small voice inside (our real professional quality control) that is saying these patients are getting nothing out of treatment—how come? Therapists are often angry at these patients for not trying hard enough, which is true, but the anger also plays on the therapist's contempt for their own not trying hard enough, and not being accountable for their own work.

In these cases, the supervision process should help formulate the therapeutic battle against the stuckness in the patient's lives. A realizable goal needs to be set. Sometimes this means introducing a decisive new life style—for example, insisting that an unemployed patient get a job, or that a family that is never together organize family meals. The goal is to make the patient(s) more responsible for the quality of their lives rather than their remaining dependent on the therapy as if the ritual of treatment itself could give meaning to meaningless lives.

Sometimes the supervisor's greatest contribution can be to inspire the therapist to trigger a dormant and overdue separation process, and the power of the separating between the too long-term therapist and the too long-patient(s) can release the energy of some measure of new growth that everyone has been avoiding because it has been too comfortable.

Worries About Getting Too Much Pleasure From A Case, Even Being In Love

Finally for this brief survey of what upsets therapists there are a whole series of sins of enjoying one's work—with some people—*too much.*

Such appears to be the charge of the True Therapist that he/she "selflessly" free others to their energies and lives, and if in the process the therapist himself/herself begins to enjoy the recipient of the services—say to the point of the therapist wanting to see the recipient more than the recipient needs to see the therapist—another serious worry rears its head.

Surprisingly, perhaps, these apparently pleasant forms of worry can trigger a fearful discomfort in therapists, especially if the pleasure is a telltale sign that something is missing in the therapist's own life that is being fulfilled by the work with this patient (Charny, 1982). Falling in love with a patient, for example, is an almost sure signal of a real deficit back home. The problem in supervision is complicated by the fact that many times it is not appropriate in a professional supervisory context to relate what is going on in the therapist's own personal life—unless, as sometimes happens, supervisee and supervisor break through to this level of work by mutual agreement.

There are, of course, the special complications that issue from the wondrous passions of sexual lust—shades of the ghost of Doctor Breuer and Anna O. and the tens of thousands of times since that Western therapists and patients have looked at each other with a deep longing and lust (let alone the thousands of times they have gone ahead, inappropriately, to consummate such lust in violation of every standard of professionalism).

However, love need not be either romantic or sexual; it can be any of a variety of forms of longing and needing and looking forward to and paying too much attention to a patient because they are giving the therapist something the latter needs for his/her own life, such as getting gratitude or admiration.

If one can listen, the true inner voice within will flag the therapist with some form of worry about holding on to the patient too much, overscheduling too many sessions or too frequently, looking forward too much to sessions, being too friendly, avoiding confrontations, or delaying steps in the process of preparation for and actual termination/separation.

Many, if not all, therapists move into some such special attraction and perhaps even "love affair" at one or more times in their work, and the responsibility of the therapist is to work his/her way out . . . as early and as artfully as possible, including sometimes sharing the problem responsibly with the patient.

If such problems are caught in time they are generally not damaging, and not at all a discredit to the therapist. On the contrary, responsible correction of such problems as they arise is a mark of a real professional, and in our work in psychotherapy—where patients are often finely tuned to their therapist's process—correction of one's own problems by the therapist at times can be turned into a positive contribution to the therapy. But unchecked, these are problems that lead to shameful consequences.

CONCLUSION

Therapists need to check with their Inner Voice about each case. Once we learn to appreciate the considerable value of all the worries that spring, uninvited, to our minds about each of our cases, we have available to us a very powerful and simple device for auditing much of our work, even without the help of a supervisor. Here is an exercise:

Write down the name of each of your cases and ask yourself: what about this case really worries me?

Perhaps you might want to go over the list with your supervisor, or with a consultant you seek out.

REFERENCES

Bross, A. (1980). The family therapist's reference manual. In A. Bross (Ed.), *Family Therapy: Principles of Strategic Practice* (pp. 218-247). New York: Guilford.

Charny, I.W. (1980). Why are so many (if not really all) people and families disturbed? *Journal of Marriage & Family Therapy*, 1980, 6 (1), 37-47.

Charny, I.W. (1982). The personal and family mental health of the family therapist. In F. Kaslow (Ed.), *The International Book of Family Therapy* (pp. 41-55). New York: Brunner/Mazel.

Charny, I.W. (1983). Structuralism, paradoxical intervention and existentialism: The current philosophy and politics of family therapy (pp. 200-215). In Lewis R. Wolberg & Marvin L. Aronson (Eds.), *Group & Family Therapy 1982.* New York: Brunner/Mazel.

Chessick, R.D. (1971). *Why Psychotherapists Fail.* New York: Science House.

Ekstein, R. & Wallerstein, R.S. (1958). *The Teaching and Learning of Psychotherapy.* New York: Basic Books.

Lang, M. Bad therapy—a way of learning (1983). In F. Kaslow (Ed.), *The International Book of Family Therapy* (pp. 447-462). New York: Brunner/Mazel, 1983.

PART II:
SUPERVISION OF THERAPY:
MODELS AND PARADIGMS

3

The Development of Professional Identity in Psychotherapists: Six Stages in the Supervision Process

Diane Friedman
Nadine Joy Kaslow

ABSTRACT. It is our view that the processes which psychotherapists undergo as they both learn their craft and develop a sense of professional identity conform to the developmental sequelae which lead to individuation and identity formation in human beings in general. In this chapter we highlight parallels in the developmental processes and delineate guidelines for supervisory practice which they imply. We have identified six stages in the learning and supervisory processes of psychotherapists-in-training and of new professionals. We describe the new trainee's diffuse anxiety, excitement, and dependency on the supervisor in the earliest stages, his or her increasing sense of confidence, competence and autonomy as they emerge in the middle stages, and, his or her emergent stability as a

Diane Friedman, Ph.D. is a Supervisor at the Cliffwood Mental Health Center in Englewood, New Jersey. Nadine Kaslow, Ph.D. is an Assistant Professor of Psychology in Psychiatry, Yale University School of Medicine, Department of Psychiatry.

The authors wish to express our appreciation to the following colleagues for their thoughtful comments and suggestions regarding an early draft of this chapter: Elizabeth Hansen, Reina Marin, Michael O'Connell, Norman Rasch, Fred Stern, and James Stoeri.

29

psychotherapist and collegiality both with peers and senior staff during the last stage.

Part of the process of becoming a psychotherapist involves developing a sense of professional identity. Once this has been attained with some degree of coherence, the professional identity serves as a stable frame of reference from which psychotherapists make sense of their work and, to some extent, the fabric of their lives. This chapter offers a description of the phases through which beginning psychotherapists pass as they learn the craft of psychotherapy and develop their professional identities. The chapter's focus is on the course of this evolutionary process as it manifests itself in the supervision relationship. The point of view expressed reflects the psychodynamic bias of the authors.

Ekstein and Wallerstein (1953/1972) point out that the

> sense of professional identity is an essential attribute in a profession such as psychotherapy, and its acquisition must be considered one of the important training goals. Professional identity is a higher form, a later acquisition than the self concept. It is an extension of the self concept. (p. 66)

These authors describe the sense of professional identity as having both external and internal components. External features relate

> to being externally *identified* as a psychotherapist, to being accepted as such by the general public and by other professionals . . . (and to) being identified as what one wants to be. The internal side has to do with the process by means of which an identity is established, the *process* . . . of identification with the teachers of psychotherapy. (pp. 77-78)

It is our belief that the "Healer identity" is an integral aspect of the professional identity. The term "Healer identity" refers to the notion of faith-in-oneself-as-Healer. In his book *Persuasion and Healing*, Frank (1961/1972) discusses in some detail the nonmedical roots of the healing process. He emphasizes the idea that the faith of both patient and therapist in the power of the latter to heal can often be instrumental in effecting the curative process.

In contrast to traditional medical sources of healing, the psychotherapeutic process is an *invisible* curative agent. The therapist, therefore, cannot easily learn to believe in its power. He or she can only attain the condition of faith through repeated experiences of conducting the process and observing its effects. Therefore, regardless of whether a psychotherapist-in-training learns his or her craft from the vantage point of psychiatry, social work, or psychology, attainment of the "Healer identity" is a significant goal of the training process. This means that even though psychiatric residents embark upon their training as psychotherapists with an already established but rudimentary medical healer identity, it is only as they learn the art of conducting the invisible "talking cure" that they develop the "Healer identity" of which we speak.

We have made it our primary task to depict the various consecutive types of dyadic supervisory relationships which trainees and new professionals form as they learn to become psychotherapists. For purposes of simplicity, we have chosen to ignore the fact that trainees, particularly in clinical psychology and psychiatry, are likely to be involved in several different supervisory relationships at any given time. These relationships will, of course, each have a different character depending upon the personalities of the supervisor and the supervisee involved. It is our contention, however, that there are identifiable, normative types of relationships which most trainees and new professionals form with one supervisor or another during each stage of their development, and it is on these normative relationships and phases that we have focused our attention.

Although we describe a variety of stage-specific supervisory problems which are likely to arise in the normal course of events, we do not address the spectrum of difficulties posed by the trainee who is identified as a "problem student." The reason for the exclusion is that students in this category manifest behavior which represents, by definition, deviation from the norm, and it is our primary task here to describe the characteristics which fall within the parameters of the norm itself. In general, it seems that trainees who are resistant to forming trusting attachments, who are highly narcissistic, or who have severe difficulties dealing with authority figures, comprise the most frequently encountered group of supervisees regarded as problematic.

In our view, there are six stages in the early learning and supervisory processes. We have labeled these as follows:

Stage One: Excitement and Anticipatory Anxiety
Stage Two: Dependency and Identification

Stage Three: Activity and Continued Dependency
Stage Four: Exuberance and Taking Charge
Stage Five: Identity and Independence
Stage Six: Calm and Collegiality

We do not see the above as discrete stages which occur once and once only. Rather, we assume considerable overlap between phases as well as a return to any of these under new or difficult circumstances. We believe that retrograde motion is inherent to learning and developmental processes and do not consider it "regressive."

Naturally, the character of supervisory relationships can never be entirely determined or controlled by the student, who is, after all, only one member of the supervisory dyad. The supervisor has an equal role in shaping the supervisory experience. It is our bias that it is the supervisor's task to assess the professional developmental level of the trainee or new professional and provide learning conditions appropriate to that stage of development. We believe that the role of the supervisor is not only akin to that of the therapist, but also to that of the mother or primary parent.

Erikson (1950/1963; 1968) has discussed in detail the process through which human beings develop the sense of a stable self. In elaborating on Hartmann's (1938/1958) concept of the "average expectable environment," Erikson (1968) speaks to the importance of the parents providing "a whole sequence of 'expectable' environments" (p. 222) in order to facilitate experiences appropriate to the child's evolving needs and abilities. Winnicott's concept of the "holding environment" (1965-b) as managed by the "good enough mother" (1965-a) is a more subtle reworking of this theme. The idea that the course of the child's identity development is related to the adult's capacity to adapt to the changing needs and abilities of his or her child is similar conceptually to the notion that the course of a trainee's professional identity development is related to the supervisor's ability to adapt to the changing needs and capacities of the supervisee.[1] Wherever possible, therefore, we have described in

---

1. There are additional parallels between early parent-child relationships and supervisor-supervisee relationships. Throughout the course of this chapter, therefore, we often draw upon the language of the former to describe the latter. In so doing, we do not mean to imply either a one-to-one relationship between the internal development of the child and that of the adult psychotherapist-in-training, or a one-to-one relationship between the parent-child experience and the supervisor-supervisee experience. In the case of the former, the similarities relate primarily to interactional processes and not to psychic content. In the case of the latter, the similarities relate only to the pattern of the process and not to the intensity, longevity, or significance of the relationship.

general terms the supervisory tasks which correspond to each of the six stages which we have delineated.

It is impossible to predict exactly how long it will take a given trainee to achieve a cohesive professional identity. Our general assumption is that the process never takes less than four years and, in fact, frequently takes many years more. This means that people who study in any of the three most common types of psychotherapy training programs (psychology, social work, psychiatry) may reach some of the later stages toward the end of their training years but will not achieve Stage Six, the period of "Calm and Collegiality" until after completion of formal training.

Not everyone who initially sets out to become a psychotherapist actually manages to master the tasks of each of the six stages. Some therapists "get stuck" in one stage or another, most often, Stage Five, the period of "Identity and Independence." These therapists are easily recognized by the fact that they never again seek close supervision after completion of their formal training years.

We have found no significant reference in the literature to the parallels between the general course of human identity development and the specific course of professional identity development in psychotherapists. However, Fleming (1953), Grotjahn (1955), Gaoni and Neumann (1974) and Yogev (1982) do propose a variety of stages of growth and learning through which psychotherapists-in-training or new therapists pass en route to becoming professionals. The models they each offer are quite consistent with one another's in the way that they address the developmental progressions of both the therapist's skill with the patient and supervisor-supervisee relationships. In terms of the former, learning is seen to occur first, through defining the psychotherapeutic role; second, through learning to explore and understand what the patient's internal processes are and imply; and third, through discovering what the therapist's internal processes are and imply. In terms of the latter, the direction of growth is from initially viewing the supervisor as teacher, to, much later, relating to him or her as senior colleague.

STAGE ONE:
EXCITEMENT AND ANTICIPATORY ANXIETY

The first phase begins when the psychotherapist-in-training initially becomes acquainted with the training agency in the capacity of student. It ends upon contact with either the first patient or information about the first patient. Depending upon either the system to which the training agency subscribes, or the new trainee's degree of reluctance to speed up the process of patient assignment, the phase may be as brief as several hours or as long as several weeks or even months.

In general, this period is marked by the trainee's diffuse anxiety and excitement. These feelings are generated by the newness and awesomeness of the long-awaited professional opportunity to become a psychotherapist. The uncomfortable feelings are maintained because the trainee has no specific task on which to focus and bind the anxiety until he or she is assigned a patient. While all of us can recall this very brief but overwhelming prelude to becoming a psychotherapist-in-training, the phase is virtually without mention in the literature. We consider the omission remarkable. So many practicing clinicians attribute considerable significance to the beginning phase of a psychotherapy venture, yet almost no one has described the analogous moments of the supervisory relationship.

The task of the new trainee's supervisor at this stage is similar to that of the newborn's parent: to provide "enough security so that the baby will be free to explore the new world on his own without feeling that he is neglected or abandoned" (Kaplan, 1978, p. 63). While the specifics of the successful holding environment will vary depending upon the personalities of the supervisor and the supervisee, the essential element consists of the supervisor's accurate empathy regarding the trainee's anxieties and vulnerabilities.

STAGE TWO:
DEPENDENCY AND IDENTIFICATION

The second stage begins as soon as the trainee is assigned a case. It ends with the trainee's first realization that he or she has had a significant impact on a given patient. Most often, this impact is experienced by the novice as having a personal rather than a professional, or healing, character. Interruptions in the treatment, whether brought about by the novice's illness, vacation, of field placement termination typically provide an opportunity for the trainee to notice the extent to which a patient has come to feel attached to or to rely on the new therapist. The patient's tears, rage, or regression all attest to the fact that at least one member of the trainee-patient dyad believes that the former is actually a therapist. Stage Two, by definition, precedes this discovery.

The trainee's lack of confidence, skill, and knowledge about what psychotherapeutic work actually entails typically leads to a high degree of dependency on the supervisor as well as to idealization of the latter's skills and understanding. Although the consistent characteristic of the supervisee's relationship with the supervisor during this stage is the dependency of the former on the latter, the visible form this may take can range anywhere from outright submission to the supervisor, to healthy, trusting dependency, to casual rejection of the supervisor's help, to a chronically rigid, counterdependent mode. Commonly, however, supervisees emulate their favorite supervisor's perceived therapeutic styles and attitudes about clinical matters, as well as, on occasion, their body postures and personal mannerisms (Barnat, 1973).

Most often, trainees seek instruction from their supervisors about how to manage specific patient behaviors such as: not appearing for, cancelling, or coming late to scheduled appointments; making numerous between-session telephone calls to the therapist; asking personal questions of the therapist; demanding concrete advice; or appearing in an intoxicated state at appointment times. In addition, trainees want to know how to respond to a patient's excessive tearfulness, psychotic productions, rage reactions, suicidal ideation, gross acting out between sessions, and difficulty separating from the therapist at the end of sessions. Questions about managing the first phone call to the patient, introducing oneself, and handling the patient's attempts at conversation in the hallway or waiting room are all of concern to the trainee during this period. Students exert considerable pressure on their supervisors to play the role of author of a *How to Perform Case Management* text while they are in this stage of the learning process.

The most fundamental question trainees have during this phase, however, is "What exactly is my job with these patients?" New trainees are easily distracted by the often complex and anxiety-provoking reality issues with which their patients present. They find it difficult to either grasp the nature of the internal problem which stymies the patient or, if they do understand it, stay fixed in their focus on the internal element. Alternately, students may perceive the "therapeutic task as being limited to a kind of detective game, at a distance from the patient, a matter of discovering dynamics and genetics, of describing pathology without doing something about it" (Fleming, 1967, p. 420).

Trainees do not usually ask their supervisors all of the questions which occur to them: some are simply too painful to articulate. Perhaps the most salient of these is: "Do I have what it takes to perform this work successfully?" Supervisees in this phase are frequently plagued by the self-doubts and ambivalent feelings which reflect both the inchoate nature of their professional identities and the minimal degree of skill they as yet have amassed with which to perform their work. Supervisors can help address the "affirmation hunger" (Barnat, 1974, p. 190) of the novice by conveying through attitude and manner a sense of warmth and acceptance. This idea is consistent with the observations of other writers that professionals who are benevolent and supportive make the best supervisors for students who are in the earliest phases of their training (Chessick, 1971; Rosenbaum, 1953).

Just as trainees do not ask their supervisors all of the questions which occur to them, neither do they tell their supervisors about all that transpires in the interactions which they have with their patients. Beginning therapists tend to disguise much of what they do with their patients when reporting to supervisors for fear of either looking silly or, alternately, not looking good enough. Although psychotherapy supervision is always fraught with potential for creating narcissistic wounds in the supervisee, at no other developmental stage are supervisees more consistently vulnerable than they are when just entering the field.

Trainees frequently express interest in understanding their patient's diagnoses, dynamics and interpersonal styles. Early on, they rarely ask for and do not seem able to digest lengthy supervisory discourses or probings regarding transference, countertransference, and more general theoretical matters (N. Kaslow and Friedman, 1984). When trainees do mention countertransference, it is usually in the form of a confessional regarding the presence of unacceptable hostile or sexual feelings about a patient. It is a rare beginner who is not disturbed by such feelings from time to time or who is able to grasp immediately, without some coaching, the extent to which such feelings provide valuable clinical information about the patient rather than solely about the therapist.

It is important that supervisors remember that trainees so often feel overwhelmed by the demands of early clinical work. Who among us does not recall the exhaustion we felt in the earliest turning phases after seeing only two or possibly three patients in the course of an afternoon. Because trainees at this stage tend to feel so emotionally drained and confused by their direct contacts with patients, the most helpful general service that the supervisor can perform is to demonstrate that there are ways of organizing and, equally important, anticipating those experiences which initially feel so chaotic to the novice. The organizing and anticipatory roles of the supervisor are basically holding functions.

It is also essential at this stage and during the one which immediately follows it that supervisors handpick patients for their students in order to screen out those who present major management problems or "hopeless" treatment prognoses. Complex management cases are to be avoided because they too quickly overwhelm and drain the novice, while "hopeless" cases impede the growth of the trainee's faith in the therapeutic process. This latter issue should not be taken lightly. It is highly unusual for a trainee to enter the field with a firmly entrenched belief in the efficacy of psychotherapy. It is therefore very much the task of supervisors and teachers to nurture the growth of the trainee's faith in the power of the healing process.

STAGE THREE:
ACTIVITY AND CONTINUED DEPENDENCY

The third phase of development may begin within several months or years after a trainee has been treating patients in psychotherapy. It is initiated by the trainee's first realization that he or she is actually being taken seriously by his or her patients, who develop faith in the "Healer" long before the "Healer" himself or herself does (assuming that the latter is a beginning-level trainee). The patients' reactions gradually convince the therapist that the latter is neither an imposter nor a fraud. Thus, the impact which the reactions of patients have on the evolving self-concept of the therapist parallels the impact which the reactions of significant others have on the child's evolving sense of self-definition (Winnicott, 1967/1971).

The direction of growth for the supervisee during Stage Three is from passivity and dependency to a more active, less dependent mode. It is a shift from being done to, to doing. This shift can be observed both in the student's supervisory relationship and in the student's therapeutic work with his or her patients: the trainee at this stage generally vacillates between being a reactor to both the patient and the supervisor and being a more active participator in each relationship.

One of the consequences of the trainee's increased activity level is a concomitant elevation in his or her sense of professional responsibility for therapeutic actions and decisions. It will be recalled that at the end of the prior stage, the novice became aware for the first time that he or she was really having an impact on patients. Now, with that awareness in mind, the new therapist fluctuates between gross overestimation of his or her therapeutic power and equally inaccurate underestimation of it. The omnipotence feelings are accompanied by considered guilt and anxiety regarding therapeutic decisions which may have to be made. A trainee at this stage, for example, may feel overwhelmed by the consequences of choosing to seek hospitalization for a decompensating young adult who may, forever after, bear the stigma of having been a "mental patient" as a direct result of this treatment decision.

Trainees frequently try to cope with the omnipotence anxieties of this stage by discussing treatment problems and strategies with an assortment of supervisors, faculty members, peers, and significant others. The primary aim of such discussions is to "spill" affect. This behavior on the part of the novice is not to be confused with the more ideationally motivated requests for consultation with colleagues and senior staff which appear at later stages of professonal development. The most helpful stance that the supervisor can assume at these points is to acknowledge the difficulty and weightiness of the new therapist's responsibilities without overstating the case and escalating the trainee's anxiety level.

Supervision continues to be characterized by its patient-focus during this phase. Although less dependent on the supervisor than before, the average trainee remains dependent enough so that the tone of the relationship is still likely to be an overtly compliant one. Unlike the diffuse anxiety which characteristized the trainee during the previous stage, anxiety is now experienced episodically, during times of crisis. It is at these moments that the supervisee is likely to slip back into the more dependent mode of the prior stage.

Trainees continue to ask questions about management, but in addition, may make beginning efforts to learn about and integrate psychotherapy theory as it relates to practice. The intensity of the student's quest for understanding, however, is rarely matched by the extent to which he or she is able to integrate the answers. Theoretical exchanges during supervision primarily serve the purpose of providing the trainee with a stage upon which to practice voicing the nouns and verbs of the profession's language. The ability to converse in a sophisticated way is not yet possible. For instance, one might hear trainees at this level say the following: "There was so much splitting going on!" or, "The patient is using so many defenses!" This is the period during which students typically diagnose anyone they know, or have ever known. Beginning piecemeal use of the psychotherapy argot is made with great gusto and is, in fact, an extremely important part of both the learning and professional indoctrination processes. However, the new words and ideas as yet have little impact on the trainee's psychotherapeutic work.

The supervisor's mirroring acceptance of the passive and active modes of the trainee's work and level of understanding enhances the trainee's self-perceptions and self-esteem. This parallels the process which occurs under optimal conditions between mother and child when the mother's "mirroring admiration . . . paints proud edges on the baby's body" (Kaplan, 1978, p.144). The basic ways in which the supervisor can convey acceptance are by limiting and focusing criticisms, setting limits judiciously, and by being predictable in affective tone from supervision session to supervision session, as well as in response to the psychotherapeutic work under scrutiny.

When the supervisor is attentive to and accepting of the trainee's needs, supervision tends to be a positive experience for the student. The supervisor, however, may or may not find this early phase of supervision to be particularly rewarding or stimulating. While it is of great value for the student's development that he or she be free to problem-solve, experiment, and make mistakes, it can be quite frustrating for some supervisors to sit back and watch this often messy and initially ineffective *modus operandi*. The supervisor's experience at this point may duplicate the mixture of pleasure and frustration felt by many parents as they watch their children's early attempts to feed themselves. Typically, food intake is painfully slow and relatively ineffectual. Because the process seems highly inefficient, it may be maddening for the parent when the child rejects help. However, as all parents know, children do eventually learn to feed themselves no matter what the degree of parental involvement has been.

Supervisors who are either unable or unwilling to perform early holding functions may create problems for their supervisees by either demanding premature movement from passivity to activity or by impeding increased activity levels as they emerge. One of the authors (NK) had the following supervisory experience during this phase of her training, when the shift from passivity to activity was prominent and the need for acceptance was primary. During the course of a family therapy practicum in which she and her supervisor were regularly doing cotherapy, NK realized that she was ready to become more active in the treatment. Prior to a family therapy session, she indicated to her supervisor that she wanted to be more active during the forthcoming interview hour. The supervisor responded by saying, "You can talk for the first five minutes and I won't interrupt as long as you don't say anything stupid." This may at first glance seem to be an extreme response from a supervisor. We include it, however, because we feel that it clearly conveys the power which supervisors can exert, particularly those who enjoy the idealizing dependency of their students, to retard the emergence of higher levels of autonomous functioning.

STAGE FOUR:
EXUBERANCE AND TAKING CHARGE

The fourth phase of development is ushered in by the trainee's realization that he or she really *is* a therapist. Previously, the trainee has observed patients improve, as many do, and has even felt instrumental in the process in some cases. What the trainee has not experienced until this turning point, however, is a basic sense of himself or herself as "Healer." Intrinsic to this aspect of the self-concept is the trainee's awareness that his or her own psychotherapeutic armamentarium is in large measure responsible for the treatment "cures" which he or she effects. It is at this stage, therefore, that trainees can be heard to exclaim with enthusiasm, "Hey! Psychotherapy really works!"

Trainees now feel more in command professionally because they know more about the treatment process, what their job is, and how likely it is that they will be able to facilitate certain changes in a given patient. The trainee's greater treatment effectiveness has come about partly in response to the amount of patient contact which he or she has accrued. But in addition, a variety of other factors have led up to this new development. By the time this phase begins, most psychotherapists-in-training have entered into personal psychotherapy, where they have accumulated perceptions about the phenomenology of being a patient as well as about the scope and pace of the treatment process (N. Kaslow & Friedman, 1984). They have also spent several years reading the literature of the field and discussing it both in class and in supervision. What happens during this phase is that all of these experiences begin to gel. One visible consequence is that trainees are now able to substantively grasp connections between psychotherapy theory and practice.

It is usually during this phase of development that the student begins to identify more personally with one theoretical orientation or another. This has not occurred before in a meaningful way (from the supervisor's point of view) because the trainee still lacked both a sufficient knowledge base of the theory in question and any stable sense of his or her own psychotherapeutic style. Now, during a time of relative security, the trainee is better able to explore and experiment with novel points of view, for it is possible to envision adding them to an existing framework of thought and behavior. When multiple theories and techniques are presented to trainees in earlier phases of their education, they lack the organizing rubric into which to fit the diverse ideas.

Supervision during this stage ceases to be primarily patient-focused. The trainee is secure enough to be ready to handle the increased anxiety which countertransference exploration engenders. He or she is also better equipped to engage in theoretical discussions with supervisors. Whereas before, trainees placed a higher premium on having supervisors who were warm and empathic, regardless of their capacities to engage with ideas in an intellectually stimulating way, they now evidence a greater preference for supervisors who are intelligent and knowledgeable about both the literature and direct practice. The supportive style which was the *sine qua non* of good supervision during the early years or months, has become a desirable but insufficient characteristic of good supervision (Rosenbaum, 1953).

By this time, the trainee is more clearly in charge of his or her psychotherapeutic work, both as case manager and as psychotherapist. Optimally, the supervisor, in response, has relinquished the more controlling role he or she had formerly played and has begun to act more like a consultant to the therapist. Because the trainee has finally begun to organize, plan, and execute the treatments he or she is conducting, these treatments take on a far more authentic cast than they have previously had. Trainees now tend to be more warmly, maturely, and genuinely related to their patients than they were before. Simultaneously, they are less intensely bonded with their supervisors.

The shift away from more dependent relations with the supervisor speaks to the solidifying professional identity of the new psychotherapist. During prior stages, the trainee responded to the supervisor in a manner which primarily reflected compliance (or, of course, non-compliance in the more negativistic student). By Stage Four, the supervisee begins to genuinely identify with his or her teachers as "Healers." This identification process is the forerunner of internalization.

Sometimes it happens that a supervisor is more interested in directing the course of a treatment than the trainee may wish. The trainee is now so invested in experimenting with and inventing the treatments he or she conducts that unsolicited supervisory advice is likely to be either resented or ignored or both. It is not a matter of a trainee's wish not to have counsel regarding patient care, but, instead, a manifestation of the increasing need to shape the terms of the supervisory and treatment relationships. The supervisor is less frequently viewed by the student as someone who is there to evaluate the student or to protect the best interests of the patient (regardless of the reality of the situation from the point of view of the supervisor), and more frequently seen by the student as a consultant who will provide help when needed. The trainee is very much preoccupied with making his or her own discoveries in a progressively independent fashion, and overinvolvement or overcontrol on the part of the supervisor is a deflating experience for the trainee which robs him or her of the creative joys of this stage.

STAGE FIVE:
IDENTITY AND INDEPENDENCE

This is the period of professional adolescence. It is most notable for the rejecting and/or devaluing attitudes which the new therapist may direct toward the supervisor. Arrival at this stage signals the emergence of the trainee's or junior staff member's new capacity to begin to envision survival without the full support of the supervisor. For most new therapists, this stage lasts for several years. It is analogous in both spirit and process to adolescent separation phenomena vis-a-vis the parents.

Major disagreements with authority figures have previously been avoided by the average trainee or new staff member because dependency needs were acute enough to muffle direct expressions of difference or anger. During this stage, however, supervisee-initiated power struggles of one sort or another can be normative. At the more subtle end of the spectrum, the supervisee may withhold a great deal of information from the supervisor about the course of various treatment cases. The motive is the supervisee's wish to feel and be more independent as a clinician; the wish to avoid looking silly, which had been the primary impetus for withholding during earlier developmental phases, is no longer the operative motive. When Stage Five is reached by a new therapist who is employed on a full-time basis in the community, a form which the struggle for independence may take might be the creation of a *sub rosa* peer supervision group composed primarily of staff members who are at the same developmental stage. While such groups meet numerous needs, the element relevant to Stage Five in the developmental process is the extent to which these groups arise in reaction to or in rebellion against the agency's or institution's formal supervision process. It is important to keep in mind, however, that just as all adolescents do not experience intense turmoil as they go through their teenage and young adult years (Offer & Offer, 1975), neither do all new therapists behave in the foregoing ways. Our view is that when and if such behavior emerges, it is best recognized as phase-appropriate.

It is important to understand that the supervisee's behavior at this stage represents a developmental achievement despite the negativistic phenomena with which a supervisor may be confronted. During earlier phases, many supervisees engage in a form of passive non-compliance whereby they pay lip-service to the wisdom of supervisory suggestions but then do not implement them in treatment. The trainee's non-compliance at these times is in large measure due to either confusion about or fear of making the suggested interventions. Now, during the present stage, the issue is quite different. The supervisee is more measured in evaluating the accuracy and quality of the supervisor's advice and may believe, in the end, that he or she knows best how to handle the treatment problems in question. The central developmental given of this phase is the fact that the supervisee now has a firmly internalized clinical frame of reference on which he or she routinely bases treatment decisions. As a result, supervisory feedback can no longer have the dramatic impact which it once had. In the main, this is a function of the increasingly cohesive nature of the professional identity which is forming.

A hallmark of this period is that the new therapist is typically quite conscious of the areas in which his or her professional or personal strengths either exceed, or seem to exceed, those of the supervisor. For example, he or she may be acutely aware of having a greater capacity to tolerate a patient's periods of silence or rage than a given supervisor has. It is not until the next phase of professional development that the supervisee will be able to comfortably accept the differential skill levels of senior staff and feel open to learning from them again despite their deficiencies. To this extent, the current developmental phase is notable for the pervasive quality of adolescent-like devaluation of less-than-perfect authority figures.

This is the phase during which the supervisee is most invested in both minimizing the impact of the supervisor and maximizing his or her own sense of professional autonomy. Some supervisors feel quite comfortable with their role during this phase, but many find it painful to either experience the loss of supervisory control or accept the more limited parameters of the teaching arena. The developmental needs of the supervisee at this point require that the supervisor support the new therapist's autonomy moves while still remaining available as a helper. The supervisor's task is complicated by the fact that he or she must create a setting which, on the one hand, allows for the supervisee's freedom of functioning, and on the other, implicitly acknowledges that it is the supervisor who carries final responsibility for the treatments which the supervisee conducts.

One of the authors (DF) had the following positive experience with a supervisor during her predoctoral internship year, when she was beginning to work through the developmental crises of Stage Five. Several months before the end of that year, DF was assigned to a supervisor whose dominant theoretical orientation was one in which DF had little interest. After several unproductive supervisory hours, DF told the supervisor that her relative dissatisfaction with the supervision process was a function of her disinterest in the supervisor's theoretical point of view. Some discussion followed, after which the supervisor quite calmly suggested a modification of the supervisory contract. He proposed that the clinical case in question be discussed on an intermittent or, "as needed" basis only. DF experienced this plan as both implicitly supporting her individuation needs and affirming her faith in her growing clinical competence.

STAGE SIX: CALM AND COLLEGIALITY

This phase is characterized both by the therapist's sense of calm and stability and by his or her feelings of collegiality with peers, senior staff, and supervisors. The sense of professional identity is by now so firmly established that risk-taking has become an integral part of the therapeutic style rather than a notable deviation from it. Therapists at this stage are more likely to re-examine and challenge psychotherapy ''truths'' than they were before and to increasingly personalize their own styles of treatment, rather than strive to emulate models to which they have been exposed. Because they have relatively stable and secure technical and theoretical bases from which they conduct treatment, therapists now feel more motivated to explore treatment modalities and issues which had prior been of less interest.

One of the reasons that the predominant mood of the new therapist is one of calm, is that self-doubts about competency issues are less intense than they have ever been: the affective highs and lows of earlier stages are considerably muted. Furthermore, the absence of the intensive monitoring and evaluation by supervisors which pervaded the training years inspires an increased sense of autonomy in the new professional, who realizes that he or she has become a trusted member of the professional community. The therapist's professional self-acceptance and the implicit affirmation of colleagues and administrators fosters independent functioning rather than the dependent style which was the *sine qua non* of the training years.

The level of integration of the therapist's professional identity is reflected in the way in which he or she views colleagues. Whereas in the early years, therapeutic expertise was presumed to lie primarily in the domain of senior professionals, there is now an awareness and acceptance of the fact that peers too are a valuable source of ideas, experiences and information. The peer supervision groups which proliferate during this stage arise out of a spirit of genuine respect among colleagues and are no longer tinged with conspiratorial feelings of rebellion against formal agency supervisors, as they were during the prior stage.

By the time therapists achieve this level of professional development, they may be involved in any or all of three different types of supervisory experiences. The first type is most similar to supervision relationships established during the training years. In this case, the therapist, now employed by an agency or institution, is likely to be subject to a form of supervision which addresses administrative as well as clinical matters. The supervisee is expected to conduct the treatments of his or her patients according to treatment plans established in concert with the agency-appointed supervisor, who carries both legal and agency-related responsibility for the conduct of the cases. The supervisor in this setting may also be responsible for formally evaluating the therapist's performance in order to determine salary increases and promotional possibilities.

Both the second and third types of supervisory relationships likely to be established by a new therapist are, in contrast to the above, voluntary in nature. The second type also takes place in the context of an agency or institution and involves the obtaining of ongoing supervision by a junior clinician from a senior clinician who is affiliated with the same facility. In this form of supervision, however, the junior member of the dyad is not obliged to act in compliance with the views of the supervisor, who is neither legally nor administratively responsible for the course or outcome of the treatments being conducted, and is not a participant in official evaluations of the supervisee. The third form of supervision is similar to the second, except that: one, the supervisor is not affiliated with the same facility that the supervisee is; or two, neither supervisor nor supervisee are affiliated with an agency of any type.

Regardless of which of these three types of supervisory relationships the clinician is engaged in, supervisors at this stage tend to be less idealized than they were during the early years of training and, equally, are less likely to be devalued as they were during the new therapist's prior developmental stage. Instead, supervisors are more accurately seen by new professionals to be as they really are: more experienced clinicians who have both personal and professional strengths and weaknesses. This is an instance in which the lines of personal identity development and professional identity development converge for the new therapist.

The narcissistic vulnerability which was so prominent during the training years and which to a large extent hindered the learning process, has by now receded into the background in most cases. A very significant result of this shift is that the new professional now comes to the supervisory relationship with a keen investment in making that relationship work. The therapist knows roughly what it is that he or she is looking for from the supervisor as well as what the strengths of the supervisor are. A fair amount of effort may be expended by the therapist to create and sustain the conditions which will enable the supervisor to be of use. This is very different from the conditions which prevailed during the early stages of traineeship. Those years were dominated by the novice's anxiety, passivity, dependency, and defensive wishes to elude the supervisor. Equally, the current picture is in contrast to later stages of training and/or early years of professional employment. Characteristic of those years were the new therapist's struggles to define himself or herself, achieve autonomous functioning, and, simultaneously, delimit the impact of the supervisor. Now, during Stage Six, these goals have been achieved, at least in a rudimentary way. Fears of the supervisor as the mother-of-fusion-and-engulfment have been minimized so that it is possible for the therapist, for perhaps the first time, to actively seek out and create the learning situations in which he or she thrives.

In the context of these supervisory conditions, countertransference becomes a prominent focus for both self-examination and supervisory interchange. Over the course of the training and early practice years, a perceptible shift in the therapist's view of the significance of countertransference has taken place. In the early stages, countertransference reactions in response to the patient were typically assumed to reveal defects in the trainee's character as well as weaknesses in his or her capacity for emotional control. The primary wish of the trainee was to exercise the ego-alien feelings. During later stages of professional development, however, countertransference reactions to the patient are viewed in a qualitatively different fashion. They are now seen as providing valuable cues about the patient's internal states and interpersonal relationships as well as about the therapist's. The therapist is both more interested in and more free to examine in a reflective and open manner his or her reactions to a given patient or to the therapeutic relationship. When this kind of self-scrutiny takes place, the supervision process may appear to be indistinguishable from the psychotherapeutic process.

SUMMARY

We have described a sequence of stages through which psychotherapists pass as they each develop their own sense of professional identity. We have not assumed that learning or identity development end here. However, we have chosen to come to rest at this plateau for two reasons. The first is that by the time the new professional reaches the period of "Calm and Collegiality," supervisory relationships no longer have the formative impact which they had in earlier years and therefore assume a qualitatively different character. The second reason is that the average psychotherapist undergoes a major transformation at about this time, when he or she begins supervising the next generation of psychotherapists. The shift in professional self-concept which is brought about by this role change is an extremely complex one, similar in nature to that which a new parent experiences, and therefore, in our view, it exceeds the scope of this paper.

The course of professional identity development which we have outlined is in harmony with Erikson's (1950) identity scheme as well as with the separation-individuation model of Mahler and her colleagues (Mahler, Pine, and Bergman, 1975). Erikson's ideas are echoed by our view of the trainee's movement from phases of industry and mastery, to adolescent-like rebellion, to identity consolidation. Erikson's supposition, as well as ours, is that the path which identity development follows leads to an individual's increased "sense of inner unity, and an increase in the capacity 'to do well' " according to one's own standards and "the standards of those who are significant to one" (Erikson, 1968, p. 92).

At the same time, our understanding of the separation and individuation processes which trainees enact with their supervisors echoes the stage-theory proposed by Mahler and her colleagues to this extent: the supervisee's growth proceeds from phases of bonding and attachment, to efforts at differentiation, to signs of rapprochement crisis, to achievement of separation-individuation proper. Individuation in this sense "refers to the taking on of those characteristics which mark the person as a person in his own right; . . . . the child individuates largely by taking into himself characteristics of significant others in his life from whom he has differentiated" (Pine, 1979, p. 226). It is our view that these similarities between the specific course of the psychotherapist's professional identity development and that of his or her personal identity development, help the psychotherapist-in-training to acquire "large portions of his own personal identity and self-concept collaterally with his acquisition of professional and therapeutic role and identity" (Ford, 1963, p. 476).

REFERENCES

Barnat, M. 1973. Student reactions to supervision: Quests for a contract. *Professional Psychology, 4,* 17-22.

Barnat, M. 1974. Some characteristics of supervisory identification in psychotherapy. *Psychotherapy: Theory, research and practice, 11,* 189-192.

Chessick, R. 1971. How the resident and the supervisor disappoint each other. *American Journal of Psychotherapy, 25,* 272-283.

Ekstein, R., and Wallerstein, R. 1972. *The teaching and learning of psychotherapy.* New York: International Universities Press, Inc., (Original work published New York: Basic Books, 1958.)

Erikson, E. 1963. *Childhood and society.* New York: W. W. Norton and Company, Inc. (Original work published 1950.)

Erikson, E. 1968. *Identity: Youth and crisis.* New York: W. W. Norton and Company, Inc.

Fleming, J. 1953. The role of supervision in psychiatric training. *Bulletin of the Menninger Clinic, 17,* 157-169.

Fleming, J. 1967. Teaching the basic skills of psychotherapy. *Archives of General Psychiatry, 16,* 416-426.

Frank, J. 1973. *Persuasion and healing.* Baltimore: The Johns Hopkins University Press. (Original work published 1961.)

Ford, E. 1963. Being and becoming a psychotherapist: The search for identity. *American Journal of Psychotherapy, 17,* 472-482.

Gaoni, B., and Neumann, M. 1974. Supervision from the point of view of the supervisee. *American Journal of Psychotherapy, 28,* 108-114.

Grotjahn, M. 1955. Problems and techniques of supervision. *Psychiatry, 18,* 9-15.

Hartmann, H. 1958. *Ego psychology and the problem of adaptation.* New York: International Universities Press. (Original work published 1938.)

Kaplan, L. 1978. *Oneness and separateness: From infant to individual.* New York: Simon and Schuster, 1978.

Kaslow, N., and Friedman, D. (1984). Interface of personal treatment and clinical training for psychotherapist trainees. In F. W. Kaslow (Ed.), *Psychotherapy for psychotherapists.* (pp. 33-57). New York: Haworth Press.

Mahler, M., Pine, F., and Bergman, A. 1975. *The psychological birth of the human infant.* New York: Basic Books.

Offer, D., and Offer, J. B. 1975. *From teenage to young manhood: A psychological study.* New York: Basic Books, Inc.

Pine, F. 1979. On the pathology of the separation-individuation process as manifested in later clinical work. An attempt of delineation. *International Journal of Psychoanalysis, 60,* 225-242.

Rosenbaum, M. 1953. Problems in supervision of psychiatric residents in psychotherapy. *Archives of Neurology and Psychiatry, 69,* 43-48.

Winnicott, D. 1965a. Ego distortion in terms of true and false self. In D. Winnicott (Ed.) *Maturational processes and the facilitating environment* (pp. 140-152). New York: Basic Books, Inc.

Winnicott, D. 1965b. The theory of the parent-infant relationship. In D. Winnicott (Ed.), *Maturational processes and the facilitating environment* (pp. 37-55). New York: Basic Books, Inc.

Winnicott, D. 1971. Mirror-role of mother and family in child development. In D. Winnicott (Ed.), *Playing and reality* (pp. 111-118). London: Tavistock Publications.

Yogev, S. 1982. An eclectic model of supervision: A developmental sequence for beginning psychotherapy students. *Professional Psychology, 13,* 236-243.

4

Growth in Supervision: Stages of Supervisee and Supervisor Development

Allen K. Hess

ABSTRACT. This essay reviews the status of supervisory models, presents an overarching schemata of stage models of supervisee development, and, finally, describes a three stage model of supervisor development. The terms "counseling" and "psychotherapy" are used synonymously, as are "trainee", "supervisee", "student", and "psychotherapist."

Various models concerning supervision of psychotherapy and counseling describe different roles and relationships which supervisors and supervisees occupy in the course of supervision (Hess, 1980a; Watson, 1973). Models generally are graphic characterizations of theoretical assumptions, and therefore are more circumscribed (Hess, 1980b) than would be a theory. These models are helpful in structuring supervision, but the conceptualization of the process of supervision often is a derivative of whichever theory and set of techniques the supervisor holds dear. For example, the psychoanalytic supervisor may examine motivations for the student-therapist's conduct in therapy, and may use the technique of interpretation and foster a process of identification with the supervisor to accomplish psychoanalytic supervision. Literature regarding client centered and humanistic approaches to supervision (Mueller and Kell, 1972; Rice, 1980) are concerned with teaching the student to

The author is grateful to John J. Mallet, Jerome Fleischer, Florence Kaslow, Cheryl Storm, Kathryn Hess, Rodney Goodyear, Celia Solomon, and Everitt Worthington for helpful comments on an early and rough draft. They might not recognize the similarity between the draft they saw and this paper due to their comments' helpfulness.

Allen K. Hess, Ph.D. is a member of the faculty at Auburn University and is in Independent Practice.

51

listen to the client, increasing authentic interaction and congruence, and fostering growth. Behavioral approaches describe the supervisor's efforts toward skill acquisition, relaxation for the student therapist, discriminative and differential responding, and imitation learning (Linehan, 1980). Several interesting consequences follow from adopting one of these orientations.

First, the work of supervision gets done, probably irrespective of the particular and favored theory of the supervisor. This occurs due to the transmission of whatever is the essence of being a therapist occurring in the context of relationship. It gets done, too, because of reality demands. If the focus of supervision misses issues important to the client or supervisee, reality, in the form of core problems of the client or therapist, will remain, and irritate the client or supervisor. If denial continues on the part of the supervisor, supervision will be unsatisfactory for the student who will engage in avoidance games (Kadushin, 1968) and seek help from sources outside this supervision. If both supervisor and supervisee avoid issues, the supervision will be unproductive. Reality, in the form of the supervisor's and supervisee's needs for an Eriksonion generativity, the client's needs, and perhaps the agency's procedures for evaluating client or trainee progress may be avenues by which reality accomplishes its salutary effects.

Second, the various theories are robust enough to have survived for decades, indicating that they must be addressing needs with some efficacy. This may occur because the essential elements of supervision (or of psychotherapy) while addressed, are being called by different names. Thus what a psychoanalytically oriented supervisor may call a supervisory alliance between supervisor and supervisee, the behaviorist will call the reinforcing value of the relationship (Delaney, 1972), and the client centered person may call positive regard. I suppose one can claim identification with the supervisor has a deeper significance than imitation of the supervisor or of one's own therapist but that remains to be proven. Thus the theories have confluences although their foci and goals do vary.

The student can become an adherent of the supervisor's orientation. If this occurs with an exposure of the supervisee to other viewpoints, and with a match with the supervisee's own proclivities, it is beneficial. If the process was purely conversional, then the student's training may be a mimicry. The theory will not have been metabolized in a way which enriches the student.

When the student is exposed to different theories which are equally and ardently endorsed by different, respected professors, or a student becomes a proselyte only to confront their belief system's limitations, confusion can result.

The student can become cynical and espouse the "nothing works" philosophy; this position is untenable for a therapist since a therapist's actions are necessarily predicated on some image of what humans are like. Either the therapist then leaves the field, adopts another theoretical viewpoint, or entertains eclecticism, the most common position of clinical psychologists (Garfield and Kurtz, 1976). Eclecticism is problematic because either one really espouses an underlying assumptive network but allows the use of techniques from other theories, or one tries to be theoretically eclectic which ultimately leads to confusion due to mixed and incompatible metaphors (cf. Hess, in press). That is, concepts that humans are quintessentially growth oriented and positive, or that they are hedonic and appetitive are distinct, and require the therapist to behave differently toward the client and to have world views of the client which are distinct.

The above discussion illustrates two supervisory phenomena. First, each theory of psychotherapy addresses important issues and can be construed to be helpful in supervision but is *not a theory of supervision*. For example, if supervision is seen as a behavior change procedure, then behavioral approaches must be helpful. But none originate nor focus on supervision per se and on supervisee needs. Second, a theory of supervision must address supervisee issues that are distinct from those of clients. While a therapist may build rapport with a client or confront a maladaptive style, or terminate with a client, one would hardly *discuss* rapport building, presentational style, or managing termination as routine issues in psychotherapy. One or another of these issues may be relevant to a particular client, but all are central to each supervision. The absence of a theory of supervision which encompasses the essential aspects of supervision is a major gap in this field. Such a theory may best be generated by first examining student or trainee needs.

STAGES OF SUPERVISEE DEVELOPMENT

Table one displays six attempts to schematically depict the supervisee's stages or needs in the course of development as a therapist. The different authors' views are denoted by numbers (Stage 1,

Table One
Supervisee Stages

	Inception	Skill Development	Consolidation	Mutuality
	A	B	C	D
Hogan (1964)	1. Insecurity-Dependency	2. Dependency-autonomy	3. Self-Confidence	4. Creativity
Delaney (1972)	1. Initial Session 2. Facilitation of Supervision Relationship	3. Goal Identification and strategy select-ion 4. Strategies - Instruct-ion, Modeling and Reinforcement 5. Termination and Follow-up		
Gaoni and Nevmann (1974)	1. Pupil	2. Apprentice	3. Therapeutic Personality	4. Mutual Consultation
Yogev (1982)	1. Role Definition	2. Skill Acquisition	3. Solidification and Evaluatio of practice	
Loganbill, Hardy, and Delworth (1982)	1. Stagnation	2. Confusion	3. Integration	
Blount (1982)	1. Adequacy-inadequacy	2. Dependency vs. Autonomy	3. Conditional Dependency vs. Individuation	4. Independent Practice and Collegial Consultation

Note: Letters A, B, C and D refer to the author's putative stages, while the numbers in the body of
the table refer to the particular theorist's stages.

2 . . .), while this author's overview is denoted by letters (Stage A, B . . .).

Stage A: Inception

Examination of the first column or Inception Stage shows the models to address a common theme with certain differences in emphasis. Delaney (1972) believes the initial session is important in setting the stage for supervision. The goal of this session is for the supervisee to adjust to supervision, in contrast to Weiner and Kaplan's (1980) goal of the initial supervisory session with the beginning student, which is to help the student adjust to meeting the client and conducting psychotherapy for the first time. Gaoni and Neumann (1974) suggest that their first stage is actually a pre-supervision stage since its focus is on specific, didactic sorts of learning. In this stage some see the therapist as a conduit between the supervisor and the patient, seeking direct advice, applying the teacher's suggestions assiduously, and serving as the supervisor's extension. Progress can be seen by the student's rapport building with clients, born of the student's optimism and even the beginner's naiveté.

Hogan (1964), Loganbill, Hardy and Delworth (1982), Yogev (1982), and Blount and Glenwick (1982) describe the feeling of being unmoored or unanchored (Hess, in press) which envelops the neophyte therapist. Hogan's level 1 describes the dependency of the apprentice, the uninsightfulness of the student not knowing his or her impact on patients and supervisors. Loganbill, Hardy, and Delworth describe "stagnation" or unawareness that an ". . . issue even exists as an issue . . . ". Narrow rigidity characterizes thought patterns, and extreme dependency is punctuated by a benign peripherality in relating to the supervisor. Yogev's role definition stage addresses the demystification of psychotherapy, the anxious expectancy of therapeutic catastrophy (I might mention "catastrophe" means "sudden change"; its root is not endowed with solely negative turns of events but certainly the trainee, while wishing for cures portrayed in the cinema and in novels, by which one unlocks a pathogenic secret, really fears saying the precisely wrong phrase thus mobilizing a full blown psychosis. This erroneous fear must be addressed in nearly every new trainee). Blount lists anxiety, insecurity and dependence, plus the ambivalent attitudes of excitement and dread over seeing one's first clients, as central to stage 1, adequacy versus inadequacy.

The various models are consistent in the type of person portrayed as a beginning therapist.

Stage B: Skill Development

This stage is highlighted by the development of skills which were germinated in Stage A. Yogev sees this in both didactic and experiential aspects. Technical skills are learned, the therapist role becomes less ill-fitting and critique is felt as non-catastrophic and can be used. Both Yogev (1982) and Gaoni and Neumann (1974) see a passivity in the student, but also increasing awareness of client dynamics, and subtleties of communication. Blount agrees, seeing the locus of responsibility for direction still residing in the supervisor.

Hogan sees the student's struggle for autonomy rife with ambivalence between overconfidence and feeling overwhelmed, from a deep commitment to psychotherapy to deep misgivings over vocational choice. Loganbill, Hardy and Delworth describe the calm after the storm, much to the supervisor and supervisee's relief. A reorganization, acceptance of strengths and weaknesses and directionality characterize the trainee's experience. Gaoni and Neumann discuss a shift in the focus of supervision from the client to the trainee. A therapist personality, spurred by self analysis and self awareness, is formed. Hogan sees a self confidence, a clarity of motivation and a deepened sharing of experiences in his stage 3. I suspect part of Delaney's stage 4, accomplishing learning skills, is relevant to the consolidation process. Blount sees the daily clinical caseload of the professional as a crucible for formation of an individuated therapeutic personality. Yogev, still seeing the student in training, describes the reverberations of clinical issues as stimulating personal issues in the therapist, which are grist for the supervisory mill.

Stage C: Consolidation

Many of the building blocks contributing to an integrated therapist personality have been described in Stage B. In some sense, a Gestalt-like emergence occurs in Stage C whereby those skills which our budding therapist does well become a hallmark of the person. One graduate school peer of mine had some early successes with hypnosis in reducing clients' weight. He prided himself on this skill, and peers sought him for advice in their attempts at hypnosis. While the evaluations of this skill development originates from external sources (professors, supervisors, peers and clients' reports), the weight of evidence allows the trainee to internalize a sense of mastery. Much like in a good gestalt, a figure emerges from an undifferentiated ground, a figure which has its own stimulus configuration (pattern of skills based on innate predispositions plus training and experiences) which is the therapist's professional personality. The emergent figure is dynamic. New skills develop. The therapist extends techniques to new client populations. The trainee moves to new settings (internships, new job positions) solidifying skills and extending one's professional identity, since the student is no longer seen as a student in the new setting. Instead he or she is seen as at least somewhat skilled, and may be given supervisory responsibilities on internships (Hess and Hess, 1983), and as a faculty member. These responsibilities can bring anxieties, which will be discussed in a subsequent section.

Stage D: Mutuality

This stage is characterized in Blount's notion of "the fully autonomous professional" who gives and receives consultation, and by Gaoni and Neumann who describe it as occurring in the sharing of opinions and advice between equals. They advocate leaderless groups since the therapist should have resolved destructive competitiveness that can occur between trainees in groups in their earlier stages of training. Hogan describes artistic, intuitive and creative therapy abetted by peer supervision. Delaney's stage 5, perhaps fitting in our stages B and C, deals with determining goal attainment in mastery of skills, best judged by the supervisor observing the therapist in the counseling setting. Loganbill, Hardy and Delworth, and Yogev are more concerned with the student in training, and the beginning therapist respectively, and do not propose a stage 4 or D.

The above schemas are heuristic devices to help understand the student but may be a function of shared fictions of the authors. One way to determine the typologies' validity is to see how students describe their experiences. While their descriptions may be influenced by the models of Hogan, Delaney, and Gaoni and Neumann which were proposed in 1964, 1972, and 1974 respectively, the work of Marshall and Confer (1980), Greenburg (1980) and Cohen (1980) concur with Table One.

Another limitation of stage models is the lack of epigenetic inevitability. That is, I have encountered students at the beginning of supervision who needed clarification of their personal issues (Stage C) and even assurance as to their potential worth as creative therapists (Stage D). Subsequently, they dealt with Stage A and B issues. Elsewhere, I describe the possibility of a spiral process by which we may see fluctuations of a student going from one to another stage (Hess, in press). Loganbill, Hardy and Delworth describe eight issues on which the student may be more or less advanced, or dealing with one issue on their Stage 1-2 level, and another on their Stage 3 level. This is at variance with all but Delaney's behavioral scheme. The others imply a more general developmental sequence in which the student passes through a stage and resolves the issues with finality.

SUPERVISOR STAGES

There exists a literature concerning supervisee stages, reviewed above, and one concerning stumbling blocks confronting beginning supervisors, but the literature is sparse regarding learning dilemmas or stages of maturation for the supervisor. It is interesting that supervision is fifth in terms of time spent on activities by clinical psychologists (Garfield and Kurz, 1976) ahead of such tasks as group psychotherapy, behavior modification and research. Yet these latter activities are prominently featured in virtually all graduate school curricula while supervisory training is offered in some 14% of graduate psychology programs. Hess and Hess (1983) report one-third of clinical psychology internships offer supervisory training, and remarkably some one third of the facilities surveyed have their interns providing supervision to others with no supervision of their rendering of this service. Perhaps a telling commentary in the area of supervision is that 24 respondents believed supervision of one's psychotherapy to be important in developing supervisors, while 19 directors of training saw supervision of supervision as important. The assumption is alive and well that it takes a therapist to be a supervisor, but training in supervision is second in importance. The assumption is unfairly made, too, since it requires the supervisor to capitalize on various and incidental learning processes as the major modality by which supervision is learned. The rationalization for not providing training takes two forms. Some respondents sympathetically said they had not thought of that type of training and either are considering adding it to their program or would add it barring time limitations in the internship year. The second, and somewhat pointed response, was that it was inappropriate to train interns to supervise; that interns were not ready. Yet the interns graduating in August will be hired in September by another facility to spend about a half day per week in supervising others' psychotherapy.

One wonders about this paradox in view of several other facts. Stanton, Sanchez and Klesges (1981) indicate 90% of their sample would have opted for a supervision course in graduate school. The Division 29 (A.P.A., 1971) standards for psychotherapy education includes Principle 9 (The faculty should be competent in the supervision aspect of teaching psychotherapy), and Principle 20 (The student should receive training in supervision of psychotherapy), as well as several principles regarding rewarding supervisory activities. The A.P.A. ethical principles (1981) advise that psychologists may only provide services in areas for which they are qualified by training and experience. When an area lacks such standards, psychologists are to "take whatever precautions are necessary to protect the welfare of their clients" (principle 2, Competence). We can conclude that there is a surge of interest in supervision training, such training is lacking, supervision is a feature of the typical psychologist's workload, and ethical principles require us to move ahead in this field. One neglected aspect in the supervision area is that of development of the supervisor. Again, seeing stages as more heuristic than necessarily epigenetic, an outline of a stage model is presented.

Stage A: Beginning

The beginning supervisor may spend some time in supervisory training, but much more common is the phenomenon of spending perhaps a month in travelling from the student's side of the desk to the supervisor's chair. The *role status changes* from being supervised to supervising, from having fellow students as one's peers to having collegial relations with senior clinicians. Naturally this change in reference group carries with it immensely demanding expectations. The neophyte supervisor's standard of comparison is not a fellow graduate student, but an experienced clinician.

This role status change coupled with the lack of supervisory training leads to a second issue in Stage A. The novice supervisor may be unaware of such supervisory issues as: the *structuring of supervision* and *techniques of supervision.* At first the supervisor may draw on such experience as having been in psychotherapy and in supervision. Naturally therapeutic techniques become the supervisor's tools and from time to time the therapy model itself is the supervision model employed. While supervisors infrequently claim to do psychotherapy in supervision, data currently being analyzed by Aldrich and Hess show supervisors and supervisees to recall parallel process incidents differently. Supervisees' reports depict supervision as being transacted like psychotherapy, and when that occurred, the experience tended to be experienced less favorably.

Whether by virtue of sensing the trainee's unease or by some other differentiating and maturational process, some supervisors experience a self-consciousness in supervision. This can be fueled by a trainee who is senior in years and experience to the supervisor. I recall a supervisee who bristled at any situation she could perceive as "one-down". In our first supervision session she cited a list of prominent therapists she claimed as her supervisors (carefully mentioning each by first name). After this recitation, the student grinned, let her shoulders slowly meet the chair back, and moved her palms as if to say, "The ball's in your court. Can you match that!"

The supervisor may be quite aware of trainee's evaluations, which is usually done by spreading the word through the "grapevine" regarding the supervisor's theoretical preferences and degree of tolerance. Given the absence of any validated measures, the clinical training director will be eager to monitor student reactions to the new supervisor, a fact which the supervisor may keenly sense.

One coping strategy is to rely on the concrete. The supervisor may be more client focused or technique oriented in supervision at this point. Teaching reflection or desensitization and engaging in differential diagnosis may be safer grounds on which to tread. My own career line somewhat fortuitously had me supervising psychodiagnostics in my first faculty position. This structured experience allowed me time to confront supervision, examine its various aspects, and develop a supervisory philosophy.

Beginning supervisors have indicated difficulties in the following areas; trainee resistance to supervision (26.7%), not knowing how to intervene (21.3%), not understanding the case (21.3%), and lack of knowledge of techniques and research (15-20%) (McColley and Baker, 1982).

Interestingly, more experienced supervisors are less likely to use trait labels. Thus their broader experience may allow the trainee more room to change by making more external and situational attributions (Worthington, 1983). Moreover, inexperienced supervisors may be better equipped to focus on technique-oriented issues with beginning therapists (Heppner and Roehlke, 1984).

Stage B: Exploration

With more supervisory experience, the supervisor can recognize better and worse sessions and more or less accomplished supervisees. Differentiation of experience is accompanied by increased feelings of effectiveness in that interventions attempted have discernible effects. The supervisor realizes his or her impact on the supervisee. Rioch (1980) describes the up-down dynamics in supervision. Supervision can take place with the supervisor telling the trainee what he or she would have done if the client were theirs. And the supervisor can perform feats such as explaining the client in ways the trainee never conceived. Sometime these acts of wizardry can be helpful in allowing the student to have insights into clients, pique their curiousity about how the supervisor, who may never have seen the client and having access only to test data or the trainee's verbal report, can describe the client in ways that could not have occurred to the trainee. Part of the learning which can be accomplished is the way the clinician can take paper and pencil markings of a MMPI and Draw-a-Person, or vignettes of a counseling session and much like a cultural anthropologist, who draws inferences about the type of culture a tribe must have developed by way of a few shards of pottery, can draw inferences regarding the mental structure and behavioral patterns of clients. I recall a student being amazed at my speculation of incest in a client who had broken wings and punctured body parts on the Rorschach, had run away from home, seemed not to be delinquent and demonstrated internal moral standards. Moreover, responses on the incomplete sentences blank and The Thematic Apperception Test allowed me to infer the identity of the family member perpetrator and the youth's age at which the assaults began. If used properly, the supervisor can use these incidents to allow the student to develop an appetite for further study, integrating research (the modal cause of runaways is family conflict and sexual abuse), clinical lore (broken wings and the body image damage concept resulting from sexual assault), and the hypothesis-testing attitude.

The supervisor comes to take supervision as a professional activity. While he or she still may keep to a firm fifty minute session and maintain many therapy-like conventions, an awareness of the importance of supervision awakens. In a real sense most poor supervisors are stuck in Stage A. By the time Stage B supervision develops in a clinician, his or her concern for supervision assures at least a modicum of success since this interest and attention on the supervisee's work necessarily impacts favorably on the trainee. The supervisor in Stage B reads supervision literature and is aware of supervisee's needs (e.g., Bartlett, Goodyear and Bradley, 1983). Perhaps the two biggest pitfalls in Stage B are when the supervisor restricts his or her supervision to one role rather than employing the role which is most apt (Hess, 1980a), and when the supervisor is too intrusive. In response to these errors, student resistances arise.

Resistance to learning can be seen in a variety of games (Kadushin, 1968) or responses. These include evidencing problems in scheduling appointment time with the supervisor, failing to prepare for the sessions even when given suggestions on how to do so, ambushing the supervisor by introducing material which contradicts advice offered by the supervisor, and trivializing supervision. Trivialization can occur by making supervision a social event by discussing off-task topics which appeal to a supervisor's interests (sports, sex, fashion) or vanity (how the supervisor's pet theory is so correct, especially in contrast to the theory's main challengers). Some chit-chat is necessary in maintaining rapport, and indeed each instant of supervision need not be highly momentous, but several sessions of off-task discussion are a warning of the occurrence of non-supervision.

Two other dimensions signal a shift in the supervisor changing between Stage A to B to C. More of Stage A supervisor's sessions are predicted on formal power or the ability to give "A" grades, or speak for or against the student's continued progress toward a degree in the institution or in the profession via a letter of reference. More supervision occurs by virtue of what the supervisor can offer in Stage B. Thus the power base shifts from the formal to informal sources (Hart, 1982).

Secondly, agenda needs shift. Student learning needs take priority. The supervisor feels less of a need to be a seer or savant and can take clinical problems facing the student or issues blocking the student from learning and give these clinical problems or problems in learning (perhaps a blind spot or a conflictful area) the priority that they merit.

Stage C: Confirmation of Supervisor Identity

When the supervisor has a consolidated identity, students tend to come for the excitement of supervision, rather than coming to supervision because of program requirements, licensing requirements, or the need to have supervision on one's resume. The supervision is built on the same level of trust and confidentiality that supports good therapy. One way I have placed supervision as a prime activity is by minimizing the assessment component. I report only general progress or lack thereof to the faculty during the semi-annual student evaluations, or in privately contracted supervision, only the client (therapist who has hired me) need be made aware of his or her progress. If the walls of the office become permeable regarding the student's issues, one can hardly expect to inspire trust or confidence in the trainee. If a trainee's conduct becomes unethical or illegal, the same limits to confidentiality in psychotherapy can guide the supervisor in taking a course of action in supervision. For example:

> A colleague supervised a trainee whose own needs to seduce prompted him to secure a caseload of divorced women and schedule them for evening sessions. Supervision is not designed to provide him a sanctuary. His narcissism provoked him to tell the supervisor who then became professionally responsible for the clients' welfare and legally an accomplice unless, as occurred, he made some direct interventions and appropriate breaching of the confidentiality.

This is not to say evaluation should not or does not occur. It must if the trainee has any judgment and has the motivation to become a competent counselor. Evaluations occur in an ongoing way. Thus the trainee makes remarks like; "I'm at a loss as to what's even the issue with this family" or "The psychiatrist said, 'undifferentiated schizophrenia' but admitted he did not know what to make of the client—and I certainly don't either!" More direct evaluations of supervision occur in comments such as;

> I saw your face, expression on your eyebrows, and finger on your lips just when I was about to be sucked in by Mr. L. again and launch on another lecture on how he just needs more confidence to get over his depression. Instead I waited, endured the silence, and was able to feel his impact on me—wow, it was a

powerful pull to give him a cheer-up talk! Finally, I intervened by asking him if he knew what impact his self-condemning statements had on me. Then I was able to tell him what behavior and feelings he elicited. I am not sure I helped him, but I did therapy, and am not exhausted over delivering my pompous moral lectures which he then used to use to confirm his self deprecations.

Of course, if enough trust is built up in supervision, the supervisor can respond to the trainee's deprecation ("not sure I helped him", and "my pompous moral lectures") and as a parallel process issue show by the supervisory intervention, how to encounter client self-deprecation, and how the client might feel about the type of encounter the supervisor has provided the trainee.

As shown above, there is less worry *about* the relationship, and more relationship per se in Stage C. The written evaluations at the end of a semester or quarter or the payment of fees in a privately contracted supervision, punctuate supervision and provide a check to see if ongoing and naturally occurring evaluation has taken place. If the supervisor's and supervisee's comments to each other provide no surprises, evaluation has been occurring. I usually ask "How can I do better; Is there something I can add or omit that would be more helpful" as a way to check that a "mutual admiration society" or a "don't harm me and I won't harm you" arrangement has not unwittingly transpired.

The attention to the student's learning agenda becomes the focus of supervision. If the trainee's needs are not productive, the supervisor's agenda of providing instruction and growth facilitating supervision is violated. Thus the supervisor's agenda can provide a check as to the legitimacy of supervision. *But the key is to focus on the supervisee's agenda.* To illustrate:

A supervisee was paralyzed by a parent's ultimatum that the therapist had "one more session to help my child." The child was a serious underachiever. The therapist was at a loss as to what to do. Two approaches were discussed. One was for the supervisee to relate her experience of the ultimatum to how the child may be feeling in response to such ultimatums. The supervisee was able to see the paralyzing and resentment-generating effect the father had and came up with several therapeutic strategies to use. Spontaneously the supervisee, who had been quite reserved in supervision, recalled how a faculty member made unreasonable demands on several students, including the trainee. The trainee remarked about the resentment the students felt but how one student was able to confront the professor in a non-threatening, reality based fashion. The professor told the students to do what they could and forget what was unreasonable. This trainee recaptured that feeling and dealt further with how to be more self-assertive. The focus stayed on the supervisee's personality as it impacts on clinical work. More personal work might best be done in psychotherapy proper. This was confirmed metaphorically by the trainee mentioning how intrusive the "bug-in-the ear" technique, which the clinic had available, seemed to her. The trainee was feeling herself out as to what were her limits of disclosure in supervision, having just been more self-revealing in supervision than she had been in several years with anyone else at the university.

Presenting the supervisee's agenda at center stage (whether the issues are known or not to the trainee) helps guarantee successful supervision. A variety of "checks" are built into the supervisory relationship as alluded to above. Rioch (1980) discusses the concept of "disciple" as being related to discipline. Successful supervision allows the disciple to construct his or her own internalized discipline and checks, making formalized evaluation redundant and non-threatening since the more crucial evaluating agent is self confirmation.

This latter point can be threatening to a supervisor who needs credit for doing good work, a Stage A or B quality. Maimonides, some seven hundred years ago, proposed eight levels of charity. Essentially the lower levels are when charity is asked for and credit for the donor's "good works" is publicized. The higher levels involve the donor being anonymous, and even the recipient not knowing they were given a gift, and not having to experience the consequent position of having had to be given to. In our contemporary terms positive self attributions can be made by the recipient who does not know of their own recipient status. Internalization of the positive role can occur. In more general terms, both donor and recipient gain in personal integrity. In supervision, the more the supervisee can work, the more professional pride and personal integrity the supervisor and supervisee will gain. Farber and Heifetz

(1981) report stressful aspects of psychotherapy include feeling personally depleted and pressured, poor working conditions, and two troublesome patient qualities, overt psychopathology and resistance. On the other hand, satisfying aspects include promoting growth and change, achieving intimacy in clients' lives, and feeling professionally respected. Good supervision provides no less.

Recently my daughter left me in her wake in a swimming race. I was surprised at the absence of bad feelings I experienced since I am typically so highly competitive in athletics. Instead my pride at her accomplishments was dominant, and I only sighed about my experiencing the limits of age and diminishing physical prowess. If only all my supervisions go that well . . .

REFERENCES

Aldrich, L. G., and Hess, A. K. (1984). Parallel process: Its prevalence, content and resolution in counseling and psychotherapy supervision. Unpublished manuscript, authors.

American Psychological Association (1981). Ethical principles of psychologists. *American Psychologist, 36,* 6343-638.

Bartlett, W. E., Goodyear, R. K., and Bradley, F. O. (1983). Supervision in Counseling II. *The Counseling Psychologist, 11,* 3-79.

Blount, C. M. and Glenwick, D. (1982). A developmental model of supervision. Part of a symposium: Psychotherapy supervision: Expanding conceptual models and clinical practices. A. P. A. Convention, Washington, D. C. August, 1982.

Cohen, L. (1980). The new supervisee views supervision. In A. K. Hess, (Ed.) *Psychotherapy supervision: Theory, research and practice.* New York: John Wiley.

Delany, D. J. (1972). A behavioral model for the practicum supervision of counselor candidates. *Counselor Education and Supervision, 12,* 46-50.

Division 29 (A. P. A.) (1971). Recommended standards for psychotherapy education in psychology doctoral programs. *Professional Psychology, 2,* 148-154.

Gaoni, B. and Neumann, M. (1974). Supervision from the point of view of the supervisee. *American Journal of Psychotherapy, 23,* 108-114.

Garfield, S. L. & Kurtz, R. M. (1976). Clinical psychologists in the 1970's. *American Psychologist, 31,* 1-9.

Greenburg, L. (1980). Supervision from the perspective of the supervisee. In A. K. Hess (Ed.) *Psychotherapy supervision: Theory, research and practice.* New York: John Wiley.

Hart, G. M. (1982). *The process of clinical supervision.* Baltimore, Maryland: University Park Press.

Heppner, P. P. and Roehlke, H. J. Differences among supervisors at different levels of training: Duplications for a developmental model of supervision. *Journal of Counseling Psychology, 31,* 76-90.

Hess, A. K. (1980a). *Psychotherapy supervision: Theory, research and practice.* New York: John Wiley.

Hess, A. K. (1980b). Theories and models in clinical psychology. In A. K. Hess, (Ed.) *Psychotherapy supervision: Theory, research and practice.* New York: John Wiley.

Hess, A. K. (in press). Learning counseling and psychotherapy skills: A challenge in personal and professional identity. In G. Sumprer and S. Walfish's (Ed.) *Clinical, counsel-*

ing, and community psychology: A student's guide to graduate training and professional practice. New York: Irvington Press.

Hess, A. K., and Hess, K. A. (1983). Psychotherapy supervision: A survey of internship training practices. *Professional Psychology, 14,* 504-513.

Hogan, R. A. (1964). Issues and approaches in supervision. *Psychotherapy: Theory, research and practice, 1,* 139-141.

Holloway, E. L. and Hosford, R. E. (1983). Toward developing a prescriptive technology of counselor supervision. *The Counseling Psychologist, 11,* 73-77.

Kadushin, A. (1968). Games people play in supervision. *Social Work, 13,* 23-32.

Linehan, M. (1980). Supervision of behavior therapy. In A. K. Hess, (Ed.) *Psychotherapy supervision: Theory, research and practice.* New York: J. Wiley & Sons.

Loganbill, C., Hardy, E., and Delworth, V. (1983). Supervision in counseling I. *The Counseling Psychologist, 10,* (1), 1-67.

Marshall, W. P. and Confer, W. N. (1980). "Psychotherapy supervision: Supervisee's perspective" in A. K. Hess, (Ed.) *Psychotherapy supervision: Theory, research and practice.* New York: John Wiley.

McColley, S. H. and Baker, E. (1982). Training activities and styles of beginning supervisors: A survey. *Professional Psychology, 13,* 283-292.

Mueller, W. and Kell, B. (1972). *Coping with conflict: Supervising counselors and psychotherapists.* New York: Appleton-Century-Crofts.

Rice, L. A client-centered approach to the supervision of psychotherapy. In A. K. Hess, (Ed.) *Psychotherapy Supervision: Theory, research and practice.* New York: J. Wiley & Sons.

Rioch, M. J. (1980). The dilemmas of supervision in dynamic psychotherapy. In A. K. Hess, (Ed.) *Psychotherapy supervision: Theory, research and practice.* New York: J. Wiley & Sons.

Stanton, A., Sanchez, V. C., & Klesges, R. C. (1981). Supervision skills: Do A. P. A. approved clinical programs teach them? Paper presented at American Psychological Association, Los Angeles, California.

Watson, K. (1973). Differential supervision. *Social Work, 18,* 80-88.

Worthington, E. L. (1984). Use of trait labels in counseling supervision by experienced and inexperienced supervisors. *Professional Psychology, 15,* 457-461.

Yogev, S. (1982). An eclectic model of supervision: A developmental sequence for beginning psychotherapy students. *Professional Psychology, 13,* 236-243.

5

The ABCX Model—
Implications for Supervision

Daniel Sharon

ABSTRACT. Both supervision and direct practice decision making processes are influenced by various elements which sometimes have an unpredictable effect. The purpose of this paper is to group and conceptualize the major variables which determine the consequences of professional guidance provided by supervision. The four key concepts which emerge from this definition are: (1) Event; (2) Perception of the event; (3) Resources to meet the event; (4) Effective change.

Supervision of a therapist's process can be defined as the professional guide facilitating the practitioner's perception of a stress-causing event in the client's life in the most objective manner to enable the most appropriate mobilization of both therapist and client's resources with the aim of bringing about effective change.

Clearly, this is an "ideal" definition of a supervisory task. In daily practice, the ideal terms by which this definition is phrased are exposed to subjectiveness, instances of inappropriateness and situations where the change obtained is neither desirable nor effective.

HILL'S ABCX MODEL*

The ABCX crisis model developed by Reuben Hill (1949) actually deals with the decision making process which determines the han-

---

Daniel Sharon, Ph.D., is a faculty member at the School of Social Work, Tel Aviv University, Israel.

*Permission to utilize material from this Model has been granted by Hamilton McCubbin (December 1984).

69

dling of a given stress potential event, resulting in a certain magnitude of experienced crisis.

The ABCX model suggests the following formula (Hill, 1949):

> A (the event) → interacting with B (the family's crisis meeting resources) → interacting with C (the definition the family makes of the event) → produces X (the crisis).

Hills' ABCX model consists of four factors: (A) The stressor or the event. According to Hill this is the more objective aspect of the crisis process. This factor manifests the hardship presented by the event, and it lies outside the family. Thus, it is an attribute of the event itself. (B) The resources available to the family when meeting crisis. (C) The manner in which the family defines the event. This factor is clearly subjected to the family's perception of the event. According to Hill, the second and third factors "lie within the family itself and must be seen in terms of the family's structure and values." He also emphasizes the C Factor as probably the most influential in the process—"The key appears to be in the 'meaning' dimension. Stressor becomes crisis in line with the definition the family makes of the event." (X) Crisis is the result of the interacting variables A, B, and C which are seen together as the crisis proneness of the family.

Adapting Hill's Ideas to Therapy and Supervision

For the purpose of adapting Hill's ideas to therapy and supervision, the X factor (Crisis) in the ABCX formula should be replaced by the concept of Change or, for mental health practice purposes, with Anticipated Treatment Outcomes. Crisis is only one form of change. The ABC interacting variables could also produce other forms of change, including growth and progression. ABC are interacting variables, which may imply that their order does not matter. Yet, for the purpose of working with these variables in supervision and therapy, the perception of the event should be discussed before an appraisal of the resources available to deal with the event is made. A logical decision making process requires that one assess the perception of the event before a mobilization of adequate resources can be implemented. By the nature of ABCX variables' interaction, the way a person perceives the availability of resources might well effect the meaning the event has for him. In other words, it would affect the extent to which he would regard the event as involving an actual threat. For example, take two families of a village struck by a tornado: the hardship attributed to the event itself (A), namely: the potential damage which could be caused by a tornado should be taken as given. The event lies outside the family and can be regarded as a constant for each tornado storm. The differences in B's (family crisis meeting resources) and C's (the definition the family makes out of the event) among two families being exposed to the same A (event) creates differences in crisis proneness—thus producing differences in terms of CHANGE. In the first family, the wife took responsibility for collecting some vital family documents, including insurance papers, while her husband saw to it that the family got to the shelter right after the tornado watch had been declared. These were some of the family resources (B's) to meet the event (A). The storm was being perceived (C) as a horror against which one should take maximum precaution and protection. Once the storm was over, there was a short period of mourning over the house ruins and the wife encouraged her husband to contact their insurance agent without further delay. The family appeared to be actively involved in planning the construction of a new house and became very excited with the idea of building a new greenhouse. Once this was accomplished, the family experienced a flourishing change, and a family member might have even said that he or she was not too fond of the previous house anyway.

The second family's reaction to the event (A) was quite different. Once the tornado watch was declared, the wife perceived the storm as a potential loss of property, grabbed her jewelry and went to the shelter. The children followed her, despite not having been explicitly instructed to do so. Negotiation between the couple had not been conducted. The husband, who perceived the tornado as an act of majestic vigourness, chose accordingly his Nikon F camera as the best (perceived) resource and went out to the field to photograph it. When the storm was over, his dead body was found in the village still grasping his Nikon F tightly. In it were the most spectacular pictures of the tornado's funnel. His wife and children faced a terrible crisis, blaming themselves for not seeing to it that the family would go to the shelter together.

The two cases demonstrate several very different possible processes which, due to different B's and C's, would lead in one case to crisis while in another—to effective change.

A	B	C	X
Family I.			
tornado touchdown	family organization; shelter; insurance policy	mortal threat to the family	damage to property.
Family II.			
tornado touchdown	individual organization; mother & kids: shelter; father: Nikon F. Camera	mother & children: individual mortal threat; father: majestic vigour & beauty	damage to property; loss of father; bereavement

In a supervisory session, an appraisal of the event (A) is brought to the supervisor—supervisee process of mutual problem solving. Such a process involves four major tasks:

The A Factor

The selection of an event (A) to be discussed in the supervisory session could become a subject of conflict. Who chooses what event may be discussed during the session based on whose set of priorities take precedence. Once supervisor-supervisee's agreement is achieved regarding the event (A) to be discussed, the event should be regarded as a constant and given entity. Using Hill's terms, the focus should be the built-in, or inherent hardship of the event. Although in reality such ideal objectivity does not exist, in order to keep the A factor constant, the inherent hardship of the event should be regarded as lying outside the supervisor's, the practitioner's and the client's emotional subjectivity. Rather, it is viewed as an attribute of the event itself. In terms of psychological theory and practice, the event is viewed as the phenomenological scientific knowledge developed for understanding the phenomena captured by the event. For example, if a case of infidelity is brought before the practitioner, there is or there ought to be a body of scientific knowledge

which provides the practitioner with a certain "value free" understanding of the marital relationship phenomena named infidelity.
This generalized understanding constitutes an attempt to standardize
our knowledge of the event, and should be kept separate from the
emotional perception of the client, the practitioner and the supervisor regarding the event's meaning or the resources they would use
to cope with it. In other words, initiating the interventional decision
making process with the phenomenological aspects of the event,
rather than with the personal perceptual ones, is what makes the
profession of mental health scientific.

The model presented here suggests that the supervisor's ability to
lead his supervisee to understand the phenomenologically inherent
hardship, which lies beyond the immediate personal and emotional
perceptions, enables a more objective problem solving process. It is
noteworthy, however, that characterizing an approach as objective
does not mean that it is value free. Our underlying assumption is
merely that professional values should outweigh personal values.
The same applies to the therapist's parallel attempt to help his client
to gain objective vision. Such a vision would enable him to gain insight beyond his narcissistic perception of the event. The client
would thus be able to gain a more systematic, phenomenological,
generalized and holistic understanding of the event. This is what is
often referred to as the educational aspect of therapy.

The B Factor

Hill's B factor refers to the resources available to the family. It
focuses on the family's ability to prevent an event from creating
some crisis or disruption in its social system (Burr, 1973). In implementing this model for supervision, the B factor could be regarded
as the helper-helpee resource network being utilized to prevent A
from becoming a crisis. In this context it refers to the resources
available for minimizing the disruption the event (A) might cause to
the client's system. Since, as noted earlier, the X factor-crisis could
be substituted for the overall concept of change, it follows that the
mobilization of the helper-helpee resources network should be
regarded as aimed at achieving the most fruitful change (X).

In human services we often face the problem of limited resources
available for problem solving (Bs' shortage). The proper utilization
of resources is a major concern of the helping professions, and is a

primary responsibility of the supervisor. The mental health problem solving process encompasses four sets of resources which have to be linked together:

(i) Client System Resources.

(ii) Practitioner System Resources.

(iii) Supervisor System Resources.

(iv) Mental Health Organization System Resources.

Frequently the practitioner and the supervisor both represent the same organization system. Yet, they might have different views as to when and how to use its resources. Often, tension occurs when the client is overdependent on the practitioner's resources and the practitioner attempts to make the client more aware of, and responsible for, using his own resources. The kind of resources to be used and the manner in which this occurs can become another area of helper-helpee conflict.

The B factor's implication for supervision is that the higher the extent of consensus among the four aforementioned components regarding the resources to be used for dealing with the event (A), the higher the efficacy of intervention and the feasibility of solving the problem.

The C Factor

The C factor refers to the manner in which the event is defined/perceived by the parties involved in the helper-helpee process: since several parties are involved in clinical practice, the situation calls for various perceptions or definitions of the event (A). In other words, the event (A) has different meanings for different participants in the process. At least three perceptions can be anticipated.

(i) The client's definition.

(ii) The practitioner's definition.

(iii) The supervisor's definition.

In additon, in couple or family therapy, several clients' perception of the event are involved. Indeed, sometimes the number of different perceptions of the event is equal to the number of family members. Different definitions of the event (A) held by those who are involved in the helper-helpee process would lead to incongruence and conflicting notions as to how to best go about dealing with the event (problem).

The implication of the C factor for supervision is that the higher the consensus among the client, the practitioner and the supervisor in defining the event, the easier it will be to proceed in selecting and using adequate resources to solve the problem and face the challenge presented by the event.

The X Factor

Hill's X factor (1948), the magnitude of "crisis" experienced by the family system, is the consequence of the ABC process. In conjunction with stress and crisis theory, it describes the level of disruption of the family's pre-crisis routines caused by the interaction of the stressor (A), the family's perception (C) of the event, and the resources being used by the family to cope with it (B).

Since disruption of certain routines can be viewed as behavioral change, it follows that crisis is merely another, yet massive, form of change. Therefore, for the purpose of applying the crisis ABCX model to the broader concept of human problem solving process, X should be redefined to mean change. However, not every ABC process ends with change. Experiencing the ABC process, while maintaining old behavioral patterns, points to a possible ABC outcome without change. Hence, for the purpose of mental health practice, the X factor should be redefined as the ABC process outcomes. Such an approach coincides with the adaptability dimension of stress theory (Olson, 1979), where the manner by which the family system reacts to change can follow two different patterns. These patterns were conceptualized by Maruyama (1963) as morphostasis and morphogenesis. System morphogenesis is a positive feedback that provides the family system with constructive system enhancing behavior, enabling the system to grow (change). Conversely, system morphostasis is negative feedback that attempts to maintain the status quo. As Haley noted (1959): "When an organism indicates a change in relation to another, the other will act upon the first so as to diminish and modify the change." Once X is broadened to include both morphogenesis and morphostasis, the term outcome should be adopted since it is more neutral than either crisis or change.

Deciding what should be the desired outcomes of an interventional process often includes, besides questions such as what and how to change, instances where the dilemma is how to merely maintain the situation. Thus, in supervisory terms, X is the pre and post intervention evaluation of treatment outcomes. It involves such questions as what are the most desirable outcomes and according to whose and what standards are these outcomes to be judged.

(Client's? Practitioner's? Supervisor's? Organization's? or the society at large?)

The model presented here suggests that the higher the consensus among the four active parties involved as to what should be the most desirable outcomes of the intervention process, (X), the higher will be the participants' collaboration towards achieving the agreed upon goals.

What stems from all the aforementioned proposed implications is that consensus among the participants, on each of the ABCX factors, might be achieved by negotiation. Negotiation aimed at achieving ABCX aggreement should be defined as the process of contract formation. All four are vital factors of a working contract. In the helper-helpee process, two interwoven contracts are actually negotiated, that of the supervisor-supervisee (therapist), and that of the therapist (supervisee)-client.

The following example is provided to demonstrate ABCX initial discrepancies in the supervisor-therapist-patient contract.

> A 15 year-old girl is brought to the attention of the protective services. Since the age of 13, she is known to have been absent from home off and on day and night. Various attempts to place her with foster families have failed, as she proved to be a chronic runaway. At the time the supervision session was held, the girl was in her fifth week of pregnancy. The session was held after she contacted a social work student regarding a possible abortion. The teen-ager's records gave testimony that this was to be her fourth abortion. When referred to the agency, the girl stated: "I have nothing to do with the man who did it to me. He put some dirt into my body and this filth is something I want to get rid of as quickly as possible." The girl seemed to discuss her previous relationship with the male who made her pregnant, as well as her previous pregnancies and abortions, as if she had no emotions regarding these events. She threatened that since she had no funds and did not wish her boyfriend's "stinking money", the social agency should arrange for her to have the cash required for a "clean and neat abortion", otherwise "she knows her ways". A neighbor of her's, known by the nickname "Flora with the knitting needles", would do it for her. The social work student was shocked by the idea, and attempted to explain that a home abortion done "by a butcher" could cause severe medical

problems and even death, as well as problems of infertility. In response to the second part of the social work student's comment, the girl uttered that for her becoming infertile is rather a virtue. The trainee then reemphasised the danger of death and suggested that the girl go to her own gynecologist whom she trusts and whose services she previously used for the same purpose. She also suggested she negotiate with the man who caused the pregnancy and who appeared to have the means for paying for a private practitioner. The student anticipated that once her client accepted her approach to the event, abortion would be administered by a professional under the most hygienic conditions, enabling her to do likewise with respect to future pregnancies and to demand that the girl's boyfriends assume some responsibilities. The girl liked the idea of using the social worker's own gynecologist. As to payment, however, she refused to either give her boyfriend's name or to contact him herself. She preferred to receive the funds from the agency while still using a private practitioner. The anticipated outcomes of such use of resources seemed ideal to the girl. She would "get rid of the filth inside her body". Also, she would demonstrate to her male, as she had done on all previous similar occasions, that she did not need his favours in order to survive and that he had no say when it came to parenthood. Finally she would receive the money from the agency, and would later be healthy enough to give birth to a child of a man who would really deserve it.

The trainee said that the girl's priorities created a problem, and that she would have to bring the matter before her supervisor. The supervisor appeared to be extremely upset with the student's stance and with the way she dealt with the event. She suggested that the student might first get a better understanding of the general phenomena of repeated pregnancies out of wedlock and the relationships with the men involved by reading Leontine Young's book *Out of Wedlock*. The supervisor stressed the distortions involved in the girl's perception of her body and her interpersonal relationships. She further stated that the agency could help the girl with the abortion process but insisted that she would have to appear before a hospital abortion committee which would approve the abortion and would see to it that she would get an IUD. The supervisor also suggested that ongoing therapy would be conducted, focusing on the girl's self-image and social relationships. The supervisor anticipated desirable interventional outcomes in terms of improving the patient's self image, body perception and interpersonal skills, and preventing the reoccurrence of unwanted pregnancies and abortions.

A *event's inherent hardship*	B *resources*	C *definition*	X *anticipated outcomes*
15 year old girl's fourth pregnancy out of wedlock			
	Client		
	agency money for private abortion	dirt to get rid of	infection; danger to life; infertility
	Student Therapist		
	man's money; Student's own gynecologist	man's responsibility; medical risk.	man assuming responsibility; safe abortion
	Supervisor		
	hospital abortion; continuous therapy; contraception.	girl's wrong perception of body, of relationship and self-control.	girl gaining a new understanding of interpersonal relations and responsibility.

ABCX Discrepancies

The above example demonstrates that the inherent hardship of the event (A), is processed to have an entirely different meaning for each of the three problem solving participants. The client perceives her pregnancy as a reminder to her distressing relationship with a man who is not different from the men she knew before. She relates to the physiological aspect of pregnancy as having to bear inside her "belly" the "dirty, sticky sperms of the one she thought to be her boyfriend." Utilization of resources is assumed accordingly. "His dirt clinging inside her body has to be uprooted" by Flora the "Knitting Needles Woman" who seems to be the proper resource— "She would quickly kill this little Ezer (the Man's name) inside me—that's what he deserves." The girl also perceives that denying her boyfriend the role of a possible resource (and father) is the best way to have revenge on him.

For the student therapist (who herself had had an abortion quite recently), the major desired outcome (X) is to prevent any medical complication. Abortion should be performed in private, hygienic conditions. Thus, the therapist's repertoire of resources (B) consists of her own trustworthy gynecologist. This is fine except that in her perception (C) the therapist denies the psycho-social meaning of the girl's pregnancy. There was only one area of resources (B) on which a consensus between the therapist and the client emerged. The agency would provide the financial support to have the abortion carried out.

For the supervisor, who did not doubt the girl's needs and right to get an abortion, the latter's pregnancy (A) had a much broader meaning. The girl's repetitious pattern of getting involved with men, becoming pregnant and not demanding any responsibility from these men suggested problems on a larger scale. The supervisor, familiar with the literature on the inherent hardship of the event, i.e., with A as a phenomenon, perceives: (1) a distorted female sexual image, (2) distorted interpersonal relationships, (3) masochistic tendencies, which include the need to be punished, (4) high dependency needs, (5) ignorance in the realm of sexual and family life education, (6) fatalism and inability to assume responsibility and control. Taken together these elements are seen as leading to a vicious circle or compulsive repetition. If the only resources to meet the event are those relevant to the termination of pregnancy, more of the same would be likely to happen in the future. Thus the supervisor's resources were much broader and implied a program consisting of a number of steps. The girl would have to appear before a committee which in turn would make her aware of the consequences of her repetitious pattern; the therapist would support her and would accompany her to her appearance before the committee; the therapist would further enhance such support by continuous therapy, thus broadening the girl's perception of what was happening to her life in total. The girl would also be provided with contraceptives, and the social worker would use her immediate support to establish further therapeutic relationships.

In terms of the ABC process outcomes (X), the girl saw her ability to get rid of the pregnancy (dirt) as the end product. By that, "she would erase the bad memories" of her boy friend. Through her particular C's and B's the girl was incapable of anticipating medical complications, even death, as Xs. She certainly could not anticipate the repetition of her destructive behavior. The therapist anticipated X as the girl recovering from the abortion and regaining her dignity. The latter is thought to be achieved by having the abortion done in a clean, professional and luxurious clinic. Due to her C's and B's of the event the student therapist is at this stage incapable of anticipating the reinforcement of the girl's psychosocial deficiencies.

Interacting variables and continuity of ABCX

Thus far the model has been presented as if A,B,C, and X are mutually exclusive variables. Indeed, the four factors interact and are largely interdependent. Such interdependence is the consequence of two processes: the interaction process and the process of the continuity of change. Hill's ABCX Model defines C as the definition one (in his example, the family) makes out of the event (A). Although not explicitly categorized as such, this pattern of interaction could be framed as C'A or the C of the A. From the two examples given thus far to demonstrate the ABCX processes, the multifaceted impact of the C factor on the determination of X seems to be quite clear. As noted earlier, factor B in Hill's model is defined as the crisis meeting resources. It refers to the resouces available to the family for the purpose of coping with what is presented by the inherent hardship of the event (A) and its external meaning to those exposed to it (C). In the context of the possible interaction between the ABCX factors, it is not entirely clear whether when using the term "Crisis Meeting Resources" Hills refers to C of X, or to C of A. The change continuation approach (pile-up) as offered by Mc-Cubbin and Patterson (1981) points out that by continuing the process one actually deals with two sets of resources: first, those dealing with the original stressor (A), and second, those dealing with the magnitude of experienced crisis (X). The latter thereby becomes a new event (A) not entirely separate from the original one, yet piled up upon the first "a". McCubbin and Patterson called this the aA Factor. The small "a" represents the stressor or the original hazardous event with its inherent hardship, whereas capital "A" represents the magnitude of Crisis (X) which becomes a pile up of stress to form a new A. Following the same rationale, continuation of resource mobilization is conceptualized as bB or existing and new resources. The cC in the McCubbin and Patterson Double ABCX Model Figure 1 represents a continuous definitional process, i.e., the manner in which one defines the original stressor combined and interwoven with the perception of the resulting crisis X which, in turn, constitutes a new A. Similar to Hill's model, the McCubbin and Patterson Double ABCX Model places great emphasis on the power of the C factor. In the Double ABCX Model, the perception factor (C) relates to the perception of the crisis (X) as the new emerging event A piled up on the initial event "a". Thus, in terms of the continuity of change, the perception or redefinition of the event further develops to become the cC of the aA. And, there is an addition element of continuity in terms of the perception of pre-crisis and post crisis resources (the cC of the bB).

In the Double ABCX Model, the pre-crisis phase includes interactional arrows between the pre-crisis "a", "b", and "c". Yet the multiperception component of all ABCX variables is only visible in the post crisis phase.

For the purpose of implementing both the Hill and the McCubbin and Patterson models to processes of intervention and supervision, the abc pre-crisis variables should be interwoven in the same manner. At the initial stage, when the stressor or the event (A) is presented to the individual or the family, a perception of this event is formed (C of A). This was explicitly stated in Hill's primary model. Two additional pre-crisis interactions should be added to Hill's model, the second of which constitutes an addition to the McCubbin and Patterson model as well.

1. C of B. Once individual definition/perception (c) of the hazardous event (a) is added to the event's inherent hardship, another perceptual process might well take place. The individual or the family exposed to the stressor may attempt to estimate the resources they have and/or may be able to mobilize in order to cope with the perceived stressor. If such estimate of available or feasible resources was entirely objective, "b" could have been regarded as given. But "b", like "a", is an objective/subjective process largely dependent on one's perception of the availability and feasibility of

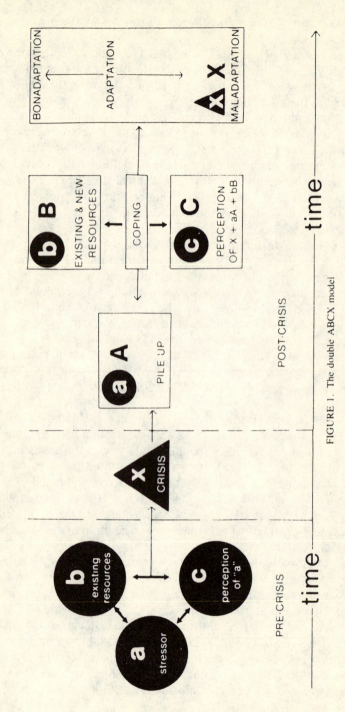

FIGURE 1. The double ABCX model

82

resources. For example, due to panic or other reasons, an individual might believe there are no resources available to him, while actually resources do exist within his reach. On the other hand, an individual might assess that resources are either accessible or can be mobilized, while in reality the opposite is the case. This process could be conceptualized as the C of the B's or the manner in which one defines the resource network available to meet the new demands presented by the event (A). One kind of misconception of the B's might occur as a result of an individual's misconception of the nature of the event or from underestimation or overestimation of the inherent hardship of the event, i.e., an erroneous C of A. When this occurs, the individual might be able to mobilize certain resources, but due to the incorrect perception of the inherent hardship of the event, these resources would prove to be inadequate. Alternatively, due to an overestimation of the inherent hardship of the event, the individual may assume that adequate resources are not available. An individual may also have an unrealistic perception of his ability to cope with the event. Under such circumstances, the individual should be made aware of his coping mechanisms—namely the resources available to him within himself.

2. *C of X.* Once the individual faces the hazardous event (A), defines the meaning the event has for him and defines the resources available to cope with the hardship entailed, he will either attempt or avoid attempting to define where the situation leads. Although the experienced magnitude of crisis (X) is often beyond human control, a certain locus of control is attributed to the process. This is due to the anticipatory factor or the human ability to anticipate certain outcomes. Terms such as "self fulfilling prophecy", and "repetition compulsion principle" are well known both in the psychodynamic literature and in daily practice, and suggest the impact of the anticipatory factor on human behavior. The individuals' ability or inability to foretell or imagine the scenario of the stress-crisis end product, could be conceptualized as the C of X.

INTERACTIONAL AND CHANGE CONTINUITY OF ABCX PROCESSES— IMPLICATIONS FOR SUPERVISION

The influence of perception (factor C) on all other ABCX factors and the continuity of change could be applied to supervision in the following manner;

I. abcx Phase

Factor "a"

(1) Event a is brought to the attention of the therapist. (2) The therapist brings it to the attention of the supervisor. (3) The supervisor discusses the phenomenological inherent hardship of the event with the therapist. (4) The supervisor may refer the therapist to the relevant literature. (5) This phenomenological understanding is being modified in order to provide the client with relevant information; the information provided is adjusted to the client's level of understanding.

Factor "c" of "a"

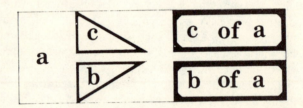

(1) The Supervisor assesses the client's and therapist's definition of the event "a". (2) The supervisor assesses perceptual gaps between the meaning the event has for the client and the therapist. (3) The supervisor discusses the meaning the event has for him/herself. (4) The supervisor negotiates perceptual changes: (i) changes which would enable the therapist to get a better understanding of his client (diagnosis) entail the supervisors' direct-intervention. (ii) Changes which would enable the client to get a better understanding regarding the nature of the problem (insight) entail the supervisor's indirect intervention.

Factor "b" of "a"

"b" is the actual implementation of the map of resources available to meet the event "a" towards achievement of "x", as being contracted through "c of b" procedures. The supervisor sees to it that implementation follows the lines of the "cb" contract.

Factor "c" of "b"

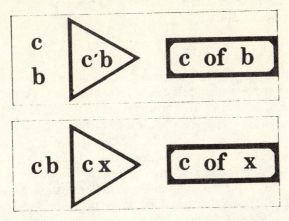

(1) The supervisor assesses the client's and therapist's perception of the feasible and available resources as well as her own perception of the distribution of resources and responsibilities. (2) The supervisor assesses gaps between the therapist's and the client's perceptions of b's. This is assessed in terms of: (a) whose resources could be utilized (the client's, the therapist's, the organization's). The supervisor negotiates directly with the supervisee and indirectly with the client, their resource network map as well as their perception of the distribution of responsibilities; (b) the manner by which resources are to be utilized, in terms of timing, techniques, and setting; (c) The supervisor also discusses his own "c of the b's", and re-assesses all parties' "c's of the b's" in terms of resource adequacy.

The concept of resources as presented here refers to therapeutic practice in the global sense. These resources include the client's strength, the family's support, its financial conditions, and its coping learned-behaviors. The therapist's resources relate to his/her skills, the intervention techniques used, the resources utilized in the therapeutic community, and the supervision available. Supervisory resources refer to the supervisor's knowledge and skills, as well as to his/her administrative standing and status within the organization. Using Kadushin's (1976, pp. 94-111) definition and conceptualization, the supervisor's resources include his/her reward power, legitimate or positional power, coercive power, referent power, and expert power. (d) The actual formation of a contract regarding the resource utilization process, based on a, b, and c criteria. This refers to two parallel contracts: Supervisor-Supervisee and Supervisee (Therapist)-Client.

Factor "c" of the "x"

The supervisor assesses the therapist's and the client's anticipatory factor, namely their perception as to: what will be the event's outcome (passive approach), the preferred end-result of the process; or, in other words, the goals towards which they prefer to invest their effort (active approach). In the therapist's terminology the weighted assessment of those two factors is defined as prognosis. Indeed the "c" of possible x's is arrived at in the following two ways: the first relates to the more intuitive and rather impulsive reaction to the event ("a"), or the interactions between "c of a" and "c of b" before knowledge of the resources unknown to the therapist and the client were brought to their attention/perception by the supervisor. The second relates to the planned and structured assessment of desired intervention outcomes, based on the supervisor's and the therapist's reassessment of the resource network brought to the attention of the therapist and the client.

The supervisor assesses gaps in "c's of the x's" between the client and the therapist and introduces his/her own perception of desired intervention outcomes. The supervisor then negotiates with the therapist the contract best suited to achieve the interventional common goal most likely to be agreed upon by the parties involved.

Once goals "c of the x" are specified and agreed upon by the supervisor and the supervisee (therapist), the latter would negotiate the c'x contract with his client, with the aim of achieving the contract closest to his supervisor's and his own perception of the most desired outcomes. In order to achieve the nearest "cx" consensus, at this stage of the abcx contracting, the therapist would most likely have to negotiate back and forth between the client and the supervisor. This places the therapist in a middle management position. Depending on the level of autonomy he/she enjoys, as well as on the organization's policy, the supervisor in a large organization may find himself in a similar situation. The supervisor has to maneuver between the practitioner's demands and the organization's limited resources ("b") and its policy "c" (i.e., the organization's macroperception). Such back and forth mental health system negotiation leads to modifications of the initial contract. Thus, both the b's and the "c's of the x" are modified until working relations and the contract achieved enable the formation of CHANGE or "x".

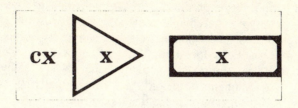

The "x" Factor

Unlike "c of x", x is the actual change produced by the factors, a,b,c'a,c'b and c'x interactions. This is the first set of actual outcomes produced by the therapist's primary supervised intervention. The outcome was forged based on the participants' closest congruence with respect to their perception of the problem/s or event/s which were dealt with in therapy ("c of a"), their perception of the resources (means of intervention to be utilized for inducing change in the problematic situation, i.e., "c of b's"), and their perception of the nature of the change desired, ("c of x"). The initial abcx process variables could then be used for assessing the outcomes, or the change induced in the client's original acute condition which led him to seek therapy.

II. The aA bB cC xX Phase

The "aA" Factor

"aA" is the new conceptualization of "x". Evaluation of treatment outcomes is a crucial issue in mental health practice. The accurate understanding of the nature of change obtained ("x") facilitates the individual's perception and understanding of events. The ability to anticipate change is based on a proper assessment of the stressor event ("c of a") and on adequate resource utilization ("c of b"). Thus, the evaluation of the outcome of the total abc process ("aA") is vital for an adaptive continuation of change.

This requires the following tasks: (1) The supervisor via the practitioner and via the client, would evaluate and compare the "x" factor, or the actual change obtained through the initial c'a, c'b, and c'x interactional process, considering the original event with its inherent hardship (''a''). This new assessment of change can be defined as the event's pile up, i.e., the original event ''a'' interacting with ''b'' and ''c''—produces ''x'', which then becomes a new ''A'' by its own inherent phenomenological hardship. However, since present and future human behavior cannot be exclusively detached from past behavior, in the ''pile up'' concept (McCubbin and Patterson, 1981), the new A actually contains new elements, yet emerges on components of the old ''a''. Conceptually ''x'' becomes ''aA''. (2) The supervisor helps the supervisee to evaluate the new emerging ''aA'' situation, and to differentiate qualities and behaviors which belong to the new A from those belonging to the old ''a''. The therapist would then follow the same procedure with his client. Such evaluation is necessary to ascertain actual interventional outcomes and to assess change. As far as possible, such change is assessed using objective attributes, which are preferably quantitative and measurable. For example, if a couple reports that since intervention began the number of outbursts and quarrels have been reduced from almost every night to around twice a week, this provides a quantitative criteria with which the change induced can be assessed. (3) The supervisor then helps the supervisee directly, and the client indirectly, to receive information on the phenomenological hardship inherent in the new emerging ''aA''. Once again, such information is taken from the more objective professional knowledge available regarding the general attributes of the event itself, and not on individual or family attributes which lie outside the event. For example, in educating the supervisee and/or the client regarding phenomena of human bereavement by pointing out the common transformation from the stage of denial to the stage of anger and self blame, the supervisor makes them aware of the attributes of the new event. Being overwhelmed with feelings of anger and guilt should then be viewed as a new ''aA'' with its own phenomenological inherent-hardship. Once the old-new emerging event ''aA'' had been identified and evaluated as a continuity of change process it becomes further exposed to ABCX interactional processes.

The ''cCaA'' Factor

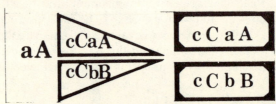

(1) the supervisor assesses the therapist's perception of "aA" or the meaning of the change from "a" to "aA" as defined by the therapist. (2) The supervisor contributes his own perception of the change from "a" to "aA". (3) The supervisor negotiates with his supervisee discrepancies in their perception of the change from "a" to "aA" (Intervention Outcomes). (4) The supervisor attempts to bridge such gaps and to obtain a consensus of perceptions regarding "a-aA" piling up changes. (Such a consensus would constitute an agreement on dynamic diagnosis). (5) The therapist assesses the client's perception of "aA" in terms of how the client perceives the change obtained from "a" to "aA". (6) The therapist then informs the client regarding his own perception of the piling up changes from "a" to "aA". (7) The therapist assesses and discusses with the client discrepancies in their perception of the pile up changes from "a" a "aA". (8) The therapist attempts to bridge such gaps and to obtain a consensus. Thus, an attempt is made to reach a mutual understanding of what has changed (been achieved) from "a" to "aA". For all parties involved, (the supervisor, the therapist and the client) this "aA" point in the process of aAbBc-CxX continuous change is where a check should be made as to whether the change achieved ("aA") fulfils the anticipatory factor—namely the Prognosis "cX" in the abcx initial phase. Such evaluation of outcomes serves, for all the parties involved, two functions: (i) An assessment of what has been accomplished and what should still be achieved (continuous cCxX). (ii) A tool for developing the locus of control skill by gaining more accurate anticipatory power over stressor.

The cCbB Factor

This factor follows almost the same procedures which were applied for the "c of b" factor in the abcx phase. However, "c of b" is expanded to "cC of bB" where "cC" refers to the multiple past and present perception, and "bB" refers to the resources already used in the abcx phase, plus the negotiation of the availability of old and new resources to be used and re-used in the aAbBcCxX continuity of change process and the distribution of responsibilities for using these resources. The major cCbB additional supervision tasks are: (1) The supervisor provides the therapist with the means of (i) assessing and differentiating continuous use of the resources ("b") which were used in the abcx phase and are still adequate for further use in the current aAbBcCxX phase. (ii) Assessing new B's e.g., therapeutical techniques adequate for the aAbBcCxX phase. (2) The supervisor informs the supervisee of methods for conducting the same differentiation with the client, regarding the latter's own resources. (3) The supervisor provides the supervisee with the means of negotiating with the client a continuous improvement of the manner by which existing resources are utilized. For example, the therapist might assess, together with his client, the coping behavior (''b's'') mobilized and utilized by the latter through the abcx phase, and reevaluate how the client might make a better use of his acquired skills in the current aAbBcCxX phase, thus transforming b's into bB's. (4) The supervisor helps both the therapist (directly) and the client (indirectly) to differentiate the availability and feasibility of resources and the distribution of responsibilities between the abcx phase and the aAbBcCxX phase. For example, if in the abcx phase the supervisor modeled for his/her supervisee a case conference with another professional regarding his/her client, now, in the aAbBcCxX phase, the supervisor can demand that the therapist be less dependent on her in the manner by which the theapist leads such a conference. Or, the therapist may ask his client to be more active in a family therapy session by addressing herself directly to her mother, and not ask the therapist to do it for her as she had done in the initial abcx phase.

The ''cCxX'' Factor

The cC of xX factor is the multiple perception of aAbBcCxX phase anticipated outcomes. With this anticipatory factor, the supervisor and the therapist are required to follow the same procedures applied in the original abcx phase (see ''c of x'' factor). However, anticipation of second phase outcomes, or ''C of X'', is believed to be affected by the manner in which the previous x was accurately or inaccurately perceived. Thus, one's confidence on his ability to anticipate outcomes, based on his previous experience in this realm, will affect his expectations regarding new outcomes. The new CX will thus aggregate with the old cx, piled up to form the cCxX. The procedure is required: (1) The supervisor assesses the supervisee's future goals, based on the latter's perception of future changes (prognosis) and on the manner in which he would like to go about producing future change. (2) The supervisor attempts to reveal obstacles in the anticipation of future changes, which stem from the interlocking of ''c of x'' in the abcx phase. Such interlocking might have been reinforced by actual negative outcomes which were piled up to form an aA negative experience. (3) Such progress inhibitors could be overcome by two ABCX techniques applied in supervision: (i) The supervisor can help his supervisee to assess changes on a continuous basis, beginning with "a" in the original abcx phase, through x in the same phase, and onto the piling up of change "aA" in the aAbBcCxX phase. This technique was already mentioned in the discussion of the "cCaA" factor.

This was defined earlier as dynamic diagnosis. Likewise, it should be reemphasized that McCubbin and Patterson's cC multiple perception factor in the Double ABCX Model, consists of the perception of $x + aA + bB$ (see Figure 1). This is also where the concept of "coping" comes into the picture. Given that "aA", "bB" and "cC" interact with each other, the original "x" could be viewed as a pile-up event ("aA) only by involving the multiple perception. Since cC consists of a multiple perception of $x + aA + bB$, the second supervision task, after changes from "a" on to "x" onto "aA" were assessed, is: (ii) the supervisor helps his supervisee to differentiate between the resources acquired in the initial abcx phase (b's), which led to one set of "c of x", and existing and new resources "bB", which ought to lead to a different anticipatory element, namely "cCxX". The above technique also holds for what the supervisee/therapist should do with his client. For both therapist and client, the technique is aimed at bridging the gap between desired change (where they wish to go) and anticipated change (where they think they can go). When this is achieved, both the supervisor and the therapist could contract the client intervention goals ("cC of xX"), based on a dynamic assessment of change and resource continuity (cC of $a + x + aA + bB$).

For implementing the McCubbin and Patterson (1981) Double ABCX model in supervision and therapy, the concept of coping should be replaced by the concept of "Case Management". For our purposes, coping is simply one form of case management. In the aAbBcCxX ABCX Model phase, coping or case management is a function of the interaction between aA, bB and cC of $x + aA + bB + xX$. Case management is thus dependent on an agreement between the participants on: cCaA an assessment of the nature of continuous change—dynamic diagnosis, cCbB an assessment of the resources network and the manner of which it is utilized, cCxX an assessment of intervention objectives.

Together, these elements of case management lead to "xX". It should be noted that there are some differences between the supervision model as presented here and the way the model was originally conceptualized by both Hill (1949) and McCubbin and Patterson (1981).

Since the ''x'' factor was broader and generalized by substituting ''crisis'' with ''change'' or ''intervention outcomes'', ''c of x'' was defined as the ability of an individual to anticipate the nature of the change to be caused by his encounter with the event (stressor) ''a''. The event itself (''a''), with its inherent hardship, introduces a change in daily routine, one that the individual must cope with. Therefore, the ''c of x'' is the ability to imagine how the changing situation would affect future changes. This further emphasizes the concept of the continuity of change. In our application of the original abcx model, ''c of x'' refers to pre-outcome anticipations. However, in the McCubbin and Patterson expansion to double ABCX, the perception of ''x'' takes place only after x has already occurred. A composite perception of both the actual ''x'' and the additional piling up stressors/events, then takes place.

By defining the process as a continuity of change, the actual multiple perception ''cC'' of events is viewed as a continuous variable. It encompasses not only defining the changes from ''x'' to ''aA'', but also the retrospective assessment and perception of events, stressors, and changes beginning with the original stressor ''a'', through the outcome ''x'', piled up on the reformulation of ''aA''. This multiple event perception could be further supported by the ''reactivation'' theory, where a meaningful event is seldom perceived as an isolated incident. It often reactivates previous memories, emotions, and various coping behaviors tied to associated and related previous events. The three parties involved in the process should perceive change or assess the pile up ''aA'' on previous ''x'' and ''a'' situations.

The ''xX'' Factor

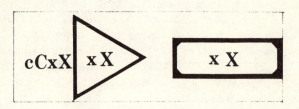

The xX factor is the piling up of the intervention process. It contains the actual outcomes of change produced continuously by both the abc and the aAbBcC phases.

The Double ABCX model (see Figure 1; McCubbin Patterson 1981) ends with the second post crisis phase, where xX stands for adaptation. Using this paradigm, it should be noted that two kinds of adaptation are possible: Maladaptation, i.e., a further crisis, or Bonadaptation, i.e., recovery and growth. This paradigm coincides with the manner in which ''x'' was perceived in the initial abcx phase, where the term ''crisis'' was replaced by the concept of ''change''. As we noted, crisis is only one form of change.

For further implementation of the Double ABCX model for supervision, the concept of adaptation should be broadened to the term treatment progress. Maladaption would suggest either lack of interventional progress or even a regression and deterioration of the client's situation.

According to the concept of change continuity, adaptive or maladaptive outcomes (xX), would continue to pile up to form a further assessment of treatment outcomes which can be symbolized by triple A's. (see the ''aA'' Factor). This is vital for planning and designing further required change. It will begin a new loop of triple event's perceptions, past and present perception and utilization of resources, and continuation of anticipated outcomes. Like continuity of change, supervision and therapy are continuous processes with the abcx factors interacting within the between phases. The decision making process in supervision and therapy based on ABCX conception flows in loops, where the abcx factors (variables) interact with one another within and between loops. Like a nuclear chain reaction it produces a continuity of change.

CONCLUSION

Supervision based on this model should yield a consensus among participants as to: (1) The event's definition. For the supervisor and the therapist, this means better diagnostic skills, and for the client it implies a better understanding of his existential being. (2) The selection of the most functional resources to bring about change. For the supervisor and the therapist this means interventional skills; for the client, it implies coping skills. (3) An accurate anticipation of outcomes. For the supervisor and the therapist this means prognostic skills; for the client, it means a sense of mastery and control. (4) Determination of desired outcomes. For the supervisor and the therapist, this means task oriented skills; for the client it means a purpose in life and a goal oriented approach. (5) Change-outcomes evaluation. For the supervisor and the therapist, this is what makes their practice scientific. It implies the production of practical knowledge (Praxis), testing it and retesting it against changing realities as well as refining and improving upon it on a continuous basis. For the client the term implies gaining further insight, namely an ability to learn from past experience and to apply it accordingly on future events. All five elements coincide with Binet's (1967) definition of intelligence, which refers to goal orientation, resource adequacy and outcome evaluation: "Intelligence is the characteristic of an individual's thought process that enables him to take and maintain a direction without becoming distracted, to adapt means to ends, and to criticize his own attempts at problem solution."

REFERENCES

Binet, A. (1967). Definition in E. Hilgard & R. Atkinson (Eds.), *Introduction to psychology*, (4th ed., p.425). New York: Harcourt, Brace and World.

Burr, W.F. (1973). *Theory construction and sociology of the family.* New York: John Wiley & Sons.

Haley, J. (1959). "The family and the schizophrenic: A model system", *Journal of Nervous Mental Disorders, 129*, 357-374.

Hill, R. (February-March 1958). "Generic features of families under stress", *Social Casework, 39*, 139-150.

Kadushin, A. (1976). *Supervision in social work.* New York: Columbia University Press.

McCubbin, I. & Patterson, J. (Spring/Summer 1983). "The family stress process: The double ABCX model of adjustment and adaptation", *Marriage and Family Review, 6*, 7-38.

Naruyama, N. (1963). "The second cybernetics. Deviation-amplifying, mutual causal process". *American Scientist, 51.*

Olson, H.O., Sprenkle, D. & Russell, S.C. (April 1979). "Circumplex model of marital and family system; I. cohesion and adaptability dimensions, family types, and clinical applications", *Family Process, 18*, (1), 3.

6

In Vivo Rotation:
An Alternative Model
for Psychotherapy Supervision

Stanley Brodsky
Harriet Hoehne Myers

ABSTRACT. Effective teaching of psychotherapy generally involves elements of didactic instruction, immediate supervision following trainee's therapy hours and some method by which trainees may observe and evaluate their own therapy behaviors. The *in vivo* rotation model of teaching psychotherapy includes these aspects, as well as the opportunity for the live observation of the supervisor and fellow trainees as therapists. Each therapy-supervision session includes a 45-minute individual therapy session with observers present, a 30-minute group discussion of the therapy with the client observing, and a 15-minute debriefing between therapist and client. Supervisor, trainee and client responses suggest that this model is an intense and productive learning experience.

Although most psychotherapy teaching is a combination of didactic instruction and one-to-one supervision, several alternative models have been developed. Thus Delk and Golden (1975) have described a *tandem psychotherapy* procedure, in which short-term clients are seen in tandem by student therapists. Two therapists are present at a time, and the client is rotated from one therapist to another, with particular attention directed toward providing continuity of treatment. Delk and Golden observe that without ''much delicate plan-

Stanley L. Brodsky, Ph.D., is Professor, Department of Psychology, The University of Alabama. Harriet Hoehne Myers, Ph.D., is Assistant Professor, Departments of Psychiatry and Behavior Sciences, College of Community Health Sciences, The University of Alabama.

The authors are grateful to Asa DeMatteo, Daniel W. McNeil and Harold W. Wolfe for their helpful comments and contributions to early drafts of this paper. Inquiries for reprints of this article should be directed to Stanley L. Brodsky, Department of Psychology, P. O. Box 2968, The University of Alabama, University, Alabama 35486.

ning, precision, and empathy", such rotation may mean that, "treating in tandem can easily become treating at random" (pp. 243-244).

Still another supervisory model has been called "through the looking glass" supervision. Gershenson and Cohen (1978) observed therapy trainees conducting family therapy through a one-way mirror. The effects of their classmates, supervisor, and teacher watching were initial stage fright, evaluation concerns, and a panicked learning situation. However as the therapy progressed, the trainees' anxieties diminished and positive experiences increased, until they concluded:

> We found live supervision to be effective, immediate, and powerful . . . We were supervised on the basis of our own work, rather than on our own subjective reconstruction of what had taken place in the treatment . . . Despite our initial discomfort with the method, live supervision eventually became a source of tremendous support and guidance. (p. 229)

When live supervision is employed, it typically takes place through one-way mirrors, although Lewin (1966) describes *in vivo* supervision. In his model, the supervisors would enter the therapy rooms 15 minutes after each session began, and occasionally would join in the session.

The development of the Interpersonal Process Recall (IPR) method and research into its effectiveness have been reviewed by Kagan (1981). This experiential process of learning therapeutic interactive skills involves a combination of supervisory techniques, including immediate videotape feedback and focused, collaborative review (with both patient and therapist) of the therapy tape by an observer. This method experientially assists therapists to *"learn to use the therapeutic relationship itself* as a case in point to help clients understand their usual interpersonal behavior and feelings and to learn to relate in new ways" (Kagan, 1981, p. 266). Studies of the IPR method indicate that both simulated experience in coping with difficult therapeutic encounters and the didactic presentation of a theoretical framework enhance the neophyte therapist's progress.

These various training and supervisory techniques generally provide a descriptive framework. However, they do not explain how trainees initially develop images of competent therapists against which their present efforts may be judged. The simplest answer may be direct observation of an experienced therapist at work. In contrast, most training models are organized around the concept of learning by doing rather than by observation. In fact, for fledgling therapists, in some programs and agencies, their wishes to "see" live therapy may be treated as illegitimate and voyeuristic.

The long tradition does exist of student therapists learning by observing movies, listening to audio-tapes, or reading therapy transcripts of experienced therapists. Most psychotherapy textbooks draw on illustrative case content in the discussion of therapeutic methods. However, all of these methods are one step removed from the immediate process of direct observation. Such distant learning devices probably do lead to cognitive acquisition of therapeutic techniques, but may not have the full impact of live psychotherapy. One close approximation has been the role-playing and simulation models summarized by Akamatsu (1981). He observed that the most effective role-playing takes place in realistic situations that closely simulate the actual therapy circumstances. Fleishman (1955), recognizing the needs of inexperienced therapists for component role models, utilized a direct observation procedure with similarities to our present one. The method involved the therapist-supervisor in action, with the students watching through a one way mirror.

If one accepts the premise of Cohen and Debetz (1977) that effective, responsive supervision necessarily includes open lines of communication between the members of the supervisory triangle (patient, therapist, supervisor), then at some point most of the previously described supervisory techniques fall short. For Cohen and Debetz the "goals, objectives and expectations of each of the participants in the supervisory triangle must be congruent." (p. 59). These specifications, taken seriously, demand a fairly radical departure from our usual psychotherapy supervision strategies.

THE IN VIVO ROTATION MODEL

We will describe here an *in vivo* model of psychotherapy that has been used for six years in a psychotherapy practicum. This model, utilized within a Ph.D. Clinical Psychology program, was developed from the perspective of the practicum supervisor (SB) and a former practicum trainee (HHM). It summarizes the experiences of approximately 20 practicum trainees during several semesters.

The model incorporates many of the positive aspects of more traditional models, as well as the immediacy of experienced therapist modeling and open communication within the supervisory triangle. This *in vivo* method combines observation, supervision, and practice of individual psychotherapy. The format involves the psychotherapy supervisor, three to four psychotherapy practicum trainees, and the individual client, in a 13-week treatment contract. The supervisor serves as the designated therapist for the first four to six weekly sessions, followed by each of the trainees in that role for several weeks. During the termination sessions, the supervisor again is the therapist. The format of each weekly session involves three phases. The session begins with 45 minutes of individual therapy with the other group members observing. The therapist of the day then joins the observers for a 30 minute discussion of the client's dynamics and the therapist's techniques; the client observes. Finally, the client and therapist spend 15 minutes dealing with the concerns and topics generated during the client's observation of the discussion.

There are no one-way mirrors, audio-visual machines, partitions, or screens in the therapy room. Only eight feet of air space separate the client and active therapist from the observers. The client and active therapist sit in reclining chairs at one end of the room while the nonparticipants huddle together in straightback chairs at the other end. There is no whispering among observers, and only an occasional flash of emotion betrays what is going on behind their professional detachment.

Provisions of the Treatment Contract

The contract with the client specifies that all supervision, all discussion, and all evaluation is to occur within the session; there is to be no trainee-trainee, trainee-supervisor, or therapist-client discussion at any time outside of the therapy room. Thus, *almost all of the group's clinical and personal opinions are accessible to the client.* Supervisees' comments are made in the presence of the client; the client's therapeutic discourse is made in their presence.

There is one other important aspect of the contract: *there is to be no cross-talk between the observers and the immediate participants.* The observers never interact directly with the client during a session and the client is never allowed to respond directly to or confront their observations. This contract, as it turns out, has powerful effects on the course of the therapy and on the functioning of the parties in it. The observer's role is rather like that of a movie critic. The observers passively experience the therapy, as a sort of *cinema verite,* and then comment on the strengths and weaknesses of the psychotherapy and on the client's dynamics. Their role is clearly evaluative and, as evaluative roles tend to be, is isolating on occasion; at the same time, however, there is a continuing and important personal investment from each about the client's welfare and the psychotherapeutic encounter. After all, each is to spend time with the client. Each is concerned that the proper groundwork be laid and that there be some continuity of approach. In good time, all are therapists; all are observers—not always and not only.

Disallowing cross-talk in effect disallows direct client feedback to the observers and vice versa, and requires that the therapist be the focus of the client's interactions. Although the final 15 minute debriefing period gives the client the opportunity to respond at least indirectly to comments of the observers, the response does not have the flow and continuity of face-to-face discourse. Generally, in the initial sessions of the therapeutic contact the observers seek to guide the sessions and the client with comments and critiques; in the end, the nature of the contract forces them to give up the attempt and settle for understanding the process of therapy. Just as the new client often moves from a cautious, evaluative mode to an understanding and trusting mode, so both trainees and the supervisor, when they are not serving as the active therapist, move from trying to guide the sessions to trying to understand and trust them. At last the roles of therapist, evaluator, and observer get sorted out.

Participants' Responses

Trainees generally see this rotating psychotherapist training model as an intense, compelling, novel microcosm—and a good training experience. Observing psychotherapy live without the interfering mediums of audiovisual recordings or one-way mirrors serves to demystify therapy while engendering a sense of respect for both clients and therapists.

Obviously, trainees experience anxiety prior to and during their turn as therapist. The awareness of being critically observed by a professor and colleagues is disquieting. The close physical proximity of the therapeutic encounter and the observers is a constant reminder that there is no hiding of slips of tongue or blatant errors under the guise of a malfunctioning tape recorder. While hesitancy to function as the designated therapist in such an exposing situation is great, each trainee has the model of the supervisor's willingness to practice in front of curious and sometimes critical others. Furthermore, the intensity of the setting seems to magnify each trainee's particular styles of interaction and therapy, making the process of examining and evaluating one's own therapeutic impact more immediately accessible.

The fact that a turn as therapist is anxiety-provoking might seem to indicate that leaving the participant role to take the more passive role of observer would be a welcome change. Not so! Indeed, participants often feel frustration and anger at having to relinquish the cherished therapist's chair. The "immediate past therapist" is observed at times to be angry at the "replacement" therapist. The departing therapist has a sense of loss, of competition, and of territoriality, which often generates excessively critical views of the performance of the therapist by whom he or she is followed. These feelings are handled in part in the discussion period of observers and designated therapist and this facilitates understanding and emotional mastery of the experience. This successful processing of loss, anger, and defensiveness of the rotating therapists serves as a mirror for the client who can then proceed to risk further processing his own feelings within the shelter of the therapy situation.

Client Feedback

Feedback from clients who have completed a semester of participation in this therapy confirms that the setting also intensifies for them the usual reactions to traditional individual therapy. They identify the anxiety of risking self-exposure to not just one, but several, people. The clients' mute presence at the supervisory groups' dissection of their therapy hours is invariably powerful for them. Just as these feelings are intensified by the setting, so is the speed with which the client gains the trust and courage necessary for increased introspection and changing interpersonal behavior. In part, it seems that the tension generated contributes to the acceleration of the therapeutic process. The accessibility of not just one, but several therapeutic styles and vocabularies may contribute, as well.

Most clients also remark on the usefulness of both same and opposite gender interactions. Initially, group observation inhibits frankly sexual or other intimate discussion. But, the experience with opposite sex therapists prompts the clients' examination of their stereotypic or seductive behavior styles and gender prejudices.

Each client must experience, in a sense, several commencements and terminations as the active therapy baton is passed between the participating trainees and teacher. Most clients view this as temporarily disconcerting but, in retrospect, they prize the unique experiences of each therapeutic relationship. This ability of the clients to experience these different alliances as useful appears to stem from their trust in the therapeutic skills of the supervisor. Clearly, for the client, the initiation and termination of the therapy is processed within the relationship with the supervisor. While the usual client concerns about abandonment by the therapist are seen, the continued presence of the supervisor in the group discussion provides stability. The supervisor is there in the beginning as therapist, is there in the middle as a concerned and involved observer, and is there at the end once again as therapist. Without question, the issue of desertion anxiety is heightened by this model. At the same time, the issue of desertion anxiety may have a much fuller resolution within this *in vivo* rotation model. The working through of the fear of being deserted is facilitated by the therapist not truly leaving, and by the opportunity for mastery of the desertion anxiety which is provided by the successive and predictable rotation plan.

Overall, the departing clients have experienced the therapy semester as stressful and useful. All express the belief that they have learned and grown. However, departing clients sometimes exaggerate therapeutic outcome as a way of demonstrating caring for their therapists and themselves. The supervisor and the students must always bear in mind that the power of the situation carries capacity for client overload as well as client growth.

Who Benefits From Participation in This Model?

Because the setting of this psychotherapy practicum is seen by trainees as more risky and more revealing than more traditional ones, they may arrive somewhat defensive and closed. Since the entire process lasts less than four months, a particularly self-conscious trainee mght spend the majority of time getting comfortable. Generally, those trainees who are able to immerse themselves into the process of the therapy and the supervision are those who have experienced fairly direct psychotherapy supervision previously—whether in the form of one-way mirrors, verbatim transcriptions, or audiotape processing.

Obviously, supervisors would not organize a psychotherapy practicum in this manner, were they not embracing interpersonal process as a theory and avenue of therapeutic change. Process-oriented supervisors will be most pleased with this model as a beneficial educational experience. Those supervisors who are adept at facilitating here-and-now processing of interaction will see the greatest acquisition of skill by the psychotherapy trainees.

There are several selection criteria for potential clients for the therapy semester. First, potential clients should be interviewed by a therapist uninvolved in the practicum for screening and orientation purposes. Clients should already possess sufficient coping strategies and an intact personality organization to tolerate the initial high anxiety generated by the setting and to assimilate the sometimes differing feedback from the several therapists. Fairly well-functioning, verbal clients who are experiencing some situational stress or who are seeking exploration and growth experiences are appropriate candidates. Also, care must be taken in the initial (screening) interview to clarify the practicum format with the prospective client. Since this is a somewhat unorthodox therapy mode, the client is usually offered referral into a more traditional individual or group therapy at the end of the semester.

CONCLUSIONS

The present model of *in vivo*, rotating therapy and supervision is not for everyone. Substantial risk-taking on the part of supervisor, supervisees, and client is required. After all, the sense of being on display and more visible than expected in such a personal enterprise can be disconcerting and harmful if careful client selection is not employed.

Nevertheless, the potential gains appear to be substantial. The supervisees show enthusiasm and sometimes light-speed improvement in therapeutic skills. The change process may be interpreted in two ways. Buss (1980) has observed that selective focusing of attention can improve both private and public self-awareness. Just as looking into a small hand mirror with instructions to meditate will promote private self-awareness, we suggest that the *in vivo* rotating supervision has a carry-over to other therapy situations in the form of increased private self-awareness. As Buss observes, "Private self-awareness furnishes a clearer picture of your present psychological status, and so you can offer a more detailed, truer picture of what you are at the moment . . . you will have clearer, true knowledge of your usual, typical behavior'' (p. 22). Therefore, increasing the frequency with which the state of private self-awareness occurs should enhance the supervisee's therapeutic use of self in treatment situations.

While longer term and less obvious benefits to the supervisees occur from increased ability to move into states of private self-awareness, the more immediate benefits accrue from enhanced *public* self-awareness. The close scrutiny and public inspection initially produce results not unlike those elicited by 3-way mirrors in clothing stores and watching oneself on closed circuit television. People feel exposed and vulnerable. Implicitly the initial reaction is that we must be doing something wrong; otherwise we would not be watched so closely. That underlying assumption is why careful scrutiny leads most of us to squirm and be uncomfortable. Thus a dual process theory of training is postulated. The initial effect on the therapist is an increase in public self-awareness, prompted by others watching the actual therapist behaviors. However, the public display is only to a few trusted others, each of whom has taken the same risks. The atmosphere is one of support, consideration, and commitment to self-improvement. Further, a desensitization to the public scrutiny effect takes place by the supervisor acting first as therapist and modeling therapeutic methods.

Thus, the second effect is a substantial diminution of public self-consciousness and an ability to generate private self-awareness. The discussions in the small group of what was felt and in what ways those feelings were handled are explicit methods that attend to internal events and private self-awareness.

The *in vivo* rotating supervision may also be discussed in terms of Kelly's (1955) personal construct theory. Hokanson (1983) has observed that one of the important tasks in therapy is to increase the number of personal constructs and perceptual categories clients use to view their worlds. We would posit that excellent therapists have a large number of constructs and perceptual structures they use to apply to therapy tasks. The opportunity to see others treating clients, treating those same clients oneself, and giving and receiving extensive feedback about the process fits closely with the Kelly personal constructs theory. Through this methodology trainees appear to increase the number of their therapeutic constructs, to be able to attend to a wider range of information, and to develop cognitive categories through which therapists' and clients' behaviors may be understood.

REFERENCES

Akamatsu, T. John (1981) The use of role-play and simulation techniques in the training of psychotherapy. In Allen K. Hess (Ed.) *Psychotherapy Supervision: Theory, Research and Practice.* New York: Wiley-Interscience.

Buss, Arnold H. (1980) *Self-Consciousness and Social Anxiety.* San Francisco: W.H. Freeman.

Cohen, Ronald J. and DeBetz, Barbara (1977) Responsive supervision of the psychiatric resident and the clinical psychology intern. *American Journal of Psychoanalysis, 37,* 51-64.

Delk, John L. and Golden, Kenneth M. (1975) Tandem psychotherapy: A model for rotating student therapists. *American Journal of Psychotherapy, 29,* 243-253.

Fleishman, O. (1955) A method of teaching psychotherapy: One-way-vision-room technique. *Bulletin of the Menninger Clinic, 19,* 160-170.

Gershenson, Judith and Cohen, Martin S. (1978) Through the looking glass: The experiences of two family therapy trainees with live supervision. *Family Process, 17,* 225-230.

Hokanson, Jack E. (1983) *Introduction to the Therapeutic Process.* Reading, MA: Addison-Wesley.

Kagan, Norman (1981) Influencing human interaction:—Eighteen years with IPR. In Allen K. Hess (Ed.) *Psychotherapy Supervision: Theory, Research and Practice.* New York: Wiley-Interscience.

Kelly, George A. (1955) *The Psychology of Personal Constructs* (Vols. 1 & 2). New York: Norton.

Lewin, K.K. (1966) Psychiatric supervision by direct observation. *Journal of Medical Education, 41,* 860-864.

7

Working in Teams:
The Pros and Cons

Brian W. Cade
Bebe Speed
Philippa Seligman

ABSTRACT. An interesting development over the last few years in the field of family therapy has been the proliferation of therapeutic teams in which three or four therapists regularly work together, often with the more difficult and disturbed individuals and families. One or two therapists work directly in the therapy room, the other members of the team observe and in a variety of ways intervene, usually from behind a one-way mirror. (However, see Olsen and Pegg, 1979; Smith and Kingston, 1980; and Kingston and Smith, 1983 for discussions of direct supervision and consultation without the use of one-way mirrors.) Advice or observer messages can be conveyed to the therapists either by telephone or by calling them out of the interview for a consultation session. The evolution of the uses of one-way mirrors has been traced by Cade and Cornwell (1983).

This chapter will concern itself specifically with peer consultation and will focus primarily on aspects of team formation and team functioning. Advantages and disadvantages of working in teams will be considered based on the experiences of the authors at the Family Institute, Cardiff.

SOME ADVANTAGES

Our development of a peer team approach evolved partly out of the use of live supervision and of one-way mirrors in our training programs. From these experiences we discovered the potential rich-

Brian W. Cade, B.A., C.S.W., is in private practice in Sydney, Australia. Bebe Speed, B.Sc., Dip Psych SW, C.Q.S.W., Dip Psychotherapy, and Philippa Seligman, C.Q.S.W., are on staff at The Family Institute, 105 Cathedral Road, Cardiff, Wales, United Kingdom. In 1969, The Family Institute was set up as the first British agency specifically with the aim of developing the practice, teaching and research of family therapy. It now functions as part of a national childrens' charity, Dr. Barnardo's.

ness of live consultation both as a way of increasing therapist maneuverability and of stimulating creativity. We differentiate between consultation and supervision, terms that are sometimes used as interchangeable in the literature. In the former, for the purposes of the consultation session, all involved are at the same hierarchical level and cooperation with a consultant's suggestions is by willing consent. Of course, it may be that one or more members may be seen as more experienced and/or their views informally and by consent accorded higher status, yet ultimately all members have an equal right to accept or reject ideas. Supervision usually takes place in a training context or in bureaucratically organized agencies. The supervisor or supervising team stands in a hierarchical relationship to the supervised and can, under certain circumstances, demand that something *must* be done, and will often carry ultimate clinical responsibility. (In some training programs, trainees are invited to bring cases from their employing agencies or private practices for a supervision group to work on. We would see this primarily as consultation offered as part of the program rather than as supervision.)

Hoffman (1981) likens the advent of the one-way mirror to the discovery of the telescope allowing for two different perspectives to be taken simultaneously, that of the participant in a process and that of an observer of and commentator on that process. She comments that "seeing differently made it possible to think differently" (p. 3). Hoffman invokes Bateson's discussions on the advantages of "double or multiple comparison" (1979, p. 87) from which new possibilities for discerning relationships and patterns can evolve. The various members of a team, although necessarily sharing certain basic assumptions, will also bring to bear a kaleidoscope of contrasting and overlapping perceptions and interpretations in regard to each case. From this potential richness can evolve perspectives and ideas for intervening that can reflect a depth of understanding not easily available to a single therapist. Each member may be able to punctuate family events in a different way leading potentially to a more systemic analysis, whereas a single therapist might more easily be "persuaded" into a particular perspective or punctuation and thus unwittingly to join in the family's "game without end". This can be particularly problematic with the more severely "dysfunctional" families. The complexities of and levels of affect in such families can quickly render a single therapist anxious, confused and hence increasingly impotent. A stance of relative detachment is more easily taken by the members of a team who can through discussion work together to avoid becoming unhelpfully over-involved with a family, or biased towards one or other family member or faction.

In addition to offering varied perspectives and greater levels of objectivity, working as a team can also lead to increased inventiveness and creativity. Ideas can be "thrown around", argued about, built on or modified; free associations and "out of the blue" ideas can be shared and utilized; seemingly irrelevant ideas can lead discussions into new and sometimes more productive directions; humour and seeming irreverence can also spark off new ideas. As Cade has observed, "Many of our more constructive and effective interventions have begun as jokes or 'silly' suggestions. It is as if the use of humour with its collisions of seemingly unrelated frameworks opens unconscious pathways in the brain allowing access to different perspectives, different associations, to lateral rather than linear patterns of thought" (1982, p. 39).

The support gained from the knowledge of the presence of a team can also lead to a greater adventurousness on the part of the therapist, a greater preparedness to take risks. Able more objectively to monitor the immediate effects of what the therapist is doing, the team is in the position to correct "errors" through intervening during the course of a session with suggestions, or through the transmission of messages or opinions, either via the therapist or sometimes directly by a team member entering the room (see Breunlin and Cade, 1981; Cade and Cornwell, 1985).

Regular observation and discussion of therapy can lead to a rapid expansion of ideas on the pragmatics of intervening and to the elaboration of theories of change and of new or expanded explanatory models and frameworks. It is perhaps no surprise that three of the most influential "schools" of family therapy in recent years, the strategic, the structural and the Milan approaches, have evolved substantially from teams working together regularly using the varied potentials of the one-way mirror.

TEAM FORMATION

It is important, particularly in its early stages, that members of a potential team share basic assumptions about problem formation and maintenance, and share congruent ideas about the nature of therapy. Although, as commented earlier, difference can lead to a greater depth of understanding and a great level of creativity, if differences are too fundamental they will tend to lead to a level of confusion and competition that can often hamper the process of therapy and the development of the team. Basic clashes can occur where, for example, one part of the team views a depressed woman's symptoms as tactics in a power struggle with her husband, while the other part of the team views it as the expression of an existential dilemma and the consequence of unresolved internal conflict. Later in a team's evolution, when basic premises have been agreed upon and have become established, when mutual respect and trust have developed, such differences in perspective can more easily be accommodated and thrown, as it were, into the melting pot. Differences become more disruptive where there are overt or, particularly, covert struggles over basic premises.

Not only are mutual respect and trust vital, but it is also important that team members' personalities fit well together in a way that allows differences in style and approach and occasional periods of conflict to be managed without serious interpersonal conflicts developing. For example, the authors, though previously knowing and respecting each others' work, needed to negotiate ways of tolerating differences such as the more serious, analytic, logical processes of one member versus the more intuitive, sometimes joking, irrational and seemingly irreverent approach of another. While the one would be sitting, carefully listening and making notes on a session, the other might be roaming around the observation room, making jokes and seemingly not paying attention nor showing any interest. At times it seemed that the more serious the one member became, the more frivolous the other became. Sometimes tempers would flare. Such differences in approach can only successfully be combined where each member's contributions, though sometimes irritating or maddening in the short term, are valued in the long term, and where the pleasures and benefits of working together outweigh the difficulties and struggles necessary to accommodate the ideas and approaches of others.

Problems can thus occur where team members, rather than choosing to work together out of mutual respect and shared interests, are expected or forced to work together by circumstances or because of agency policy. For example, when the authors of this chapter decided to work regularly together as a team, the other members of our small agency were left to work in relative isolation for a significant part of each week or to form, as they subsequently did, a second team.

Talking of her experience working in a district psychiatric centre, Palazzoli comments,

> teams working together in public agencies are formed by some external authority according to purely administrative criteria . . . the decisions about institutional assignments are taken by the higher echelons without the slightest consideration for the theoretical models adopted by the practitioners who must "co-operate" . . . a team which is prone to divisions and internal quarrelling is bound to suffer and cannot achieve its objectives (1983, p. 168)

In such settings, choices about who to work with can be minimal; team members may know little about each other's work or personalities and only subsequently find the team unworkable because of profound theoretical or personal disagreements.

Problems can arise in any team where members have or are perceived as having differing levels of experience and expertise. This can lead to the development of an informal hierarchy with "senior" members' ideas carrying greater weight to the extent that their word can become "law", and more "junior" members often deferring to and even becoming dependent upon them. Some teams can fail to progress beyond this point, particularly where a "senior" member is particularly forceful, has considerable "charisma" or is held in high esteem either inside and/or outside of the agency.

As the more "junior" members gain in experience and begin to seek or demand equal status, increasing levels of stress, competition, even rebellion can ensue. Factions can develop; the "junior" members can be seen as lacking in respect for or rejecting the ideas and experience of the "senior" members. Sometimes such differences can be resolved only by the team breaking up and perhaps forming two parallel teams (or by giving up the idea of working in teams).

When working through such issues it is important to face them as a whole team and to avoid the tendency towards covert meetings between members of a particular "faction" and the forming of coalitions against other team members. Such coalitions are not necessarily consciously formed. For example, two members can find

themselves increasingly though subtly rejecting, not taking seriously, or even deriding the ideas of another, yet claiming that all team
members' contributions carry equal weight.

Over the evolution of our team, some of the issues around which
such coalitions formed were as follows . . . the more experienced
"strategic" therapists against the less experienced; the "feeling"
therapists against the "tactical"; the serious and logical against the
"frivolous"; the theoretical thinkers against the intuitive; the
systemic thinkers (Milan approach) against the strategists. At times
such struggles became intense and threatened the stability of the
group. It is impossible to avoid coalitions, but vital, if a team is to
become and remain effective, to avoid their becoming permanent.
As with families, the covert and denied coalition will be potentially
the most destructive.

For our team, one difficulty arose out of an imbalance formed by
the different levels of contact between members outside of the formal team meetings. One member who subsequently dropped out of
the team (but stayed involved with our research project) spent one
day each week with us, being employed the rest of the time as a lecturer in a University social work department. The rest of us worked
together full time at the Family Institute. The inevitable increasing
imbalance in experience led to growing tensions and to an increasing
feeling of being "deskilled" on the part of the "outsider".

In such a situation those members who more frequently meet
together outside of formal team times can inadvertently exclude the
others by discussing cases or theoretical issues or by making decisions in their absence. The team can seem increasingly split into the
"real" team and the "visitors". Such problems can be alleviated
partially by restricting team business, as far as is possible, to when
all members are present, or, where necessary, contacting absent
members by telephone if emergency decisions have to be made.

Problems of status in a team can arise where the team's informal
status hierarchy conflicts with the formal agency status of team
members. In an earlier team at the Family Institute, set up to develop the use of strategic approaches in family therapy, the elected con-
venor of the team found himself in constant conflict with a team
member who was of higher rank in the agency's formal hierarchy
yet less skilled in strategic therapy. In such struggles it was not
always easy to unravel whether the agendas being pursued were
those of the team or those of the agency. Conflicts over the team's
basic theoretical or practical premises would become struggles

about who had the power to change agency procedures or overall policy, or what was the "right" image to be projected to the outside world.

Problems can also arise where different professional disciplines are represented in a team. For example, in the team an older male psychiatrist may be expected to accept the guidance of a younger female nurse or social worker who has considerably more experience as a family therapist, yet earns a fraction of his salary. It may take some time before the members of such a multi-disciplinary team can feel themselves as equal in status in respect to the team's functioning. This can be further complicated when other members of the agency or the wider community confer more power and authority onto one member by virtue of his or her higher professional status; for example, where a team member is also the consultant psychiatrist in charge of the agency. Such issues can be particularly difficult to resolve where it is claimed that all have equal status in the team yet a covert and often denied rule exists to the effect that "some are more equal than others".

It is difficult to say what the ideal size of a team should be. Generally, a team of two is likely to agree more quickly on basic premises and to establish functional procedures yet it may also tend towards over-accomodation such that difference and creativity is minimized. A team of three may be faced with the problems of triangulation and coalition, some examples of which have been elaborated upon earlier. A team of four may subdivide into two parts. Larger teams may tend towards chaos. How these potential difficulties are managed will, in part, depend on the personalities involved as well as on the various status and agency agendas that need to be resolved.

SOME ASPECTS OF TEAM FUNCTIONING

It can be particularly helpful for a new team clearly to articulate and elaborate some basic rules to facilitate its functioning and to minimize the potential disruption of issues and agendas such as those referred to earlier.

Basic to the success of a team will, of course, be the commitment of each member to attend regularly on the agreed upon day or days and for the agreed upon stretch of time. If a team member cannot give such a commitment or subsequently is found to be undependable, his or her membership in the team should be seriously questioned. Rules governing pre-interview discussions, consultation etiquette and post-session analysis should be discussed. Some issues needing consideration include: does the therapist have the final say where agreement cannot be reached? Is a telephoned message a suggestion or an instruction? What should the therapist do if he or she does not agree with a telephoned message? Is it best to carry on or come out immediately to seek clarification or to declare the disagreement? What is the optimal number of "interruptions"? Who in the observing group has the right to telephone through? Should one person be elected for each session and all ideas fed through that person? Under what circumstances can a team member make a spontaneous intervention without discussing it with the other members of the team, for example, if he or she thinks that to delay might mean the "right" moment will be lost?

Such apparently trite issues can often be highly symbolic and, if ground rules are not established, lead to considerable tension. For example, in our team, issues of dependence and independence became, at one point, extremely important as we struggled to move from operating relatively independently to operating as a unit. The tendency of a "senior" member (that is, one who saw himself, and to an extent was perceived by the others, as more experienced in the approach being used) to make unilateral decisions to telephone through, caused numerous heated arguments until a "rule" was agreed upon.

A major advantage for the therapist, particularly when struggling with a difficult family problem, is that the responsibility for coming up with ideas about how to proceed is a shared one. At times the therapist can concentrate totally on collecting information, joining with family members, or even on survival, in the knowledge that the team will be working on how best to understand and to intervene.

However, when a therapist comes out for a consultation, it is important that he or she have an immediate opportunity to express thoughts and feelings about the interview and the direction it is or should be taking (even if it is only to say "I'm lost" or "I have no idea what to do next".) Being immediately bombarded with ideas, however good they are, can lead rapidly to confusion, frustration, and a sense of being disqualified. The rest of the team will already have had time to discuss ideas and thus to devise potential interventions. The therapist will often need time to "disengage" mentally and emotionally from the family before feeling able to consider what the team has to offer. The advantages of multiple perspectives can become disadvantages if the therapist becomes swamped with ideas, particularly where these are conflicting ideas arising out of conflicting frameworks.

We realized in our team that it was thus important to set aside time for discussions and even fights over theoretical and practical issues. We found that, if this was not done, then such issues tended to be fought over in respect to particular families such that consultation sessions could become rather stormy and, at times, the therapy would be adversely affected.

Unresolved and covert team differences can, of course, leave a team more susceptible to becoming caught up in a disturbed family's "game without end". Team struggles can mirror struggles in the family. Team members can take sides, over-identifying with particular members or factions or with particular themes in the family. It can sometimes be difficult to disentangle whether family or team agendas are being pursued. At such times it becomes important to set aside time for working on the team's problems, if necessary by involving an outsider as a consultant to the entire team.

The authors were fortunate, during a period of some difficulty, to be offered a consultation by Luigi Boscolo and Gianfranco Cecchin of the Centro Milanese di Therapia della Famiglia. They pointed out that, in any team, there is a constant tension between the carrying out of the team's primary task, the *therapy,* and the needs of the members for support, validation, dependence and independence.

Where the emotional needs of the team members tend to take precedence over the primary task, the team becomes more like a family, existing primarily for itself and the needs of its members. When this occurs it becomes necessary for a team to re-articulate the reasons for its existence, to re-address itself to its primary goals. It was pointed out to us, by Boscolo and Cecchin, how we had become overly preoccupied with the team's relationships and its internal processes and had, to an extent, lost sight of the reasons we had originally joined together as a team. We had become a dysfunctional family rather than a therapeutic team.

A particular problem which our team experienced, particularly during its formative period, arose with the advent of visitors coming to view us at work. During such visits competitiveness between members of the team, or between the team and the visitors, could lead to considerable tensions arising. Visitors seen by us as of high status or as potentially critical could adversely affect our functioning. Sometimes we would try to be "on our best behaviour" and present a united front. We would deny or avoid dealing with differences in the presence of the visitors. Consequently, they would often become all the more apparent. The more we were preoccupied with being seen as competent, the less competent we seemed to become. It appears that it may be important for a team to limit the number of visitor observers until such time as it feels confident in its ability to function adequately under the scrutiny of others.

AGENCY RELATIONSHIPS

A well-functioning team may pose a considerable threat in an agency, particularly within a more traditionally organized setting. Much of the tension may be founded on straight-forward and legitimate ideological or theoretical difference. However, there may be other factors involved. The evolution of our team led to tensions developing elsewhere in the agency. In retrospect, we had paid insufficient attention to the implications for other staff members. Although it is necessary for a team to be sufficiently freed from the constraints of its wider setting in order that it can develop, it is also necessary to keep alive the relationships between the members of the team and the rest of the agency staff lest a destructive insider/outsider dynamic develop.

Also, by challenging many of the conventional wisdoms upon which an agency may have been based, a team can considerably threaten other staff. Their angry and defensive responses can lead to a 'siege' mentality in the team which can lead to a more hostile response from the others, which in turn can lead to a greater level of defensiveness in the team, and so on.

Many teams have, through the combined efforts of their members, acquired significant resources such as interviewing suites, one-way mirrors and video-tape equipment, as well as the time to pursue their interests. Such facilities are not always equally available to other staff, particularly those working in public agencies. Often non-team-member staff, with justification, feel they are struggling with equally demanding workloads yet with less recognition and with considerably less support.

A mystique can develop around what a particular team is "up to". Other staff feel "put down" or patronized when in discussion with team members who can somehow convey that they are in possession of "the truth." Hoffman (1981) has highlighted the problems of envy which can arise when a team is perceived as exclusive and effective. This can be further exacerbated where the team, or members of the team, begin to be invited to give lectures and workshops on its ideas and its approach, outside of the host agency.

CONCLUSIONS

As with Heraclitus' river, a team is a constantly evolving phenomenon; each day, in a sense, a different team. Over the life of our team it is possible to identify three stages. First, the early experimental stage when, though we struggled together frequently and sometimes angrily, we did some exciting and effective work and created some original ideas (see, for example, Cade, 1980; 1982). Then came the middle stage when procedures and ideas became more formalized. Certain kinds of interventions were seen as appropriate, others as not appropriate. We had decided to do research on our therapy (Speed; 1985) and thus it became important to articulate the approach clearly and to be consistent in what we did. At this stage, at times, the team seemed to become more delimiting and less creative. Rather than encouraging adventurousness and risk-taking, the team began, at times, to feel like a source of potential disapproval or criticism, concerned more with ensuring that the "right" things were done according to the "rules". Not all members of the team reacted to this period in the same way. To one member it was a period of consolidation and her more positive approach was reflected in a number of positive therapeutic outcomes. To another it was a period of relative boredom and constraint and this more negative attitude was reflected in a number of poor therapeutic outcomes in his work.

The third stage, following the consultation with Boscolo and Cecchin, involved a loosening of the team's structure. The boundaries became more permeable; others could be invited in; rules about what was "appropriate" became more flexible; greater differences could be more easily tolerated without it becoming an important issue that such differences be "resolved". This period was again one of greater levels of excitement and creativity. Perhaps a team needs to be beginning or ending to do its best work. Once it has become established it becomes more concerned with its internal processes. As Haley observed, "It is in the nature of organization that it crystalizes what is there at the moment, thus preventing new developments . . . Generally, it seems that organizations develop when innovations are dying" (1984, p. 5). It was, interestingly, not very long after the publication in English of "Paradox and Counter-paradox" (Palazzoli, et al., 1978) and the growing international interest in *the* Milan method, that the Milan team began to split up.

Looking back over the last four years, there are many ways in which working as a team has been crucial to our development. The continuing challenge, feedback and support provided by the direct exposure to each other of our work and our thinking has led to a sustained period of creativity and mutual learning. The immediacy of the consultation was extremely valuable. Although we experienced struggles and sometimes fought, what sticks most in our memories is how much we laughed. Important to us also was the two hour wind-down period in the local pub (a uniquely British institution sadly unavailable to most teams outside of the United Kingdom) which followed our late clinic evenings. The authors still frequently work together, though no longer as a formally constituted team. In many ways we continue to build upon what we had learned when we were working so closely together. Each of us is now pursuing different areas of interest. It seems that *any team has a limited creative life span.* One way this can be extended is by the addition of new members. At times, our flatter periods could be lifted and new enthusiasm injected through exchanges with other teams. For example, we very much valued regular contact with Luigi Boscolo and Gianfranco Cecchin and also with The Team from The Brief Therapy Centre, Milwaukee.

Though it is our firm belief that a team approach is an effective way of doing therapy, particularly with the more disturbed and dysfunctional families, this belief seems at present to rest almost entirely on subjective experience. As far as we know, no systematic research has yet been published that can justify the use of teams in family therapy. However, as Speed et al. (1982) have commented,

support so far comes from clinical experience alone; a sense of increased effectiveness. It may be that this belief itself is a powerful ingredient of any such effectiveness. Rosenthal (1966) has shown that the beliefs and expectations of interviewers strongly affect their behaviour and hence outcome. If working in teams helps to generate a sense of optimism about the possibility of change, then arguably change is more likely to occur. It is probably true to say that working in teams has developed not only because teams engender optimism about effectiveness but also because the process of achieving any such effectiveness is more satisfying. Family therapy is always difficult, sometimes nerve-wracking and sometimes depressing; working in teams can be creative, highly supportive, challenging and very often fun. (p. 283)

REFERENCES

Bateson, G. (1979). *Mind and nature.* New York: E.P. Dutton.

Breunlin, D.C. & Cade, B.W. (1981). Intervening in family systems using observer messages. *Journal of Marital & Family Therapy,* 7, 453-460.

Cade, B.W. (1980). Resolving therapeutic deadlocks using a contrived team conflict. *International Journal of Family Therapy,* 2, 253-262.

Cade, B.W. (1982). Humour and creativity. *Journal of Family Therapy,* 4, 35-42.

Cade, B.W. & Cornwell, M. (1983). The evolution of the one-way screen. *The Australian Journal of Family Therapy,* 4, 73-80.

Cade, B.W. & Cornwell, M. (1985). New realities for old; Some uses of teams and one-way screens in therapy. In D. Campbell & R. Draper (Eds), *Applications of Systemic Family Therapy.* London, Academic Press.

Haley, J. (1984). Marriage or family therapy. *The American Journal of Family Therapy,* 12, 2: 3-14.

Hoffman, L. (1981) *Foundations of family therapy.* New York: Basic Books.

Kingston, P. & Smith, D. (1983). Preparation for live consultation and live supervision when working without a one-way screen, *Journal of Family Therapy,* 5: 219-233.

Olsen, U. & Pegg. P.F. (1979). Direct open supervision: A team approach, *Family Process,* 18: 463-469.

Palazzoli, M.S. (1983). The emergence of a comprehensive systems approach, *Journal of Family Therapy,* 5, 165-177.

Palazzoli, M.S., Boscolo, L., Cecchin, G. & Prata, G. (1978) *Paradox and counter-paradox,* New York, Jason Aaronson.

Rosenthal, R. (1966). *Experimenter effects in behavioural research.* New York: Appleton-Century Crofts.

Smith, D. & Kingston, P. (1980). Live supervision without a one-way screen, *Journal of Family Therapy,* 2: 379-387.

Speed, B. (1985). Evaluating the Milan Approach. In D. Campbell & R. Draper (Eds), *Applications of Systemic Family Therapy.* London: Academic Press.

Speed, B., Seligman, P.M., Kingston, P. & Cade, B.W. (1982). A team approach to therapy. *Journal of Family Therapy,* 4, 271-284.

8

Supervision of Cotherapy

David G. Rice

Psychotherapeutic treatment with two therapists has become a popular and accepted modality. A summary of the advantages and disadvantages of cotherapy can be found in Dowling (1978) and Roman and Meltzer (1977); therefore, these will not be reiterated here. Instead, the present chapter will focus on issues of supervision with cotherapists.

Hoffman and Hoffman (1981) give a brief history of cotherapy. To recapitulate, Alfred Adler apparently first used what he referred to as "multiple therapy," i.e., two therapists treating a single case (Dreikurs, 1950). Multiple therapy is still utilized in treating seriously disturbed individuals whose ego fragmentation places great demands on the therapist's clinical and personal resources. Mullan and Sangiuliano (1960) describe such a treatment format with a variety of individual patients, as well as with groups and families. The present author believes that multiple therapy is the "treatment of choice" for inexperienced therapists treating patients with borderline and schizotypal personality disorders. Such patients show prominent use of "splitting" as a defense, e.g., seeing one therapist as "good," the other as "bad" (Rinsley, 1977). A case study illustrating supervision where cotherapists are being "split" will be presented later in the chapter.

Although "multiple therapy" is clearly a form of cotherapy, the term cotherapy usually applies to two therapists treating a couple, family or group. In the author's experience, the more complex the system, the more advantageous it is to have a cotherapist. In this sense, group therapy represents a more complex treatment form and much of the literature on supervision of cotherapists deals with group therapy (Coché, 1977; Dies, 1980). Many articles on

David G. Rice, Ph.D., is a professor at the University of Wisconsin Medical School and Director of the Psychology Internship Program.

cotherapy highlight the relationship between the two therapists as perhaps the most important factor in successful treatment (McGee & Schuman, 1970; Roman & Meltzer, 1977). In supervision much attention is focused on the cotherapist relationship.

From a study of the empirical literature, one can not conclude that two therapists produce better results than a single therapist. However, it is probably safe to infer that this variable has not been tested completely. In perhaps the most carefully controlled study to date, Mehlman, Baucom and Anderson (1983) investigated the effectiveness of behavioral marital therapy for 30 couples, comparing when it was (a) conducted by a male-female cotherapy team versus each therapist working individually and (b) using immediate treatment versus delayed treatment (utilizing a waiting list). Couples were seen for 10 successive weeks; the first five weeks focused on training in problem-solving and communication skills and the last five on training in quid pro quo contracting. The results indicated the treatment to be effective, as documented by self-report and behavioral change measures. However, the "cotherapy team and the single therapists were equally effective in producing treatment changes" (p. 258). There were no significant differences between couples seen immediately and those who were treated after being on a waiting list for 10 weeks.

Although the Mehlman et al. study (1983) represents a well-controlled and much needed test of cotherapy versus treatment with a single therapist, there are difficulties in generalizing the results, particularly to non-behavioral marital and family therapy. The highly structured treatment format may not require the two therapists to take different in-therapy roles. The short treatment period (10 weeks) does not necessarily lend itself to full utilization of the cotherapist relationship. Behavioral marital therapy typically does not deal with the patients' transference distortions, and their manifestations in the co-therapists' relationship, an important focus in much of co-therapy (Berkman and Berkman, 1984).

Taking into account the lack of empirical support for cotherapy, it is sometimes hard to justify the additional economic and time costs of using two therapists instead of one. Group therapy would be an exception, as cost can be less of a determining factor, given the greater number of patients. There does appear to be a general preference for utilizing cotherapists in a training setting (Davis & Lohr, 1971; Yalom, 1970), where beginning therapists are learning to treat difficult cases. Sometimes treatment is conducted by an experienced-inexperienced therapist pair (Kaslow, 1977). In such a case, the experienced therapist usually functions partly in the role of a supervisor. For many reasons, including the likelihood that the inexperienced therapist will feel "one down" and the blurring of "supervisor" and "therapist" roles, this may not be an optimal learning format (McGee, 1968). The more typical training situation involves two inexperienced trainees serving as cotherapists and a supervisor who reviews their work. Much of the present chapter deals with this type of supervisory format.

SELECTING A COTHERAPIST— IMPLICATIONS FOR SUPERVISION

The cotherapy literature consistently stresses the importance of a good cotherapist match (Roman & Meltzer, 1977). Some training programs prefer to do the matching, in order to assure cotherapist compatibility (McGee & Schuman, 1970). This type of matching process is likely to require more omniscience than most clinicians possess (though many aspire to). Empirical documentation of cotherapist interaction dimensions leading to favorable treatment results is just beginning to appear in the literature. Piper et al. (1979) compared six outpatient therapy groups treated by twelve relatively inexperienced cotherapists over a five month period. Using measures of in-therapy behavior, each cotherapist pair was classified as "consistent" or "inconsistent" and "similar" or "dissimilar" in type of content responded to both within and across sessions. Results indicated that "consistent/dissimilar" cotherapist teams may be the most clinically effective. It was felt that these dyads communicated greater clarity of goals and modeled different but complementary role behaviors while minimizing competition between the therapists. Such studies will hopefully provide future guidelines for cotherapist matching. In the meantime, a more naturalistic selection process is likely to take place in most agencies and training facilities.

The author's observations suggest that better cotherapist "matches" are made by individuals who have had experience with one another in a variety of settings and interactions. It seems particularly helpful if the two therapists have been in a therapy group together and learned about each other's personal struggles, family background, modes of self-presentation and sensitivities (Dies, 1980; Yalom, 1975). Several writers caution about the cotherapists' vulnerability to sexual feelings and potential intimate involvement as the result of working together (Bowers & Gauron, 1981; Brent & Marine, 1982; Dunn & Dickes, 1977; Kaslow, 1980). When these feelings are generated in therapy and then acted upon, the cotherapists will likely start attending more to one another and less to the clients. However, closeness and friendship between cotherapists may facilitate their working together.

A number of years ago, the author was supervising male and female third year psychiatric residents who were working together as cotherapists for the first time. Their clinical interaction was unusually synergistic and change-producing with a difficult family. When the supervisor expressed some surprise at how well the two therapists were working together, the woman resident said: "Well, it might help you to know that we dated each other during most of last year." The supervisor was indeed surprised, since he knew this resident was currently involved with another resident in her class, and had assumed it was a long-standing relationship. The supervisor found himself curious about the break-up of the cotherapists' prior relationship, but did not quite feel comfortable asking about this. Fortunately, the male cotherapist volunteered: "We've remained friends, however, and there don't seem to be hard feelings left for me." (To cotherapist) "How about you?" She replied: "I agree." This experience taught the author the possible value of prior cotherapist contact and experience with one another in different contexts. Although potentially the cause of cotherapist conflict (e.g., competitiveness, jealousy), prior experiences seem generally facilitative of effective naturalistic cotherapist selection.

Another prominent goal stressed in the cotherapy literature is the achievement of an equalitarian co-therapist relationship. Getty & Shannon (1969) define such a relationship as having three essential ingredients: acceptance, mutual sharing of responsibility, and equal cotherapist participation. The latter quality is probably more realistically conceived of in terms of equity, i.e., the perceived fair distribution of participation by the two therapists, including both verbal and non-verbal behavior. The goal of equity in cotherapist participation takes into account natural differences in preferred activity level and usually does not lead to "score-keeping" on the therapists' part to make sure everything is equal.

Weinstein (1971) states that the three most important variables in cotherapist selection are, in order of importance: (1) trust, (2) understanding and recognizing differences in personality between the two therapists, and (3) equal ability, real or potential. Potential ability is perhaps the most difficult of these qualities to assess. Respect for the less experienced individual's potential ability does seem a necessary ingredient for therapists with different levels of experience and/or perceived status to work together successfully. Rice and Rice (1975) discuss status issues in cotherapy and recommend that the cotherapists deal with these factors openly and forthrightly, either alone together or in the context of supervision. Friedman (1973) surveyed third year psychiatric residents and found that the preferred ideal cotherapy team consisted of a male and a female therapist with equal perceived status. Interestingly, "equal status" was seen as more important than having therapists of opposite gender.

MODES OF SUPERVISOR INTERVENTION

At one extreme model of supervision, the supervisor is not involved in any direct observation of the cotherapists' work. In this format, the therapists present their observations of the treatment session(s) via oral report and/or written notes. Many supervisors feel self-report is subject to a great deal of therapist distortion, selectivity of data, and defensive cover-up (Birchler, 1975). One exception is Nichols (1975) who feels that, if the supervisor develops a trusting relationship, the cotherapists will bring their "mistakes" into supervision.

An intermediate position, favored perhaps by the majority of supervisors, is reviewing of audiotaped or, preferably, videotaped sessions (Liddle & Halprin, 1978). This post-treatment session supervisory format offers a chance to stop and review carefully the clinical interaction. Disadvantages to such a procedure include feelings of inhibitedness on the patients' or therapists' part from being "on camera." Also, a certain degree of electronic sophistication is needed, e.g., split-screen video capability is usually necessary to monitor both the patient's and the therapists' behavior.

At the other extreme of involvement, the supervisor watches (either via a one-way mirror or actually sitting in the room) and participates actively during the therapy session or gives feedback immediately after the session. Active intervention can also be facilitated via a telephone line or earphone connection into the treatment room or by the supervisor entering the room and becoming active in the therapy. The supervisor may or may not consult with a group of observers before intervening. A book edited by Whiffen and Byng-Hall (1982) contains several chapters discussing the pros and cons of these different methods of supervision. The main disadvantage appears to be the cotherapists' felt intrusiveness of the supervisor's active interventions. On the other hand, supervisors feel it is very advantageous at times to be able to intervene *in vivo* and actively direct or redirect the course of treatment, sometimes adding the interpretive weight of "the (unseen) observers agree that . . . "

To the present author, active intervention by the supervisor during the actual treatment session blurs the distinction between "supervisor" and "cotherapist." The supervisor in this mode appears to be acting more as a third therapist, albeit one whose mode and timing of interventions are different from the two therapists present in the room for the entire session. Thus, such methods of treatment should perhaps be called "triadic therapy" rather than "supervision of cotherapy."

WHICH SUPERVISORY MODE . . . AND WHEN?

Given the types of supervision available, how does one pick and choose the most appropriate and effective procedure? A developmental model would suggest that different modes of supervision may be needed for different levels of cotherapist experience. Nichols (1978) indicates that close or intensive supervision is needed by inexperienced therapists with the supervisor gradually moving into the role of a "consultant" as the therapist(s) gain experience.

Other formulations describe a series of developmental stages that occur over time when two therapists work together. Dick, Lessler & Whiteside (1980) describe the relationship evolution of two male therapists who worked together over a several year period doing weekly open-ended group therapy. They identified four cotherapist developmental stages: (1) *Formation*-during which intrapsychic issues between the two therapists (e.g., competency, performance anxiety) are salient and the "two leaders together do not add up to one whole, fully functioning therapist" (p. 277). They found this period lasted three to six months. (2) *Development*-in which the interpersonal relationship between the cotherapists is the focus. During this period, the relationship becomes complementary, utilizing each therapist's strengths and with each making up for the other's perceived deficits. Dick et al., believe supervision and outside consultation are necessary in these first two stages (3) *Stabilization*-during which the therapists' energy and attention is directed primarily toward the patients and less toward one another. The cotherapists may also begin to air and resolve within the session some theoretical and practical differences. (4) *Refreshment*-a stage reached occasionally in cotherapy in which "effective and efficient treatment flourish almost without effort" (p. 280).

Dick et al. (1980) demonstrate the degree of harmony two experienced therapists can achieve by working together with a variety of clients over time. However, most therapists who treat couples and families (and many who see groups) do not have the opportunity to see their clients over long treatment periods (Gurman & Kniskern, 1978). To achieve Stages III and IV in the Dick et al. model, many of the relationship issues between the cotherapists would need to be worked through quickly and the pair are likely to require intensive cotherapy supervision. The supervisor will find this task easier if there has been careful selection and pairing on the part of the cotherapists.

Hoffman & Hoffman (1981) also describe a four-stage cotherapist developmental process, in this case for two experienced therapists married to one another. The stages were (1) *Preparing*-a four to six month period of talking about and anticipating the experience of working together prior to actually doing cotherapy. (2) *Polarizing*-a period of variability in performance during which it felt as if the two therapists at times pulled together but at other times worked against one another. (3) *Integrating*-a period of greater tolerance of differences and open dealing with conflict within the treatment session (similar to Dick et al., Stage III) and (4) *Stabilizing*-a period of more comfortable risk taking, greater use of self and more flexible, less gender prescribed role behaviors. Brent & Marine (1982) likewise use a four stage process to describe the development of their cotherapy relationship, in this case involving a relatively experienced female therapist and a relatively inexperienced male therapist. The stages were: (1) *Encounter*-characterized by a sense of mutual dependency, inability to "click" and, at times, too great a focus on the cotherapists' relationship to the exclusion of the patients. (2) *Power and control*-in which some discordance may prevail as each therapist struggles for a sense of personal autonomy, with behavior somewhat characteristic of a sibling rivalry. (3) *Intimacy*-characterized by more spontaneous interchange but also a period in which "flaws in the therapists' style are accepted and more easily discussed as therapeutic issues rather than experienced as personal attacks'' (p. 72) and (4) *Separation*-during which a sense of sadness at the ending of the treatment experience is shared and worked through.

Those cotherapists who ascribe to a developmental model tend to believe that such stages occur in sequence regardless of the theoretical model(s) of treatment held by the cotherapists. One's theoretical stance may affect treatment length and thus result in the truncation of some stages. One implication of a developmental model is that cotherapists are more likely to need direct, active supervision in the early phases of working together. This is also the time when they are likely to feel the most insecure and sensitive to any critical supervisory comments.

When one works in the early treatment phases with the "supervisor" as one of the cotherapists, this format is likely to reinforce the inexperienced therapist's feelings of inadequacy and incompetence. Indeed, a study done by the author and his colleagues (Rice, Fey & Kepecs, 1972) found subjectively rated effectiveness of treatment lower for a group of experienced-inexperienced cotherapist pairs than for either experienced-experienced or inexperienced-inexperienced cotherapist pairs. Gurman's study (1974) supported this finding of a negative relationship between cotherapists' different levels of experience and treatment effectiveness, as measured by marital dyad attitude convergence in marital therapy.

Many therapists would agree that the opportunity to work with an experienced cotherapist can be beneficial (Nelson, 1978). However, this pairing is likely to be more profitable if the inexperienced therapist has previously had a positive cotherapy experience working with a peer, and thus some confidence in him/herself as a cotherapist. It is also helpful for the beginning cotherapist to have had some experience in doing individual therapy. This is useful for gaining a sense of how much individual change can be expected to occur in therapy, what kind of transference and countertransference relationships the therapist can expect, and some discussion of how splitting the transference might impact on the course of treatment.

In summary, working with a supervisor in supervision and having a supervisor as a cotherapist are two distinct experiences. For the present author, the preferable sequence is for an inexperienced therapist to first work as a single therapist with individual patients, next to do supervised cotherapy with another therapist of comparable status and experience and then to work with an experienced cotherapist in a relationship characterized by mutual trust and respect. All three formats can provide useful learning experiences. This sequence also helps minimize the inexperienced therapist's anxiety and promotes a developing sense of competence.

WHICH THEORETICAL POSITION . . . AND WHY?

The cotherapist issues that a supervisor attends to are likely to be dictated in part by his/her theoretical preferences (Liddle & Halprin, 1978; Winokur, 1982). Everett (1980) points out that "significant theories of supervision remain essentially nonexistent" (p. 372). Cleghorn and Levin (1973) present a therapist skill analysis that focuses on generic perceptual and conceptual objectives and executive skills that cut across theoretical lines. However, this approach is unlikely to be adopted by the majority of supervisors, given the diversity of theoretical proclivities. For example, many marital and family therapy supervisors stress the need for therapists to be aware of the concept of circular causality (Bateson, 1979). This concept is in contrast to a linear cause and effect model and is central to understanding the behavior of systems. Whiffen (1982) states the task as follows:

> One of the most difficult tasks in teaching a systematic approach to family therapy is to help the trainee move from the causal-linear way of thinking to a cybernetic-circular approach. The opportunity for observing minute details of interchange between family members and the order in which this happens, allows the trainee to see that each event was in response to the previous one and that in time the sequence comes full circle, the same order being repeated over again. This enables the trainee to see that each part of the system contributes to the chain of events and that attributing cause to one incident in a cycle is inaccurate and often misleading (p. 40).

This epistomological model is quite different from that used by psychodynamic or behaviorally oriented supervisors, who are likely to focus on different aspects and levels in any given clinical interaction.

The present author prefers an object relations model that focuses on cotherapists understanding and dealing with couple and family dynamics, as mirrored in the therapists' own interaction. Becoming a therapist involves ultimately meshing "what one does" with "who one is." To achieve this goal, it is important to gain experience with different therapeutic modalities and to be supervised from a variety of theoretical viewpoints, as well as to possess a high degree of self-knowledge and insight.

COMMON PROBLEMS IN COTHERAPY: SUPERVISORY STRATEGIES

Davis and Lohr (1971) discuss a variety of cotherapist problems, as manifested in psychodynamically oriented group therapy. The authors provide clinical vignettes demonstrating the need for supervisory input. They do not give transcriptal material illustrating the supervisor's specific response to such problems. In this type of group therapy, the authors indicate that the most serious problems involve transference-countertransference phenomena. They cite certain extrinsic problem areas for cotherapists, likely to be salient at the beginning of treatment: (1) gender, particularly the sex-role expectations ascribed to each therapist, (2) age, particularly if quite different, (3) race, (4) discipline, "title" and level of experience, and (5) physical appearance, especially if different from the "norm."

Davis and Lohr also elaborate the following personality factors, in which cotherapists may differ, leading to difficulties in treatment: (1) activity-inactivity, in regard to verbal behavior; (2) activity-passivity, including both verbal and nonverbal behaviors; (3) affect, in terms of level and amount; (4) reality focus, including amount of social "chatter" engaged in and amount of personal information each therapist chooses to reveal; (5) timing and frequency of interventions; and (6) cognitive styles, that is, a therapist who is primarily "supportive" in interventions paired with one who is "investigative."

A third classification of differing cotherapist behaviors described by these authors relates to unconscious personality factors and includes: (1) defensive patterns, particularly when similar and resulting in mutual "blind spots" in treatment; (2) competition, which may lead to a struggle for dominance of the relationship; and (3) self-esteem, as illustrated when a sophisticated group of patients make the therapists feel inferior or inadequate.

Supervisors who work from an intrapsychic or object-relations model point out additional dynamic factors that pose potential hazards for cotherapists, such as splitting and unconscious mirroring of core conflicts present in the family or group (Berkman and Berkman, 1984; Dowling, 1978; Muntz, 1965; Rubenstein & Weiner, 1967). For example, cotherapists treating a fragmented, poorly organized family may find themselves becoming confused about treatment goals and then avoiding necessary post-treatment session meetings that would allow for exploration of and agreement on how to proceed. The cotherapists in this example begin to "mirror" the family's disorganization. Other writers have pointed out that the cotherapists form a group themselves, a "group within a group," and manifest structural and process issues similar to the group or family being treated (Holt & Greiner, 1976; Levine & Dang, 1979). For example, the cotherapist dyad may subtly resist the supervisor's efforts to change their behavior, preferring to "do it our way," much as the couple, family or group resists the therapists' efforts.

In summary, much attention in supervision is likely to focus on the cotherapists' relationship. Careful naturalistic selection of cotherapists, based on factors discussed earlier, can make the supervisor's task easier. Given two therapists of comparable status, who have chosen to work together based on some prior knowledge of one another's behavior, in the author's experience the following clinical issues are likely to be addressed most often in supervision. Excerpts from supervisory sessions are presented to illustrate how certain of these issues might be handled.

Splitting of the Cotherapists

As indicated earlier, this is a frequent issue in individual or multiple therapy with very disturbed patients. Splitting also occurs in family and group therapy (Dowling, 1978; Yalom, 1970). In such instances one therapist is seen as "good" (caring, rescuing, providing insight) and the other therapist as "bad" (rejecting, judging, insensitive). Supervision in such cases focuses on helping the cotherapists to avoid colluding with this defensive process, and thus to not behave along the lines of the patient's projections. This task requires the cotherapists to work together and to be flexible in their role behaviors. Through this process, the patient learns to accept contradictory parts of him/herself, without experiencing disruptive anxiety and the need to project such feelings onto others. This experience eventually helps the patient to complete the developmental process of individuation, by reconciling and accepting inevitable ambivalent feelings toward the significant others in one's life. By way of illustration:

Two women therapists (a second year psychiatric resident and a post-doctoral clinical psychology trainee) were treating a nineteen-year-old woman diagnosed as having a severe borderline personality disorder. The patient voiced numerous suicidal threats and had been hospitalized on two occasions, once following an overdose of anti-depressant medication and again after cutting her wrists and arms. She had "latched on" to one of the therapists (Dr. White, the psychologist) whom she idealized as capable of "doing no wrong." this was the opposite of the way the patient saw her mother, whom she blamed for many of her problems. She saw the other therapist (Dr. Black, the psychiatrist) as more businesslike but also more powerful. She viewed Dr. Black quite ambivalently, much as she acknowledged feeling toward her father. In some ways both therapists liked the way they were seen by this patient. They realized they had been "split" when each therapist attempted to do something that was "reserved" by the patient for the other therapist. An excerpt from a supervisory session reviewing an audiotape approximately six months into therapy illustrates this phenomenon and its management:

Patient: I was feeling real scary last night. I tried to call Mary (Dr. Black) several times. I was hoping you might be willing to give me some pills. It was real frustrating when I couldn't reach you. I was pissed.

Dr. Black: Sorry I wasn't there when you called.

Dr. White: (to patient) So what did you do?

Patient: Well, eventually, I went to bed. I went through the medicine cabinet. There wasn't anything there that would help. I didn't sleep very well but I did remember I'd be seeing you today and that helped a little bit.

Supervisor (stops tape): Did you consider asking her why she didn't attempt to call Jane (Dr. White)?

Dr. White: Well, she did mention later on in the session that she wondered if I was out last night too. If I'm honest, I'd have to admit I was glad she didn't bother me.

Supervisor: But she (patient) knows the contractual arrangement. Right? (both therapists nod "yes") If she needs to get in touch with her therapist, she is to try and reach either one of you.

Dr. Black: Yes, we've encouraged her to alternate.

Supervisor: It seems in this incident that she has succeeded in splitting you. Mary (Dr. B) is once again the "bad guy," who doesn't come through for her and toward whom she can then be angry. Jane (Dr. W) gets to once again be the "good guy" who in fantasy could come through for her but is not really tested to see if this is indeed true. If she is able to keep splitting you, over time, I suspect each of you could end up resenting the other. Mary will resent Jane because Jane doesn't get called at night. Jane will feel less important because it's clear when she (the patient) really needs someone, she turns to Mary whom she believes will be able to give her something more powerful—in this case, medication.

Dr. White: Well, what should we do to head that off?

Supervisor: In the instance we just heard, it would have been good to reiterate the "rules." That if she can't get one of you she should try the other. And, this is important, make it clear once again in therapy that you two are both in agreement on that. That you both believe the other is capable of handling her requests. You do agree that's true. Right?

Dr. Black and Dr. White: Yes (both smile)

Supervisor: She (the patient) has got to see that sometimes Jane (Dr. W) won't be able to come through for her. She's got to put that to the test. She needs to come to accept that she will feel ambivalent toward both of you, but that's healthy. Otherwise, she'd never leave therapy. Why leave somebody you believe is all good?

Competition Between Cotherapists

Coché (1977) states that competitive feelings are more likely to occur between therapists with comparable perceived status. However, any two therapists can become competitive. Even if the two individuals do not feel a need to compete, the family or group can subtly place the cotherapists into a competitive struggle. This phenomenon is somewhat similar to splitting the cotherapists and probably derives from the common childhood experience of learning to get one's way by setting one parent up against the other. ("Daddy,

Mommy says I can have a quarter if it's ok with you?'') There can be healthy competition within the dyad, with each therapist attempting to do his/her best job, or destructive competition, where one therapist's needs work against the other. The latter issue needs to be addressed in supervision. An example follows:

Two male second-year psychiatric residents (Drs. Jones and Smith) were treating a group of male and female college students, most of whom showed mild to moderate neurotic or characterological interpersonal problems. The therapists had worked hard to carefully select a homogeneous group. They began the supervision session following the fifth group meeting with Dr. Jones saying that he had felt uncomfortable toward the end of the session for reasons he could not pinpoint. Dr. Smith reported that he had been surprised to learn during the post-session conference about Dr. Jones' uncomfortable feelings. He had not felt anything particularly different in this regard, compared to the other sessions. The supervisor asked to listen to the audiotape for the approximate ten minute period before Dr. Jones sensed his uncomfortable feelings. In the excerpt, the group had been talking about how hard it was to risk getting to know someone new of the opposite sex. After several minutes of this, the following interchange occurred:

Pt. A (Judy) I'm so tired of the bar scene. But it seems like it's the only place where people go when they're unattached.

Pt. B (Fred) I'd certainly go along with that.

Dr. Jones (to Judy) The only place? (pause)

Dr. Smith: I can think of a variety of other places, at least from what I've heard. (to Judy) Are you sure the issue isn't that you're scared to risk trying out something new—taking a chance on meeting someone in a less well known and predictable place.

Judy (attracted by Dr. S's forthright manner): Gee, I never thought of that. I think you're probably right.

Supervisor (stops tape): (to Dr. J.) How did you feel when Jim (Dr. S.) came in there?

Dr. J: Huh? Well . . . ok, I guess. I said what I was going to say.

Supervisor: Except, if I heard it right, you really wanted Judy to deal with her own feelings, and not have Jim take over and tell her what he thought she was feeling, and why.

Dr. J. (protecting his cotherapist): Well, he's probably right in what he said there.

Supervisor: I agree, but it sounded like he stepped in and took over for you. We all know you're capable of following through in the direction you were going. Right? (both nod "yes") So I find myself wondering if you didn't have some sense that Jim was competing with you, taking over when you were going along just fine. If I were to guess, that sort of thing might have led to your uncomfortable feelings . . . after a while.

Dr. J: You may be right—that hadn't occurred to me.

Dr. S: I know I do have a tendency to jump in, even when I'm in agreement with what Bill (Dr. J.) is doing. Its hard for me to hold back at such times.

Supervisor: I know. It's hard for me too. Although it's usually helped to have my cotherapist "call" me on it. If you (Dr. J.) had sensed that was going on in the excerpt we just heard, you might have said something like: "Hang on a second, Jim. I'd like to get more of Judy's thoughts about what she just said, ok?"

Supervisory strategies for dealing with cotherapist competition focus on reinforcing both therapists' competence and emphasizing the valuable though different skills that each brings to therapy. In this sense, one communicates to the therapists that competing destructively with one another is likely to end in a "draw," with the patients as losers and no winners.

Dealing With Cotherapist's Unresolved Personal Issues

Sometimes therapy gets too close to unresolved issues in the therapist and makes him or her anxious. Such issues often relate to conflicts within the therapist's present significant relationships and/or family of origin. Cotherapists are usually acutely aware of one another's moments of anxiety. At such times, the natural response is to change the subject at hand, even though important to the patient(s), in order to protect one's cotherapist and the "image" of the dyad as psychologically competent (Byng-Hall, de Carteret & Whiffen, 1982). Supervision in such instances stresses the need for a nonverbal (in-session) agreement between therapists to "take over" for one another, until the "anxious" therapist's psychological equilibrium is restored. In this manner, the flow of treatment is not interrupted and the competence of each therapist is respected. An example from a marital therapy session is presented below:

Male and female cotherapists, both experienced individual therapists, were treating a difficult, somewhat rigid couple in their 50's who came to therapy complaining of diminished time spent together and feeling emotional distance in their marriage. The husband blamed his wife for their presenting problem. He believed she was spending too much time and energy dealing with her terminally ill mother, who lived in a local nursing home. The cotherapists had been feeling frustrated with the lack of meaningful interaction in the sessions and had sought consultation with an experienced marital therapy supervisor, who asked them to videotape the next (fourth) session. In this session, the wife explained how painful it had been to visit with her mother during the past week-end. Reviewing the videotape, the supervisor noted about one-third of the way through that the usually verbal and active female cotherapist became strangely silent. Her appearance changed and the male cotherapist was noted to be watching her carefully. There was also an increase in the level of tension in the wife's voice. The supervisor stopped the videotape at this point and inquired of the cotherapists:

Supervisor: What's going on? Something seems to have changed.

Male Therapist: Everyone seems to have gotten tense all of a sudden.

Female Therapist: What Alice (the wife) was saying really got to me. (pause) I began to remember my own mother's painful death from cancer . . . it was just four years ago. I thought I had worked it through but something Alice said brought those feelings back— I was afraid I was going to cry.

Supervisor: What would have happened if you had said something about that, maybe to Ron (the male therapist), in the session.

Female therapist: Well, I don't think that would be fair. He could handle it but I don't think it would be appropriate to lay that on Alice. I mean she's having enough trouble keeping control.

Supervisor (to male therapist): Did you know what Jane (the female therapist) was going through?

Male therapist: Well, I knew something was up. I was watching her and it looked "heavy." I didn't connect it with what Alice was saying. But it was clear I wasn't listening much to Alice when I sensed Jane reacting to something.

Supervisor: Exactly. But since Alice was talking about a very meaningful experience, it would have been helpful if you (Ron) could have supported her, until Jane got her "sense of equilibrium" back.

Female Therapist: Yeah, that would have been nice. As you'll see on the tape, after a while I was fine.

Supervisor: It would be a good idea for you two to work out some sort of "code" for when one of you would like the other to "take over."

Male therapist: We could use semaphores. (laughter)

Supervisor: I had in mind something not quite so dramatic. Why don't you work out a "high sign" that you can use for such moments. I assume you've both felt a need for that?

Male therapist: Yeah, I get pretty anxious when Ed (the husband) expects me to come up with answers I don't have. I would be good if Jane could focus then on why, for example, he puts us in the position. At least until I can come up with the answers. (laughter)

In this example, it was important for the supervisor to respect Jane's vulnerability and not expect that she (or Ron) would always be in control during the treatment session. It was important to convey that such moments of felt "weakness" would even out over time and that each therapist needed to respect one another's vulnerabilities as well as strengths. The supervisor then encouraged the cotherapists to talk about some limited within session self-disclosure that could have effectively communicated empathy for what Alice was going through. This suggestion was in keeping with the finding that experienced cotherapists, both male and female, reported greater levels of self-disclosure than inexperienced cotherapists (Rice, Gurman, and Razin, 1974).

Supervising Cotherapists With Different Activity Levels

Different cotherapist activity levels can reflect variations in theoretical orientation, personality traits, or a need by one therapist to dominate the other, in response to power and control needs and/or to competitive feelings. One therapist may be a more verbal and/or more extroverted person. As Davis and Lohr (1971) note, differences in activity level become a problem if either the therapists or patients feel discomfort in response to greater overt participation on the part of one therapist. If everyone feels comfortable with this difference, obviously there is no need to address it in supervision. If problematic, the supervisor can encourage the cotherapists to talk about the disparity and bring up the issue in therapy, thus addressing the patient(s) discomfort directly. If the cotherapists are basically different in preferred activity level, it is helpful for the supervisor to focus on how both "active" and "inactive" interaction styles can be valuable in therapy. This concept can then be buttressed with examples from treatment sessions. If differing activity levels reflect felt power and control needs and/or competitive strivings on the part of one or both cotherapists, this issue can be dealt with in the manner discussed previously.

Dealing With Felt Supervisor Preference for One Cotherapist

McGee and Schuman (1970) indicate: "It is not infrequent that the supervisor is accused of favoring one cotherapist over the other . . . " (p. 34), partly as a manifestation of differential cotherapist-supervisor transference feelings. This issue is often a correlate of the "divide and conquer" strategy, alluded to earlier as a frequent learned behavior from childhood. The present author believes that supervisors should be careful to deal with both cotherapists in an equitable manner. If care has been taken along these lines and one cotherapist has a sense of favoritism, it likely reveals more about that therapist's personality (either overvaluing or undervaluing oneself) than about the supervisor's intentions. If the issue is divisive between the therapists, the supervisor needs to take the initiative in bringing up the issue and dealing with it during supervision. Supervisors can be "set up" in this regard, e.g., by acceding to a request from one of the therapists to go ahead and meet for a supervision session when the other cotherapist cannot attend.

Supervising an Unfavorable Cotherapist-Patient Match

Sometimes a well-functioning cotherapist team is poorly matched with a particular couple, family, or group. This often reflects social value incompatability. For example, cotherapists by virtue of their professional training and identification are usually career oriented. They may serve as better role models for dual-career than for "traditional" families (Rice, 1979). In such cases, the wife may sense an inability to identify with the woman cotherapist and may feel outnumbered and/or isolated in the therapy sessions. Likewise, the "traditional" husband may feel pressured to change his belief system, even though the spouses agree that the type of marriage they have is what both want.

In supervision it is important to point out the functional aspects of the family's belief system, even though it may differ from the therapists'. The supervisor can remind the cotherapists that no one family "style" has cornered the market on happiness and stability. Continued monitoring is necessary during supervision to determine the degree of value alienation felt by the patients.

With supervision, cotherapists can usually develop greater tolerance for differences between themselves and their patients. Along these lines, cotherapists may tend to project their own intimacy needs onto their patients. When this happens, patients may experience a sense of failure in not living up to the therapists' expectations. The supervisor needs to point out that individuals and families differ markedly in their "level of preferred intimacy." It is important to help the cotherapists set realistic goals in this regard. The clinicians also may be responding to their own increased feelings of intimacy from working together.

Dealing With Cotherapists Attraction to One Another

Dunn and Dickes (1977) indicate that the development of erotic feelings between cotherapists is a frequent concern, particularly in the practice of sex therapy. They state: "People learn that if someone is sexually attracted to them, they are in less danger of being criticized and hurt. Therefore, one or both therapists may offer subtle seductive cues to their cotherapist to increase sexual interest" (p. 207). Dunn and Dickes indicate that attraction between therapists can have positive benefits, in terms of enhancing their interest in working together effectively. However, acting out of sexual feelings can frequently complicate not only the therapy but also the therapists' personal and professional lives. They believe that: "The supervisors should work to create a supportive atmosphere in which therapists can feel free to raise their concerns about any sexual issues. Discussion is best directed to the origins of the arousal and the effect upon the patient rather than the presenting therapists'' (p. 210).

In the author's experience, this sensitive issue is rarely brought into supervision, even when a trusting supervisor-trainee relationship has been established. It is more likely to be talked about indirectly in the course of therapy, often along the following lines:

Male and female second year psychiatry residents were treating a young couple who were not married but had been living together for approximately two years. They came to therapy because of differing opinions about wanting to have children, and the implications of this issue for whether they would get married. Neither therapist was married. The patients reported that they had seen the therapists having lunch at a restaurant some distance from the clinic where the therapy sessions were conducted. This led to fantasies about the cotherapists' involvement. This segment of the eighth treatment session was presented by audiotape to the supervisor:

Bob (male patient): Hey, did you know we saw you guys eating lunch together last week? Cathy (female patient) and I were wondering . . . you know . . . (defensively) if you do that often?

Male cotherapist (to female cotherapist): I think they're asking whether we're involved with one another.

Female cotherapist (being coy): Before we answer that, let's get their ideas

Cathy: That's not fair. Besides it really isn't any of our business.

Bob (to Cathy): But you do have to admit that you're curious.

Cathy: Well, yes.

Male cotherapist (to patients): Do you think we'd get along . . . as a couple?

Bob: Well, I don't know. Diane (female cotherapist) doesn't take any crap. (laughter) You'd have to stand up to that.

Cathy (embarrassed): Bob!

Bob: Well, that's the way I see it . . . it's just my opinion.

Female cotherapist: I rather like his characterization of me. (to Cathy) What do you think, about John's (male cotherapist) question?

Cathy: Well, you seem to work with each other in a way that's comfortable. I mean you seem to get along.

Female cotherapist: Well, the truth is, we're not involved seriously with one another. We are good friends . . . and we do like to work together. And we both like to eat lunch. (laughter)

Supervisor (stopping the tape): I think you both handled that well. were you uncomfortable dealing with the issue?

Male cotherapist: I was surprised . . . that they saw us . . . outside. But I wasn't uncomfortable about being seen by them. (Female cotherapist nods agreement)

Supervisor: Can you tell anything about some of their personal issues from the fantasy material they came up with?

A discussion followed in the supervision session regarding Bob's concern that Cathy would not budge in regard to her wish to have children. He feared this would mean the eventual end of their relationship. His own traumatic childhood included taking care of his very ill mother following her divorce from his father when Bob was ten. These experiences had left him very ambivalent about the amount of caretaking that being a parent would require. To his credit, he did not expect that Cathy would assume more than her share of parenting responsibilities. Bob's perception of the female cotherapist's assertiveness (and the implications of this for the male cotherapist in relating to her) can be seen in part as a projection of his own struggle with himself and with Cathy. Perhaps his fantasies about the cotherapists' relationship outside therapy represented his wish to learn how a strong man might "stand up to" a strong woman. The supervisor did check out whether the cotherapists had honestly answered the couples' question by asking: "That is correct? You're not involved seriously with one another?" Both therapists said that the female therapist had been honest in her reply. This example reveals a common way that the issue of attraction between cotherapists is presented and discussed in supervision.

SUMMARY

Cotherapy is a useful procedure for training therapists. A variety of supervisory formats can be employed, with varying degrees of supervisor involvement in the actual treatment process. A cotherapist developmental stage formulation suggests different types of supervisory input will likely be needed as the therapists gain experience working with one another. A strong emphasis has been placed on carefully choosing a cotherapist, with comparable levels of status and experience seen as desirable in achieving and modeling an egalitarian relationship. Compatible theoretical preferences and complementary personal "styles" facilitate cotherapy. A variety of issues commonly addressed in supervision are discussed, such as patients' attempting to "split" the therapists and the management of competitive feelings. Several excerpts from supervisory sessions are presented to illustrate strategies for dealing with these cotherapist problems.

REFERENCES

Bateson, G. (1979). *Mind and nature*. New York: E.P. Dutton.

Berkman, A.S. & Berkman, C.F. (1984). The supervision of cotherapist teams in family therapy. *Psychotherapy, 21*, 197-205.

Birchler, G. (1975). Live supervision and instant feedback in marriage and family therapy. *Journal of Marital and Family Counseling, 1*, 331-342.

Bowers, W.A. & Gauron, E.F. (1981). Potential hazards of the co-therapy relationship. *Psychotherapy: Theory, Research and Practice, 18*, 225-228.

Brent, D.A. & Marine, E. (1982). Developmental aspects of the cotherapy relationship. *Journal of Marital and Family Therapy, 8*, 69-75.

Byng-Hall, J., de Carteret, J. & Whiffen, R. (1982). Evolution of supervision: An overview. In R. Whiffen & J. Byng-Hall (Eds.) *Family Therapy Supervision: Recent Developments in Practice*. London: Academic Press.

Cleghorn, J.M. & Levin, S. (1973). Training family therapists by setting learning objectives. *American Journal of Orthopsychiatry, 43*, 439-446.

Coché, E. (1977). Supervision in the training of group therapists. In F.W. Kaslow (Ed.) *Supervision, consultation and staff training in the helping professions*. San Francisco: Jossey-Bass.

Davis, F.B. & Lohr, N.E. (1971). Special problems with the use of cotherapists in group psychotherapy. *International Journal of Group Psychotherapy, 21*, 143-158.

Dick, B., Lessler, K. & Whiteside, J. (1980). A developmental framework for cotherapy. *International Journal of Group Psychotherapy, 30*, 273-285.

Dies, R.R. (1980). Group psychotherapy: Training and supervision. In A.K. Hess (Ed.) *Psychotherapy supervision: Theory, research and practice*. New York: Wiley.

Dowling, E. (1978). Co-therapy: A clinical researcher's view. In S. Walrond-Skinner (Ed.) *Family and marital therapy: A critical approach*. London: Routledge and Kegan Paul.

Dreikurs, R. (1950). Techniques and dynamics of multiple psychotherapy. *Psychiatric Quarterly, 24*, 788-799.

Dunn, M.E. & Dickes, R. (1977). Erotic issues in cotherapy. *Journal of Sex and Marital Therapy, 3*, 205-211.

Everett, C.A. (1980). Supervision of marriage and family therapy. In Hess, A.K. (Ed.) *Psychotherapy supervision: Theory, research and practice*. New York: Wiley.

Friedman, B. (1973). Cotherapy: A behavioral and attitudinal survey of third year psychiatric residents. *International Journal of Group Psychotherapy, 23* 228-234.

Getty, C. & Shannon, A. (1969). Co-therapy as an egalitarian relationship. *American Journal of Nursing, 69,* 767-771.

Gurman, A.S., (1974). Attitude change in marital co-therapy. *Journal of Family Counseling, 2,* 50-54.

Gurman, A.S. & Kniskern, D.P. (1978). Research on marital and family therapy: Progress, perspective and prospect. In S. Garfield & A. Bergin (Eds.) *Handbook of psychotherapy and behavior change* (2nd Ed.) New York: Wiley.

Hoffman, L.W. & Hoffman, H.J. (1981). Husband-wife co-therapy team: Exploration of its development. *Psychotherapy: Theory, Research and Practice, 18,* 217-224.

Holt, M. & Greiner, D. (1976). Co-therapy in the treatment of families. In P.G. Guerin, Jr. (Ed.) *Family therapy: Theory and practice.* New York: Gardner Press.

Kaslow, F.W. (1977). Training of marital and family therapists. In F.W. Kaslow (Ed.) *Supervision, consultation and staff training in the helping professions.* San Francisco: Jossey-Bass.

Kaslow, F. (1980). Some emergent forms of non-traditional sexual combinations: A clinical view. *Interaction, 3,* 1-9.

Levine, C.O. & Dang, J.C. (1979). The group within the group: The dilemma of cotherapy. *International Journal of Group Psychotherapy, 29,* 175-184.

Liddle, H.A. & Halprin, R.J. (1978). Family therapy training and supervision literature: A comparative review. *Journal of Marriage & Family Counseling, 4,* 77-98.

McGee, T.F. (1968). Supervision in group therapy: A comparison of four approaches. *International Journal of Group Psychotherapy, 18,* 165-176.

McGee, T.F. & Schuman, B.N. (1970). The nature of the cotherapy relationship. *International Journal of Group Psychotherapy, 20,* 25-36.

Mehlman, S.K., Baucom, D.H. & Anderson, D. Effectiveness of cotherapists versus single therapists and immediate versus delayed treatment in marital therapy. *Journal of Consulting and Clinical Psychology, 51,* 258-266.

Mintz, E.C. (1965). Male-female co-therapists: Some values and some problems. *American Journal of Psychotherapy, 19,* 293-301.

Mullan, H. & Sangiuliano, I. (1960). Multiple psychotherapeutic practice: Preliminary report. *American Journal of Psychotherapy, 14,* 550-565.

Nelson, G.L. (1978). Psychotherapy supervision from the trainee's point of view: A survey of preferences. *Professional Psychology, 9,* 539-550.

Nichols, W. (1975). Training and supervision. Audiotape #123, American Association of Marriage and Family Counselors, Claremont, CA.

Nichols, W.C. (1978). Supervision and training in marriage and family therapy. Paper presented to annual meeting of Gulf Coast Association for Marriage and Family Therapy, Auburn University.

Piper, W.E., Doan, D.B., Edwards, E.M. & Jones, B.D. (1979). Cotherapy behavior, group therapy process and treatment outcome. *Journal of Consulting and Clinical Psychology, 47*(6), 1081-1089.

Rice, D.G. (1979). *Dual-career marriage: Conflict and treatment.* New York: Free Press.

Rice, D.G. Fey, W.F. & Kepecs, J.G. (1972). Therapist experience and "style" as factors in co-therapy. *Family Process, 11,* 227-238.

Rice, D.G., Gurman, A.S. & Razin, A.M. (1974). Therapist sex, style, and theoretical orientation. *Journal of Nervous and Mental Disease, 159,* 413-421.

Rice, J.K. & Rice, D.G. (1975). Status and sex role issues in cotherapy. In A.S. Gurman & D.G. Rice (Eds.) *Couples in conflict: New directions in marital therapy.* New York: Aronson.

Rinsley, D.B. (1977). An object-relations view of borderline personality. In P. Hartocollis (Ed.) *Borderline personality disorders: The concept, the syndrome, the patient.* New York: International Universities Press.

Roman, M. & Meltzer, B. (1977). Cotherapy: A review of current literature (with special reference to therapeutic outcome). *Journal of Sex and Marital Therapy, 3,* 63-77.

Rubenstein, D. & Weiner, O.R. (1967). Co-therapy teamwork relationships in family therapy. In G.H. Zuk & I. Boszormenyi-Nagy (Eds.) *Family therapy and disturbed families*. Palo Alto, CA: Science and Behavior Books.

Weinstein, L. (1971). Guidelines on the choice of a co-therapist. *Psychotherapy: Theory, Research and Practice, 8*, 301-309.

Whiffen, R. (1982). The use of videotape in supervision. In R. Whiffen & J. Byng-Hall (Eds.) *Family therapy supervision: Recent developments in practice.* London: Academic Press, 1982.

Wiffen, R. & Byng-Hall, J. (Eds.) (1982). *Family therapy supervision: Recent developments in practice.* London: Academic Press.

Winokur, M. (1982). A family systems model for supervision of psychotherapy. *Bulletin of the Menninger Clinic, 46,* 125-138.

Yalom, I.D. (1975). *The theory and practice of group therapy.* (Second Ed.) New York: Basic Books.

9

Seeking and Providing Supervision in Private Practice

Florence W. Kaslow

ABSTRACT. Before an individual goes into private practice he is expected to possess the required graduate or professional degree in his discipline, several years of postgraduate clinical experience in an institutional setting under supervision, and to become licensed and/ or board certified. Once he/she has passed these milestones, he is usually considered eligible to practice independently. Yet, sometimes the individual practitioner runs into a particularly difficult case and becomes stymied. Other times they experience an impasse because of counter-transference phenomena. Occasionally one is confronted with a symptom or problem they've had little experience with. In these instances they may want to voluntarily enter into an arrangement for supervision or consultation. This paper focuses on selecting a supervisor, working out arrangements, the special aspects which accompany the decision to seek and purchase supervision and the benefits to be derived. Vignettes from supervisory practice in this context are used illustratively.

Part of the aura surrounding the idealized concept of the private practice of psychotherapy is that it signifies the clinician's arrival at some mysterious level of expertise and professional maturity where independent functioning is legally sanctioned. Yet, although the current criteria are necessary—they may not be sufficient.

The point of readiness is usually derived quantitatively in terms of (1) a terminal graduate or professional degree in one's chosen field—the shorter programs leading to an MSW or MFT/MFC and the longer ones to an MD and Residency Training in Psychiatry or a PhD/PsyD including a year of internship and maybe a post doctoral year or two in Clinical Psychology; plus usually (2) two years post

Florence W. Kaslow, Ph.D., is Director of the Florida Couples and Family Institute and in private practice in West Palm Beach, Florida. She is an Adjunct Professor of Medical Psychology in Psychiatry at Duke University Medical Center, Durham, N.C.

degree experience under supervision in an agency setting in all specialties except psychiatry—since upon completion of a residency their discipline deems them "ready" for private practice; and (3) licensure in those states and professions which require this as another criterion or proof of one's mastery of the field's knowledge base sufficient to serve the public directly and privately. Rarely, if ever, is one's clinical skill evaluated in vivo by a certifying group at the point of entry into independent practice.

Nor does this occur when coveted "Fellow" status is bestowed upon someone by a professional organization. Rather this latter distinction is awarded either based on self nomination or colleague nomination accompanied by the submission of impressive paper credentials attesting to one's research, publications, and other significant contributions to the field; and of letters of reference from outstanding peers. For example, in the American Psychological Association these credentials are evaluated by a specially designated Division Fellows Committee and if approved, forwarded to the (National) A.P.A. Membership Committee for approval or rejection. A different procedure is followed by such organizations as the American Association of Marital and Family Therapy. Here the Fellows Committee selects candidates for fellow status from those recommended by board members, Fellows Committee members and the executive staff. There is no clinical screening process. It is only at the level of "diplomate" that prestigious groups like the American Board of Professional Psychology (ABPP) and the American Board of Forensic Psychology (ABFP) require an in-person oral examination and a demonstration of one's actual clinical practice skill.

Thus there are no qualitative milestones to be demonstrated before entering private practice. Once this occurs, the clinician is free to function autonomously and in relative isolation without any further supervision or consultation. This poses an interesting spectrum of possibilities. For example, someone graduating with a B.A. at age 22 and completing an MSW or MFT program two years later (age 24), and following this with two years in a mental health clinic or family service agency is able legally to go into private practice by age 26—often lacking the depth and breadth of clinical acumen that accrue from a wide exposure to different kinds of cases and supervision in diverse settings over time. They may be the persons least likely to be invited to serve as clinical or adjunct faculty at a local university and so will be remote from centers of learning, dialogue and peer critique. At the other end of the spectrum are the analysts who usually have their B.A. at 22 years, followed by 4 years of medical school (if consecutive—they graduate at 26 years of age) and then take a 4 year residency. At the youngest, they finish this at 30 years of age—having been exposed to life and death tragedies in their medical training and psychiatric in-patient rotations. Analysis and analytic training with control cases carefully supervised may take another 4 to 5 years before the analyst is considered "ready" to practice totally on his/her own (at the tender age of 35). And there is a strong likelihood that the person will become engaged in teaching/supervising or consultation activities in the community and remain involved in the Analytic Society or Institute. The sequence followed by PhD psychologists who become analysts is similar.

Some decide on their own to stay in institutional settings for many years—preferring the safety, security, stimulation and collegiality such a context provides. If they gradually move into private practice, first part-time and later full-time, they are likely to have acquired a broader clinical knowledge of process and technique in treating a wide range of patient personalities and symptomatologies. They are also more apt to have gained a grasp of the business, financial, and ethical aspects of setting up and running a solo or small group practice.

The portrait of the independent practitioner is multidimensional. He or she can be anywhere from 26 years of age to 75 years of age—a mental health counselor, school psychologist, marital and family therapist, social worker, psychiatric nurse, clinical psychologist, psychiatrist or psychoanalyst. The practitioner can have graduated from a superb medical school and residency program or a high standard psychology graduate program—or—a non traditional university without walls semi-correspondence program. He or she may have had excellent mentors, fine supervisors and continuous exposure to top notch continuing education courses and staff training seminars. Or the clinican may have had poor to mediocre teachers, little post graduate stimulation and may reside in a state that does not licence his/her profession and therefore requires no continuing education. Thus, few generalizations can be drawn. One that can is that regardless what one's background and discipline of training—every therapist has some cases over time which are particularly difficult. Where do they turn for guidance?

IS SUPERVISION/CONSULTATION NECESSARY?

Probably and sometimes definitely. When a therapist feels "stuck" in treating a patient—there are several avenues of recourse open. The first is to transfer the case to another practitioner. This may be advisable, and at times urgent, when one finds that during the therapy something has come to the fore that they didn't anticipate and about which they know little or practically nothing. Until they have time to learn enough to deal with it competently, at the least they are short changing the patient, and at the worst, something disastrous might occur.

Two vignettes come to mind to illustrate this point—both drawn from my private practice in which I treat many therapists (Kaslow, 1984). Occasionally particularly perplexing cases are brought up in the therapeutic context around feeling inadequate or overwhelmed, angry at a supervisor, or by way of also utilizing the therapist as a mentor.

The Case of Continuous Regurgitation

Mrs. A. was a social worker who had received her MSW three years before entering therapy. After graduation she had worked primarily in the drug and alcoholism field and had administered an employee assistance plan. A bright, assertive and independent woman, she decided to go into private practice although her clinical experience was limited, when her husband suffered financial reverses and she thought being on her own would be more remunerative than her agency salary. This career shift had occurred shortly before she entered treatment and building her practice and her self confidence for this venture were among the major themes in therapy. Since her fees were relatively low and her practice was building slowly, she had made no arrangements for supervision or consultation—even on an "as needed basis".

About two months after her therapy commenced, she came in distressed about a female client who had been referred to her for young adult adjustment problems. It turned out this included severe bulimia—about which Mrs. A had known nothing. Since I am committed to the American Psychological Association Code of Ethics which states in Principle 2:

> The maintenance of high standards of competence is a responsibility shared by all psychologists in the interest of the public

and the profession as a whole. Psychologists recognize the boundaries of their competence and the limitations of their techniques. They only provide services and only use techniques for which they are qualified by training and experience. (APA Ethical Principles of Psychologists, 1981, p. 2)

I suggested that she might consider transferring the case and then begin to do some reading about and attend some workshops on the dynamics and treatment of eating disorders to prepare for handling such cases in the future. She was loathe to give up any client and perceived having to do so as a narcissistic injury to her fragile self esteem. Since my primary role was as her therapist and not as her supervisor, I had no authority over her behavior and instead focused on helping her explore the meaning of her choice and its potential consequences for her and her patient. I also encouraged her to make arrangements to purchase supervisory time—but she was not ready to realistically face her own limitations or make this investment in her practice. (Given that she was not a psychologist, she was not governed by the same code of ethics and did not seem to have been reared with this governing principle of professional behavior).

In the second case, I was seeing a psychiatrist and his wife for marital therapy. During a brief period of time when his wife was out of town, he came in alone—mostly to focus on their deteriorating relationship with his children from a previous marriage and how he could repair it. One day he wanted to talk about:

A Bewildering Case of Sexual Dysfunction

He had been treating the D's for several months because of Mr. D's "secondary impotence"—something recent in their marriage of fifteen years. The onset had seemed sudden and Dr. X had ruled out some of the usual causes of impotence including alcholism, diabetes, medications for hypertension and repressed anger. He had done some psychodynamic marital relationship therapy to no avail and wondered if I could suggest anything.

I asked if he had considered the possibility that the problem might be one of disorder of the desire phase (Kaplan, 1979; Aroaz, 1982) rather than performance phase (Kaplan, 1974) and he asked "What's the difference?" When he explored this further he revealed he had had no training in treating sexual dysfunction and had just "happened into" marital therapy. He enjoyed a fine reputation as an administrative psychiatrist and as a clinical psychiatrist treating individual patients but clearly he did not have adequate background for treating this particular syndrome. Since he thought it would be humiliating for him as a senior psychiatrist to pursue the option of seeking consultation from one of his peers, he asked instead to borrow some of my books on this subject and indicated that if this didn't suffice, he'd refer his patients to someone else—probably who was credentialed as a sex therapist.

These and other similar experiences have reinforced my contention that everyone who is in independent practice should make arrangements for supervision or consultation either on an ongoing or "as needed" basis depending on numerous factors. These include but are not limited to: (1) the depth and breadth of their knowledge and clinical experience and the gaps in same; (2) the need for a sounding board for verification and critique; (3) the periodic need to recognize and work through transference and countertransference issues; (4) the need to expand one's assessment and treatment repertoire and refine one's skills; (5) and to counter professional isolation and the stress associated with carrying the burden of hearing problems for many hours per week without access to a therapeutic support and discussion system.

CHOOSING A SUPERVISOR OR CONSULTANT

In independent practice a relative beginner or person with several years experience may want to contract with a well respected clinician for supervision. The strict meaning of "supervision" embodies recognition by supervisor and supervisee alike that the former carries the responsibility for and therefore assumes some authority over the latter. While this is quite explicit within an institutional hierarchical context, it often is not crystallized in a private arrangement, but it is important that it should be. The two individuals contemplating a supervisor/supervisee pairing need to jointly explore the conditions of and parameters surrounding their potential collaborative arrangement.

One of the critical issues which Slovenko (1980) pointed up cogently is that a supervisor carries "vicarious liability" for a supervisee. Thus, if a supervisee/trainee is sued, the supervisor may also be held accountable and named in the suit. This is a weighty responsibility in all circumstances and all the more so in independent practice. It has been pointed out during 1984 (see for example—APA Monitor, December 1984, p. 15) that the number of malpractice suits against psychologists has spiralled upwards. This in all probability means the cost of malpractice insurance will rise sharply in the near future. Thus, before agreeing to supervise anyone, the supervisor in private practice must carefully evaluate the pros and cons of entering into such a contract. He or she should make sure they add coverage for supervision on their insurance policy at the maximum level available and that each supervisee also has taken out a policy for the highest amount of coverage. Not all insurance companies will permit one to purchase coverage for members of other professions (for example—a psychologist to name a social worker as someone for whom he/she is carrying responsibility) so this should be checked before one embarks on a cross-discipline arrangement.

The legalities surrounding the responsibility of a consultant seem to be less clear. When one seeks consultation, they are entering into an arrangement that has a "take it or leave it" quality. Traditionally in an agency setting the input of a consultant is sought much more voluntarily on the basis of wanting another opinion and some guidance. The consultant does not carry any authority for making evaluative judgements on quality of performance nor does he/she make recommendations or decisions regarding promotions, retenion or firing. In the realm of private practice, it may be that when one seeks supervision, implicit in the potential relationship is a hierarchical interaction in which the supervisee is requesting that the supervisor oversee his work, critique and correct it, enhance his diagnostic and treatment skills, and carry a back-up responsibility for it. Conversely, when one asks for a consultative arrangement, one is seeking a professional dialogue with a respected colleague but is not endowing that person with authority over his/her work as they are much freer to reject it in part or in full if they disagree. It is in the realm of "another opinion" rather than of "this is how I think it should be done". Thus, one wonders if a consultant is less apt to bear vicarious liability than that of a supervisor for a consultee.

Another matter to be checked before embarking upon an interdisciplinary arrangement is whether supervision by a member of a different profession is acceptable when one is applying for clinical membership in a professional organization or attempting to accrue the requisite supervisory hours to become eligible for licensure. Sometimes such supervision is not counted and it is wise to know this before commencing to avert later disappointment and frustration.

There are numerous factors to be considered in addition to whether the potential supervisor or consultant, whichever one is seeking, is of the same or a different professional discipline. Probably the overriding consideration is whether the individual is well respected, ethical, emotionally sound, competent and an experienced clinician and supervisor. Some of the same factors enter into the selection process when therapists seek a therapist for themselves. (Fay & Lazarus, 1984; N. Kaslow & Friedman, 1984). A criterion elucidated by Grunebaum in the selection of a therapist (1982, p. 22), which I believe is equally significant in the choice of a supervisor, is that the person appreciates, respects and affirms the patient (or supervisee).

If one has lived in a community for several years or more, they will have heard about various senior professionals through the local grapevine. This "hearsay" is only a beginning point. Specific credentials in terms of education, date of degree, and current job can be ascertained by checking listings in directories of such organizations as American Psychological Association, National Association of Social Workers, or American Psychiatric Association. These also usually indicate if one holds fellow and/or diplomate status. One organization, the American Association for Marriage and Family Therapists, even designates its own approved supervisors and this is indicated in the directory listing. Another avenue is to contact officers of one's regional or state professional association and ask for recommendations for an expert supervisor. It is likely several names will be received repeatedly and this consensual validation as to "who is good" might lead one to place these names at the top of the list.

There are some additional items that might merit consideration before one makes the initial phone call exploratory overture for an appointment. Do such demographic factors as the person's race (Royster, 1972; Calnek, 1970), class or ethnic background (Kutzik, 1972; Gardner, 1980), or sex (Brodsky, 1980) matter to the person desirous of supervision? Do they believe specific similarities or differences in these variables will facilitate or impede formation and utilization of a beneficial supervisory relationship? What of age? For some these factors might be insignificant. For others they may be salient.

If the telephone inquiry goes well, it should be followed by an exploratory interview. At this time the potential supervisee/supervisor dyad should ascertain if there is a "resonance" between them similar to the one there needs to be between therapist and patient (Givelber & Simon, 1981), a "goodness of fit" that permits a joint exploration of the trainee's strengths and weaknesses and a shared adventure in expanding and enriching these strengths. When such a rapport or resonance is lacking, it is unlikely that supervision will be fruitful or rewarding and it should not be commenced. If underway and frought with non-resolveable conflict, ("bad vibrations"), it should be terminated.

One might also want to inquire about a potential supervisor or consultant's theoretical orientation. For some clinicians it is vital that the supervisor be a purist and share their orientation en toto—that is, a therapist of psychoanalytic persuasion may only be able to respond to a psychoanalyst. No matter how competent a supervisor is, if he/she is a cognitive-behaviorist, the practitioner-supervisee seeing an analyst would be resistant to him/her and the entire experience is likely to be unsatisfying and possibly even disastrous for both. Students in graduate programs may have to "submit" to being supervised by someone who holds radically different beliefs and utilizes interventions at odds with their own in order to "broaden" their perspective and to not antagonize anyone with high rank in the establishment. But in private practice, one is free to pursue supervision with someone who is equally orthodox in their theoretical stance and should, if this is their predilection. A supervisor's theoretical persuasion initially can be checked through the informal grapevine, through reading his/her publications, and/or through attending his/her lectures or workshops. If these avenues are not available, when the exploratory phone contact is made one should ask directly, yet politely, what the supervisors' theoretical orientation is.

Conversely, there are others who wish to use the supervisory experience as a way to expand their horizons and thus grapple with and absorb additional conceptual frameworks and accompanying intervention approaches. For example, a family therapist steeped in Bowenian theory (1977) may be pleased to be supervised by a structural (Minuchin, et al., 1974) or systemic (Selvini Palazzoli, et al., 1978) theoretician/practitioner. In fact, he/she might consider it a privilege to have an opportunity to train with someone who holds another viewpoint and thereby to fill in some of the gaps in his/her own knowledge base and skills armamentarium. Therefore, whether one prefers a supervisor of same or different theoretical persuasion, determining which is an important element in the final choice.

SCREENING POTENTIAL SUPERVISEES AND CONTRACTING FOR SERVICE

Just as someone seeking a supervisor needs to make a selection that is judicious for them, the person being approached to supervise also has to exercise some judgement as to who to accept. The most obvious concern revolves around whether the candidate has the minimum formal education and degrees required by the supervisor—particularly if the supervision is to be counted toward organizational membership or licensure. Other important considerations are likely to encompass the trainee's personality (will they be compatible in their interactions), interpersonal skills, level of intelligence, theoretical orientation and underlying flexibility or rigidity, level of maturity, ability and willingness to take risks in therapy sessions, and stage of moral and ethical development.

It is often wise to agree to a short trial contract for three or four supervisory sessions. If all goes well, the agreement can be extended for a given time period (six months to a year) or for x number of sessions. Frequency and length of sessions should be specified as should cost and time of payment. The supervisee's goals and expectations should be clearly articulated at the outset and redefined periodically.

The cost aspect warrants additional attention. Individuals who have practiced within an institutional setting receive supervision as an often mandated necessity that seems to be a continuous right. Sometimes it is sparse and of inferior quality and the supervisee may "grin and bear it" because of passivity or expediency or may ask to be transferred to another supervisor. Other times it becomes supervision ad nauseum—too frequent for an experienced therapist who only needs occasional consultation. Ideally, it is timed well and of good quality—changing over time as the supervisee becomes more confident and proficient. But always it is part of the employment package—*there is no charge.* Thus, when one enters private practice and has to purchase supervisory time, it comes as quite a shock. Good supervision is costly; it constitutes a major investment in one's ongoing education and a professional commitment to maintaining some objectivity about one's work.

Generally most therapists I know who do private supervision charge the same for a supervisory hour as they do for a therapy hour. They derive a portion of their income from this activity and allocate a certain number of hours for supervision. They structure the supervisory session to be confidential and uninterrupted—viewing it as a parallel process to therapy and a therapy of the therapy—not of the therapist—thus modelling good form (Abroms, 1977). If they agree to do small group supervision of two to four people, they usually extend the time frame and raise the fee by 25% to 50% depending on the number of participants who will be dividing it. Supervising three people *is* more time consuming than supervising only one—as when there are records to read and videotapes to view in preparation for sessions. And if one adds all supervisees to their malpractice insurance coverage, this too is a cost that needs to be absorbed somewhere.

Trainees who want pro bono or discounted supervision might well examine whether such requests or feelings of entitlement relate to their own dependency needs, exploitative behaviors or non-recognition of the business and professional aspects of theirs and the supervisors' private practices.

By way of illustration of some of the above phenomena:

Several years ago I began doing staff training and case consultation for a medium size private practice group. Two of the women in the group approached me about wanting supplementary more in-depth consultation—always focused on their cases rather than rotating turns with 10 others. For the following reasons it was agreed they would come together. My office was a long drive from theirs and they could come and go together and share ideas en route; they were at about the same level of professional development and could learn from listening to the discussion on each others cases; the cost would be more manageable if they could share it.

The first session went exceedingly well. At the second session K announced this would be her last—that she realized she had never before paid for supervision nor had she travelled and been inconvenienced to acquire it. Instead she decided that if she were stymied, she'd prevail on a colleague for whom she had done a favor to "chat" with her about it over lunch—for free, or at most, for the price of lunch. She was banking on the fact that her colleagues would find it difficult to say no.

In pulling out, she seemed unconcerned about the impact of her behavior on N. She had broken a commitment to her (and to me) for a minimum three month period of bi weekly sessions. Nonetheless, N wanted to continue as she recognized the greater value of formal over "catch as catch can" supervision so we renegotiated the time frame and cost of the seasons.

In a very different vein, one or two focused supervisory sessions can break a deadlock, unhinge a countertransference reaction, and quickly reenergize a faltering therapy. In accordance with what is articulated by Friedman & Kaslow in terms of stages of development in the supervisory process (Chapter 3), it is important that the supervisor assess accurately the supervisee's developmental level, maturity, knowledge base and clinical skill. Then he or she should home in on the focal issues that constitutes the impasse—determining: is it lack of understanding of the problem/syndrome/personality or interaction, is it a deficit in determining and utilizing an intervention strategy, or is it an interpersonal transference or countertransference issue? Once this is done, the supervisor can either guide the person toward uncovering for himself/herself the core of the impasse, or can directly and tactfully communicate his/her interpretation of the difficulty and make some suggestions as to how to work it through or overcome it. Which of these or other valid supervisory paths are pursued will depend on the personality, style, orientation and needs of both supervisee and supervisor. There is certainly more than one right way!

In another supervision with me:

Betty was a masters level marriage and family therapist. She was troubled by Mr. T, a patient of hers who was a Ph.D. psychologist. He had been referred to her because she had a reputation for being an effective therapist with recovering substance abusers and he had been "doing drugs" heavily. His progress was erratic and Betty often felt unnerved by him.

In supervision we dealt with her covert desire to go back for her Ph.D. and her feelings of inferiority with people who outranked her academically. She was surprised and flattered by his willingness to come to her, but always slightly uneasy when he played "one upsmanship games" with her. In addition, he was quite seductive and occasionally queried why she was so cold and inaccessible indicating that "many women find me attractive and would be flattered by my interest". His implication was that there was something wrong with her; that she lacked warmth and couldn't be very sensuous as she was impervious to his overtures.

She was irate and thwarted. In supervision we zeroed in on her particular vulnerability to his patterns. First, she herself wanted her doctorate and believed this higher degree does signify greater competence and accomplishment. Having Mr. T as a patient exacerbated her sense of inadequacy regarding credentials. We explored the reality of her ability to go back to graduate school at this time and worked out a plan for her to return part-time the following fall and switch to full-time the year after. I also reinforced her ability to claim the many areas of knowledge and skill she already possessed. We validated the fact that she had been an effective therapist for many patients in the past and bolstered her sense of professional adequacy by touching on some very difficult cases in which her interventions had led to a positive difference in people's functioning. In terms of the therapy, it seemed that perhaps it would be fruitful for therapist and patient that she raise the question of why he sought her services given the more usual pattern of seeking a therapist with greater rather than fewer formal credentials. This might enable him to examine his motivation and need to be in the power position though ultimately this could sabotage the therapy.

The second arena of concern was Mr. T's seductiveness and quips about her coldness. We looked at this as inappropriate behavior on his part—cognitively as a psychologist he knew his therapist's Code of Ethics precluded any sexual involvement. But emotionally, along with his addictive personality he was extremely narcissistic and destructive. He wanted to know he could have any woman he wanted—and the more status he ascribed to a woman, the more he saw "having" her as a victory. Once he made his conquest, he would first demean and then abandon her.

At this point in time Betty was emotionally and physically disengaged from her husband and considering separation. He too had been accusing her of being an "ice queen" and so similar taunts from her patient had stirred her up immensely.

In supervision we considered her self concept regarding the qualities of warmth, empathy and sensuousity. She saw the patient as both an undesirable and taboo love object. She confronted her dislike for her husband and that she was decathecting from him and on a pathway to separation. But she did not feel cold, barren, or unsexy.

Thus we agreed that she should do "bad therapy" (Lang, 1982) and confront him about his pattern—using his behavior with her as a case in point and adding it to numerous others he recounted directly pointing out his need to conquer and be destructive with women; his asking her to transgress professional ethics, and in doing all of the above—violating his AA recovery program. This was to be done calmly, nonjudgmentally, yet with conviction. Once she was freed from feeling "put down" by his criticisms and had worked through her angry counter-transference, she was able to move ahead and deal with his pathology—without wanting to inflict further narcissistic injury to his fragile masculine ego.

PROCESS AND METHOD

The "flow" of the supervisory process and various contemporary methods have been dealt with intensively and extensively in other chapters in this volume. Thus, to do so again would be redundant.

Suffice it to say here that within the context of private practice supervision, the processes and methods utilized should be predicated upon the therapist/supervisee's level of development and proficiency, the number of sessions to be allocated for supervision, the flexibility and range of techniques possessed by the supervisor, and the availability of technical equipment. Certainly there should be some supervision based on process recordings—especially with a relatively recent private practitioner who is not ready to risk fuller self disclosure. And with a very advanced practitioner with whose work the supervisor is conversant, a summary record accompanied by verbal highlighting may provide enough data for the supervisor to move in and untangle an impasse. On other occasions, utilization of segments of audiotape and/or videotape comprise important avenues for hearing and seeing the therapeutic interchange in all its nuances and subtleties of voice tone, length of articulations, gesture, seating arrangement, therapist demeanor, etc. The more direct approaches of co-therapy, observation through a one way screen and calling in or going in to the treatment room to intervene all have their merits and should be utilized when and if appropriate. Only by observing someone in action does a supervisor ever really know what it is that their supervisee does. To the extent that the supervisor has or can arrange to utilize video equipment or a one way mirror, this broadens the range of supervisory possibilities. If the course of supervision is to run for more than a few sessions to break a stalemate on a particular case, or on an occasional as needed basis, then it is probably advisable to employ two or three different methods over time as each approach is likely to heighten different awarenesses in the supervisor and lead to additional kinds of critique, feedback and reinforcement for the supervisee.

CONCLUDING REMARKS

Up until the last decade private practitioners were utilized primarily as therapists and as consultants to agencies and organizations (Cohen, 1977). Their utilization as supervisors, sought out voluntarily by other practitioners, is a recent development. As a group they constitute a rich resource since they are a repository of much experience in both the clinical and business aspects of independent practice. The fact that private practitioners, who tend to value their autonomy greatly, are voluntarily seeking expert supervision from competent therapists at their own expense is a testament to their desire for continual learning and increased diagnostic acumen and intervention skills for the sake of improving the quality of practice. Another valid and practical motivation, though perhaps slightly less noble, is to acquire supervised hours credited toward licensure and/ or organizational membership. Perhaps such supervision also might have positive implications for the peer review process. No matter what the motivation, the contract should be clear and mutually acceptable and upheld by each party to it, and their working relationship should be compatible. Only then can the process be valid and fruitful.

REFERENCES

Abroms, G.M. (1977). Supervision as metatherapy. In F.W. Kaslow (Ed), *Supervision, consultation and staff training in the helping professions.* San Francisco: Jossey Bass.

American Psychological Association (1981 revision). *Ethical principles of psychologists.* Washington, D.C.: American Psychological Association.

American Psychological Association (December 1984). *The Monitor* (p. 15). Washington, D.C.: American Psychological Association.

Araoz, D. (1982). Clinical hypnosis in treating sexual abulia. In F.W. Kaslow (Ed), *The international book of family therapy.* New York: Brunner/Mazel.

Bowen, M. (1978). *Family therapy in clinical practice.* New York: Jason Aronson.

Calnek, M. (1970). Racial factors in countertransference. *American Journal of Orthopsychiatry, 40,* 39-46.

Cohen, E. (1977). Private practitioners. In F.W. Kaslow (Ed) *Supervision, consultation and staff training in the helping professions.* San Francisco: Jossey Bass.

Fay, A. & Lazarus, A.A. (1984). The therapist in behavioral and multi-modal therapy. In F.W. Kaslow (Ed.), *Psychotherapy with psychotherapists.* New York: Haworth.

Gardner, L.H. (1980). Racial, ethnic and social class considerations in psychotherapy supervision. In A.K. Hess (Ed) *Psychotherapy supervision.* New York: Wiley.

Givelber, F. & Simon, B. (1981). A death in the life of a therapist and its impact on therapy. *Psychiatry, 44.*

Grunebaum, H. (1982). A good therapist is hard to find. Mimeographed paper.

Kaplan, H.S. (1974). *The new sex therapy.* New York: Brunner/Mazel.

Kaplan, H.S. (1979). *Disorders of sexual desire.* New York: Brunner/Mazel.

Kaslow, F.W. (Ed), (1984). *Psychotherapy with psychotherapists.* New York: Haworth.

Kaslow, N.J. & Friedman, D. (1984). The interface of personal treatment and clinical training for psychotherapist trainees. In F.W. Kaslow (Ed), *Psychotherapy with psychotherapists.* New York: Haworth.

Kutzik, A. (1972). Class and ethnic factors. In F.W. Kaslow (Ed), *Issues in human services.* San Francisco: Jossey Bass.

Lang, M. (1982). Bad therapy—a way of learning. In F.W. Kaslow (Ed) *The international book of family therapy.* New York: Brunner/Mazel.

Minuchin S. (1974). *Families and family therapy.* Cambridge: Harvard University Press.

Royster, E. (1972). Black supervisors: problems of race and role. In F.W. Kaslow (Ed) *Issues in human services.* Jossey Bass.

Selvini-Palazzoli, M., Boscolo, L., Cecchin, G., Prata, G. (1978). *Paradox and counterparadox.* New York: Jason Aronson.

Slovenko, R. (1980). Legal issues in psychotherapy supervision. In A.K. Hess (Ed), *Psychotherapy supervision.* New York: Wiley.

10
Peer Supervision in the Community Mental Health Center: An Analysis and Critique

Steven A. Roth

ABSTRACT. This chapter is divided into three major sections. The first part delineates six models of supervision that are frequently used in a community mental health setting. The second section spells out some of the possible administrative considerations and concerns regarding supervision in family service agencies, mental health centers, social service organizations, and similar counseling environments. The last segment of this chapter describes a novel supervision model which I have called "peer supervision carried to the extreme". This model has been used in a community mental health center in the Rocky Mountain region. This model is analyzed and its advantages and disadvantages are explicated. It is the conclusion of this author that the "peer supervision carried to extreme" format is viable, but only under certain specific conditions which in the short run may make the model less attractive to community mental health centers.

FREQUENT MODELS OF SUPERVISION

Most community mental health centers provide some form of supervision for their clinical staff. Hess, in his excellent chapter "Training Models and the Nature of Psychotherapy Supervision" (1980) describes six types of supervision models which I will adapt to the community mental health setting, as all of them are used at one time or another. His definition of supervision is a "dyadic human interaction with a focus on modifying the behavior of the supervisee, so he or she may provide better service to a third person."

Steven A. Roth, Ph.D., is Assistant Director of the Florida Couples and Family Institute and in Independent (private) Practice at 2617 North Flagler Drive, West Palm Beach, Florida 33407.

Most mental health centers still utilize more one-on-one supervision than other approaches.

Hess designates the first type the *lecturer model.* Here, the Center would invite an expert to come and speak to its staff about his/her theories, techniques or approach to treatment. The goal of the lecturer is to educate and to share his/her views and at times to do some subtle proselytizing. Staff attend the lecture to meet a person whose work they have read about, or to learn new skills or techniques. This approach has many advantages including that it may be cost effective as many people can attend, it serves as a stimulus to discussion, and the lecturer may impart new skills for participants to try out on their own clients. The lecturer may also generate excitement in a relatively staid and in-bred staff, especially in rural areas. The disadvantages of this model are that each individual's own questions and agenda items may not be addressed. Secondly, if the lecturer does not stimulate the audience, a relatively useful tool may never be tried. Lastly, a naive audience member may get the impression that they are also now an expert and may try techniques without being fully aware of the consequences of their actions.

The *teacher model* can be adapted to a community mental health center when administration decides to offer a seminar or course either on or off center premises to select staff who show interest in becoming more adept in a particular area such as family therapy, gestalt techniques, or behavior modification. In this setting the group is usually smaller than in the lecture model and there is time for presenting both didactic and current clinical case material. The course should be tailored to the needs of the community mental health center, as well as to the level of the individuals participating in it, yet be taught in a fully professional manner. The teacher and the "trainees" need to both be aware of the goals and tasks involved in the course.

The third approach, the *case conference* or case review, where ongoing difficult or unresolved cases are discussed by a total staff, is used very often in the typical mental health setting. The goal of this means of supervision is to clarify and aid in the decision making process for the case presenter, and to give the patient the benefit of the knowledge of an entire multidisciplinary staff. What often happens in a community mental health center setting is that this method of supervision starts off well, but over time (three to six months) dies a slow death. What appears to be going on is that new ideas are not often appreciated and as the old ways start to be questioned the senior staff make it subtly and not so subtly known that the deviations are not appreciated and are not to be shared. Sometimes the presenter is boring, the case moves slowly, and attendance drops off.

Conversely, some of the potential, albeit rarely allowed to bear fruit, benefits from the case conference method of supervision are: (1) to learn which staff members are tuned in to the same wave lengths as you are, (2) to help in the management of cases which are difficult and frustrating, and (3) to gain practice in presenting one's viewpoint and therapeutic process in a concise and convincing manner. When the case material is gripping in and of itself and the presenter raises the really critical diagnostic and treatment issues, this approach can be thought provoking and enriching.

Many mental health centers have the *collegial-peer* method of supervision whether or not it is formally explicated in policy. It just seems to evolve when people of the same discipline are housed in the same surroundings and have similar responsibilities. This is usually a rather informal model and its goals are often unstated, rather than being formally spelled out. Just having someone with whom to air a case, to go over a procedure or technique, often clarifies one's concept of how to proceed. This particular form of supervision does not usually cause any problems in a community mental health center unless the two individuals lock other professionals out of their relationship and refuse to participate in any kind of supervision other than the one in which they are involved.

The *monitor model* of supervision is the one that probably would be most unappreciated by the staff of a mental health center. The role of a monitor is primarily to see that no harm is done in providing services to patients. This leaves out any chances for innovation as innovation involves risk. It also leaves out room for favorable feedback as the monitoring function is one of external censor and evaluator with its goal being the provision of minimally acceptable psychotherapeutic practice. This is unfortunate, as often minimally acceptable is what is achieved, but at least there are no waves or risks. Center staff seem to have an instant aversion to anyone looking over their shoulders and telling them what to do or not to do.

The last (sixth) model is one in which the supervisor also becomes, in effect, the therapist for his supervisee. Even though one might expect to see this often in a community mental health center setting, it has been this author's experience that just the opposite is the case. The notion of "therapizing the therapist," or don't "social work the social worker'' holds on strongly in an agency setting where there is potentially a feeling that there is a great deal to lose by revealing too much about oneself. The goal of helping the therapist grow is a noble one, and it is easy to see how a supervisor who is also a therapist would tend to slip into the role of a therapist in order to help his supervisee. The right to comment on the therapist's mental health is not usually spelled out in the supervisory contract (Abroms, 1977). In a community mental health center even if this right to comment is explicated, there is no real guarantee that the supervisee will not take the commentary as a criticism. When this occurs it creates a negative impact on both the supervision process and the therapy being supervised. Abroms (1977) further states ''supervision is a therapy of therapy...'' ''The patient is clearly neither the supervisee not the supervisee's client but rather the therapeutic relationship between them.'' If a supervisor feels that personality change is necessary if his supervisee is to function at his/her optimal level, then referral to an independent therapist away from the agency is recommended.

Many mental health centers experiment with many models of supervision until they find the one that seems to work for them, and to meet their needs at any particular time. In human service settings, in general, the model has most often been that one receives training and supervision from senior, more experienced members of one's own profession (Kaslow, 1977). Given the relatively small size of many mental health centers this is not always possible or practical, and does not fit in with the egalitarian philosophy of the community mental health movement.

ADMINISTRATIVE CONSIDERATIONS

Supervision as an activity is difficult for many mental health centers to justify to their community boards since it is a non-reimbursable, non-revenue-producing activity. The business structure of a non-profit center requires effective utilization of staff hours in order to generate the funds needed to carry out the mission of the center. Fees are usually based on a sliding scale with no one turned away because of inability to pay. Fees of $2.00 to $10.00 are not uncommon, and rarely go above $50.00 to $55.00 per session. One has only to look at the structure of time available to provide services in order to see the dilemma which many centers find themselves in when trying to determine how much time to allocate for supervision. Most centers provide salaried positions for their clinical and business office staffs. For clinical staff, salary ranges are determined by degree (Ph.D., Ed.D., MSW, MA, BA, non-degreed), profession (psychology, social work, education, mental health worker, psychiatric nurse) and, to a lesser extent, degree of responsibility and additional quasi-administrative duties. Clinical staff normally receive their salary every other week or once monthly whether they are involved in the provision of direct clinical services eighty percent of the time or forty percent of the time. Fees and consultation and education contracts and activities provide the main sources of outside income for centers. This is, of course, in addition to state, county, city and federal grants which for many centers comprise the bulk of their funds. Mental health centers, like many other businesses, are involved in activities which are non-revenue producing. Some of these non-reimbursable time consuming activities are staff meetings, committee meetings, report and case note writing time, phone calls, conferences with collateral contacts (can be reimbursable, but most often are not), coffee breaks, reading and research, and supervision.

Let's look for a moment at how time is spent in a mental health center in order to understand better the concern over time allocated for supervision. In a usual year there are 262 days (Monday through Friday) available to provide services. A mental health center may offer (and this is not at all unusual) its clinical staff the following:

1. one month vacation (20 working days)
2. twelve days sick leave
3. one week conference or staff development time (5 working days)
4. ten paid holidays

This totals to 47 days out of 262 when a clinician may not be available to provide service, leaving 215 days available to provide client services. In percentage terms the days available have been reduced by 17.9%. If one assumes that a very good therapist is able to use 30 of the 40 hours in the week or 75% of their time to provide clinical services (which this author believes is definitely a high estimate and it is thought to be closer to 55% or 60%) then this means that there are now 161 person days per year available to provide services. Comparing this 161 days to the original 262 it is seen that the number of days available to provide service has been reduced by 39%. It is not that uncommon to have a community mental health center provide 50% to 60% direct treatment services which would translate into 106 and 129 days respectively that are available for reimbursable activities. Is it any wonder that supervision, or for that matter, any non-reimbursable activity is constantly being questioned when centers are only able to provide at a maximum potential of 60%?

Supervision becomes one of those non-billable activities which mental health center administrators seem to always be trying to reduce in order to raise the hours available for reimbursable activities. Experienced, senior staff normally would be capable of commanding the highest fee from clients and are expected to be most efficient in their use of their time. These are also the individuals who are called upon most often to be supervisors. Depending upon the size of the staff these individuals may spend anywhere from 10 to 20 hours a week providing supervision.

PEER SUPERVISION IN THE EXTREME

One method of supervision which appears to be different from any of those described by Hess which has been tried because it meets both the egalitarian nature of the community mental health center and maximizes the available time of the more experienced staff is what I will call peer supervision carried to the extreme. What is involved in this method of supervision is that all staff are involved as both supervisors and supervisees. Each staff member supervises one other staff member and in turn is supervised by (in most cases) a different staff member. The decision as to who supervises whom is made without respect to longevity, experience, professional discipline or ability as a therapist or supervisor. Administrators, who in many cases are themselves at least part-time clinicians, make the decision as to the supervisor-supervisee pairing. The resulting dyad may involve a mental health worker supervising a psychologist, an MSW social worker supervising another MSW social worker with five years more experience, or the more conventional dyads of more experienced supervising less experienced and more capable supervising less capable. These supervisory pairs will usually last for six to ten months and then the system switches totally. These dyads meet once a week for one hour and thus all staff spend a maximum of two hours a week in supervision.

There are many assumptions made when attempting this method of supervision. They include that:

1. All staff are capable of being supervisors.
2. This method is more effective from the standpoint of time and manpower than other forms of supervision.
3. Over the long haul everyone will have received some quality supervisory experience.
4. The ability to supervise is not a separate skill, but one that all people possess in greater or lesser quantities.

Let us consider each of these assumptions separately and in some depth. The first assumption is true, if it is expanded upon. Yes, all staff are probably capable of being supervisors but only *if* they are given training to be supervisors, have the experience to draw upon and knowledge to impart positive and negative criticism, and the skill and tact to retain some distance between themselves and their supervisee during the supervision process, even though they may be good friends outside of this process. This is no small order and the likelihood is great that the above activities will not be carried out, and that not all staff meet the qualifications for experience nor have the skill and tact necessary to be effective supervisors. If the primary goal of supervision is just to have another staff member be aware of the clients in another therapist's caseload, and share responsibility for them in that therapists absence, then all staff are capable of being supervisors. If the goal of supervision is to let all staff experience what it is like to supervise someone else without worrying about the quality of that supervision then yes, everyone is capable of being a supervisor.

If time is a primary consideration in the supervisory process, there is no great saving in actual time by using this peer supervision model. If one has ten staff members it makes no difference to the total time expenditure whether one person spends ten hours supervising ten people (total of twenty hours of staff time) or each of the ten staff people spend two hours each, one hour supervising and one hour being supervised for a total of twenty hours of staff time per week. More time may be wasted if staff do not find their supervisor satisfactory. The chances are good that they will seek additional supervision from another staff member (often a staff psychiatrist or senior psychologist or social worker) thus actually using considerably more than the two hours allocated. To further make matters worse, the staff member may feel guilty about what he/she is doing and share one or two cases with this staff person, one or two cases with another and fractionate their available time to see patients even further defeating the intent of the peer supervision.

It is potentially true that over a two year period of time using the peer supervision model all staff will have had at least one good supervisory experience. Some staff will have had more than one while some staff will likely just have the one good experience. The newer, less experienced staff are the ones that are likely to suffer the most as they need quality supervision experience for their own professional growth, as well as to gauge their appropriateness and fit within the larger organization. Their models for supervision are often limited so that when they supervise an individual they are just as likely to model some of the negative, punitive aspects of their own supervisors as they are to model some of the more positive, caring aspects. The other group which gets hurt by this system is the center's top quality therapists. They seemingly have profited and grown from past supervisory experience and may come away from a peer supervision experience feeling somewhat burned out rather than enervated, and feeling that the organization has cheated them. (Many mental health centers have in their personnel policies the provision of supervision to all staff).

What seems to be happening with the peer supervision system is a push to mediocrity—the really talented, solid staff person as well as the new, naive staff person are the ones that get hurt most. This development toward the "mean", middle, and mediocre has done a great deal over time to damage the reputation of mental health centers. Many centers, in addition to the assumption that all staff are capable of supervising, also assume that all staff are generalists and can handle any case that walks through the door, that all staff are able to consult with outside agencies, and that all staff can handle emergency situations with the same degree of efficiency. This striving for total equality of function and purpose tends to create an impression of being neither very good nor very bad as not all people are capable of doing all things equally well. The staff who mess up, create litigious situations, give a bad impression by their lack of abilities in specified areas are compensated for by the staff who present a positive, well considered front to the community, but the overall impression becomes "fair to middling" or "not bad, but not good either". It is felt that propagating the idea that all staff are also capable supervisors just goes one more step to pushing a community mental health center to the brink of mediocrity, or less.

Not to be totally negative about the idea of peer supervision, there is some potential for success *if* care is taken in setting up the system. Training would need to be provided for all staff, and at least initially some supervision of supervisors. The training of staff should take into consideration the needs of staff members, and guidelines are needed to provide at least a modicum of uniformity in the supervision process. The process needs to be taken seriously with a commitment from center administration to change if things are not going well. If all of the above criteria are met one can envision some good coming out of the process of peer supervision. It is a democratic process with no member of any discipline having to feel more or less capable or qualified to supervise (*if trained well*), just by virtue of their professional affiliation or educational background. This can go a long way in boosting staff morale as a good clinician is a good clinician whether they be a doctoral level psychologist, a masters level psychologist, a social worker or a mental health worker. No one profession holds the key to quality of supervision and this can also be recognized through a peer supervision system. The long time staff member may be surprised (hopefully, happily so) by some of the enthusiasm and fresh ideas and techniques of a relatively newly trained supervisor staff member leading to an expansion of their own repertoire. This can lead to a lowering of burn out and further feelings of competence. The new staff member gets an immediate feeling of belongingness, and their feelings of self worth are also enhanced by their capability of sharing some of their education and knowledge with the ''old-line staff.'' The long-time staff member who has grown little over the years is somewhat forced out of his/ her complacency when new staff are immediately put in a position of responsibility. The over-inflated ego starts to lose some of its air when a young ''whippersnapper'' with some obvious skills is placed in a supervisory position over them. One key result of the peer supervision process can be more tightly knit staff with a heightened feeling of mutual respect within the various mental health professions.

CONCLUSION

In summary, the ''peer supervision carried to the extreme'' model is sometimes workable and potentially good for the image and ongoing functioning of a community mental health center. At other times it is destructive, time consuming, and a flag bearer for perpetuating the perception of mental health centers as lacking excellence or even it's pursuit. The critical variables appear to be the time spent in organizing, the thought given to individual pairings, and most importantly, the amount and type of training in the supervisory process given to all staff members.

If a particular center is viewing peer supervision as a time-saving or short cut method of supervision they will only be doing their staff and their own image a disservice by pursuing it any further. Initially there should be a large expenditure of time devoted to training and to planning. Ongoing training and at least initial supervision of supervisors involve further expenditures of time. No staff member should be forced into a supervisory role if they are adamantly against it, so that an alternative supervisory process may need to be organized. Time, in a community mental health center, (as well as many other social service organizations) is literally money as time is the commodity being sought by clients and "sold" by the agency. It would take a financially sound center, highly committed to exploring new avenues of and skill in supervision, to be willing to expend the time in a non-revenue producing activity to make this model function soundly. Hopefully, there are some organizations which meet these criteria, and which are also willing to devote the time and energy necessary to do some research into the efficacy of this model for community mental health centers.

REFERENCES

Abroms, G.M. (1977), Supervision as metatherapy. In F.W. Kaslow (Ed.), *Supervision, consultation and staff training in the helping professions* (pp. 81-99). San Francisco, California: Jossey-Bass.

Hess, A.K. (1980). *Psychotherapy supervision: Theory, research and practice.* New York: Wiley.

Kaslow, F.W. (1977), Community mental health centers. In F.W. Kaslow (Ed.), *Supervision, consultation, and staff training in the helping professions* (pp. 268-281). San Francisco, California: Jossey-Bass.

PART III:
TRAINING TO IMPROVE
THE QUALITY OF PRACTICE

11

Family Therapy and Systems Supervision With the "Pick-a-Dali Circus" Model

Judith Landau Stanton
M. Duncan Stanton

ABSTRACT. This chapter describes supervision within a team model in which the whole team usually remains in the room with the family and, often, the referring person(s) and family friends. The method involves an active, flowing process and the development of metaphors and enactments that are often surrealistic in nature, at times becoming a "theatre of the absurd." The general idea is to explicate and validate all opinions within the system, including those of the extended family, referring persons and other helping professionals, and to integrate these views into a composite whole from which the family can then make a choice without being unduly triangulated. Use of this model in training is discussed as it applies to (a)

Judith Landau Stanton, M.D., and M. Duncan Stanton are both on the faculty of the Department of Psychiatry at the University of Rochester Medical Center and are involved in running a family therapy training program.

This is a revision and expansion of a paper entitled "Aspects of Supervision with the 'Pick-a-Dali Circus' Model", published in the *Journal of Strategic and Systematic Therapies*, 1983, *2* (2), 31-39.

169

inexperienced trainees as team members, (b) inexperienced clinicians as "identified" therapists to the family, and (c) experienced family therapists who have no prior experience with the model. It is proposed that this form of multi-faceted supervision can be utilized as a primary mode for training beginning family therapists.

The approach that we have come to call the "Pick-a-Dali Circus" was developed by the first author (JLS) in the mid 1960s—although it has undergone modification and improvement during the ensuing years. It started as an informal team of professionals from different disciplines meeting more or less haphazardly together with families, rather than as a formalized "training of family therapists." It was necessitated by the frequent number of cases which involved multiple treating and helping systems. Knowing that a patient and family have to return to their natural environment and support systems when they depart the treatment setting, it seemed wisest to intervene in a way that would be least disruptive of these multiple systems so that they would not neutralize changes induced in the therapy. The approach taken, therefore, was to empower, validate and avoid alienating members of the extended family, other helpers, and "external" systems involved, by representing, and even expanding, their views within therapy sessions.

The training facet of the Pick-a-Dali Circus (PDC) evolved parallel to its emergence as a treatment approach. This was partly for reasons of practicality, in that some of the training of would-be family therapists that the author was undertaking occurred in centers which had no one-way mirrors or videotape equipment. Another factor was that the work took place in a developing country—South Africa—in which there were great numbers of trainees to be concurrently brought to a similar level of competence, along with an urgency to train supervisors. As will be described, this model, in addition to showing therapeutic efficacy, has evolved into a highly effective training method (Landau and Stanton, 1983).

THE METHOD

In Pick-a-Dali Circus various spatial, metaphoric, and kinetic features can be introduced by team members as they interact with the family and each other within the therapy room itself. Since the method is described in greater detail elsewhere (Landau and Stanton, 1985) it will be only briefly presented here, greater emphasis being given to the training and supervisory aspects of the experience.

Team methods using live supervision are not new to the field, most notably beginning with Multiple Impact Therapy (MacGregor, Ritchie, Serrano, Schuster, MacDanald and Goolishian, 1964) and family networking (Speck and Attneave, 1973). Teams have also been employed by the Milan group (Palazzoli-Selvini, Boscolo, Cecchin and Prata, 1978), Goolishian and associates in Galveston, Olson and Pegg (1979) in England, various groups at the Ackerman Institute (e.g., Papp's [1980] "Greek Chorus"), Todd (1981), the Brief Family Therapy Center in Milwaukee (de Shazar, 1982), Damman and colleagues in Atlanta (Berger and Dammann, 1982), Heath (1982), and others, including various groups at the Philadelphia Child Guidance Clinic—in several of which the second author (MDS) participated (Morenas, 1983). While PDC shares a number of similarities with these, and has been influenced by several of them, it also embodies a rationale and many operations that differentiate it from them.

In many ways, PDC is like theatre of the absurd. Team members respond singularly, in couples or small groups, or in unison in an ongoing, flowing way during the session. They may physically situate themselves at different places in the room, change their positions, leave the room alone or in groups to observe through a one-way mirror, and so on, in accordance with the therapeutic strategem of the moment. The general idea is to first view the family as stuck at a point of transition, with its various members dispersed in their positions along one or more dimensions (e.g., emphasis on nuclear family demands versus those of the extended family). Conflict is seen to arise as attempts are made to resolve the disparities among family subsystems (Landau, 1982; in press; Landau-Stanton, Mason and Griffiths, 1982). Some of the other major dimensions across which family members distribute themselves are: closeness (joining)-distance, safety-danger, sanity-craziness, strictness-lenience, leadership-submission ("one down"), anger-nurturance (gentleness), dependence-independence, optimism-pessimism, sadness-happiness, authority-ignorance, humor-seriousness, teasing (mocking)-empathy. Different families will, of course, show greater intra-family disparity on some dimensions than others, and family themes will tend to gravitate selectively toward particular dimensions in a given family (e.g., enmeshed versus disengaged; depressed-happy; noisy-quiet; disorganized-regimented).

Knowing this, the therapy team also distributes itself along the various dimensions, both mirroring the family spectra and exaggerating, amplifying or polarizing their dispersions. The team, moving from a specific, common position, might proceed to spread itself out along a given spectrum, thereby reflecting the actual (often hidden) ambivalence in the family. This establishes a new, workable reality, injecting flexibility in the family and perhaps decentralizing one member. Hidden conflicts and family secrets are mirrored, exposed and prepared for resolution, often through the use of humor, play and teasing (which are acceptable in this context because someone else in the room provides a steady counterbalance of solemnity and empathy). Such a process commonly leads to an active, swirling, surrealistic portrayal of the family conflict—the team picks or fashions an appropriate Dali-like metaphor or enactment for the family and spreads it before them.* This could lead to various team members "running away" (e.g., rapidly leaving the room) from a family with a runaway child or being crazier and more psychotic than a family in schizophrenic process (Landau and Stanton, 1985). Often it is a method of introducing a "relative contrast" to the family pattern (Stanton, 1981c) much like that used by Andolfi, Menghi, Nicolo and Saccu (1980).

Conversely, the team members, being "distributed" along a given dimension, might suddenly converge, concertina-like, on a particular point and exert pressure (push) only at that point. This may occur (a) spontaneously (usually with an experienced team that has worked together), (b) under the explicit direction of the team leader, or (c) following a pre-planning session in which such a decision had been made *a priori*.

In therapy with a single therapist it is often difficult for the clinician to see more than one or two dimensions at a time. However, with the introduction of a team, one gets a multi-dimensional, moving view in technicolor. The complexity of the process takes one beyond the "bi-cameral view" (Bateson, 1979; Hoffman, 1981)—the difference is like that between a black and white Mercator map and a full-color, spinning globe of the world within its celestial context.

Another advantage of this method, as Heath (1982) has pointed

---

*Like most analogies, the Dali comparison is limited, in particular because Dali portrays his surrealistic metaphors on a two-dimensional canvas, while the PDC addresses a myriad of other dimensions in kinetic, three-dimensional (spatial), verbal, experiential, proprioceptive, temporal and other realms.

out in drawing from the social psychology literature, is that a group of therapists is more liable to take risks and inject greater creativity into problem solving than is a single therapist. This is the "risky shift" effect first noted by Stoner (1961), a phenomenon that ubiquitously occurs in many group or team settings (Kelley and Thibaut, 1969). Such risky shifts are particularly useful when dealing with stuck or intransigent cases.

Sessions usually require 90 minutes. The first five to ten minutes are used for orienting to the family (for an initial interview), reviewing the previous session and subsequent relevant events, and perhaps designing a strategy for the present session. Following the 60 minute session, 20-25 minutes are normally devoted to a postmortem discussion and planning for the next meeting.

Commonly in PDC a structural map of the family is constructed and such structural techniques as joining, establishing leadership, tracking, unbalancing, enactment, etc. (Minuchin, 1974) are employed. These are combined or integrated with compressive (Stanton 1981c; 1984) strategic techniques such as paradox, reframing (e.g., through humor), positioning, restraining, etc. (Rohrbaugh, Tennen, Press and White, 1981; Stanton, 1981a; 1981b).

Due to the inherent expense of team methods (and, of course, disregarding the issue of cost-effectiveness, since the expense of team work is minimal if beneficial change is brought about in cases that are very costly to society) we tend to use the PDC with difficult, rigid, intransigent cases. Frequently they are families in which the therapist and the therapeutic system are stuck or stymied. However, this is not always the case. As noted earlier, the first author has used this approach with regularity in a multitude of settings, especially those which involve primarily inexperienced therapists and in contexts which are conducive to, and supportive of, teams of this sort.

Team Roles

While therapists working with PDC may assume a variety of different, often transient, roles, three primary roles are dictated by the structure of the model: Supervisor/team leader, "identified" therapist to the family and team member. The interplay between the people in these primary roles is crucial to the success of the therapy. For instance, usually the family's "identified" therapist (IT)* is most intimately joined and openly aligned with the family—on the

---

*As in "You're IT."

joining dimension or spectrum he or she anchors one of the poles. This provides protection against losing the family and also permits the team leader or supervisor the most authority and leverage for change. Because of the safety provided by the IT, the supervisor can exercise greater latitude in initiating interventions which challenge the family's tendency toward homeostasis (remaining the same).

Concerning a team that includes trainees, a clear hierarchical structure exists, with the supervisor/team leader at the top and the other, more experienced members, in middle positions (Haley, 1976; Heath, 1982). With more experienced team members, the structure becomes somewhat more democratic and egalitarian. However, even in the latter case the team needs leadership and the supervisor/team leader is the fulcrum around which the interventional process revolves.

It would appear that such a fast-moving and often bizarre process as PDC can make considerable demands on team members to be spontaneous, playful, challenging, etc., at different points and to tune into their own primary processes when necessary. While this is so, we would also hasten to point out that the craziness and confusion sometimes experienced by team members makes implicit sense when viewed afterward. Videotapes reveal a logical clarity threading through the process.

ASPECTS OF SUPERVISION

The remainder of this paper will discuss the training process within the PDC model, with particular attention to the inclusion in the team of (a) inexperienced trainees, (b) inexperienced clinicians as identified therapists to the family, and (c) experienced therapists who have not previously been exposed to this kind of work. Discussion will also cover the use of this form of multifaceted supervision as a primary mode for training beginning family therapists.

The Inexperienced Trainee as Team Member

One might think that a person with little or no family therapy experience, upon entering a team process such as this (even if only as a team member rather than as primary therapist for the family) would experience nothing but abject terror. However, while this might sometimes occur, it is our experience that more typically the trainee's reaction is not terror at all but, after the first few moments, one of comfort and exploration. Why might this be?

We can begin to answer this question by reminding ourselves of some of the primary issues faced by new therapists. Commonly, they are confronted by personal dilemmas such as: "Who should I be in therapy (what side of myself is to be shown)? How should I handle the family? Who should I join? How should I join?" Often they do not know when or if they are properly joined with a family or a member. Even before they get into specific interventions they encounter problems with leadership ("How and when do I take charge of the session?") and with ways for bringing about and/or handling intensity.

In the PDC the novice team member has a built-in cushion provided by the team member who is the family's therapist and the team member who is the supervisor/team leader. The trainee can be "in" the session at times and "not in" at others. He/she can throw out the odd comment and gauge the family's response to it—a kind of measured testing (rather than necessarily following one's primary process). The trainee can then alter his/her position or not, as seems fitting. Since the inexperienced trainee is frequently at sea as to who and how to be, PDC provides an opportunity to be "natural," to "be oneself," without taking undue risks. The family's therapist is joined with the family, thus providing safety—including a greater guarantee that the family will not bolt from therapy. Conversely, the supervisor is present to provide security if the trainee makes a "mistake"—i.e., a "master hand" is running the show and preventing matters from running amok. Thus the new trainee can experiment with (a) ways of mirroring the family's dimensions, and (b) his/her own personal reactions, even if they are clearly subjective and loaded with countertransference. Guidance and support from the supervisor allow the trainee to practice different maneuvers and "play" with various facets of him/herself in relation to the total therapeutic system, such as becoming angry, provocative, sexy, regressed, funny, crazy, scared, overinvolved, supportive, or "one-down," and by such exercises as attempting to run away, test collusions, make attacks, take control, and the like. The supervisor facilitates this by encouraging the trainee to first exercise skills and propensities already possessed—both as a therapist and in terms of his or her overt "personality." For instance, a quiet, submissive person is encouraged to start from the one-down position or a dominant personality is encouraged to take an authoritarian, leadership role. From this solid and secure base the trainee eventually develops enough faith in him- or herself to take chances, tip-toeing out with different postures, new roles and an expanded repertoire.

The trainee is also permitted to withdraw from the action if the intensity of the session surpasses his/her limits. Consequently, the trainee can begin to participate without having to bear the load of responsibility, since these are assumed by therapist and supervisor. This engenders enormous relief in the trainee—relief in being allowed the freedom to "be oneself" without great risk. For these reasons the PDC is a safe way to introduce inexperienced therapists to family processes and the interventional strategies that are designed to alter them. Obviously it also enjoys the advantages outlined by Haley (1976), Heath (1982) and others of training people in a group. In sum, the experience for trainees becomes comfortable, non-threatening, fun, rewarding and informative.

The Inexperienced Clinician as Identified Therapist

It is often the case that a relatively inexperienced therapist will bring a case to the team. This therapist thus has at least two obvious roles—that of "maintenance" or "identified" therapist (IT) to the family and that of a team member. In such instances the supervisor wants to initially bind the IT and family very tightly, especially if it is the initial session and such joining has not already occurred. The supervisor encourages the IT to assume those ends of the various spectra or dimensions mentioned earlier which are most consonant with the family, in a sense almost making the IT a member of that family within the total therapeutic system. For instance, if the couple or the family wants to break up or separate, the therapist advocates the split.

This done, the supervisor (along with other team members, in accordance with their facility and PDC experience) assumes the responsibility of identifying the polar opposite to the family position, e.g., pressuring the splitting family to stay together or the separating couple to hold a new wedding ceremony. The supervisor then commences to dance back and forth between the extremes, first reinforcing the IT's position, then assuming an opposite posture. Other team members may (a) follow suit, (b) ally themselves with one pole or the other, or (c) assume intermediate positions along the spectrum.

With clinicians at this level, and during this stage in therapy, the supervisor is very central, serving as conductor. He/she determines whether, when and how to reflect or mirror the family's opposing views and collusions, such as by evoking Yea-Nay votes, constructing male-female coalitions, contrasting youngsters and oldsters, etc., within the total therapeutic system of family and team. Both subtly and openly the supervisor shapes the process by directing inexperienced members to assume particular postures. (At this stage the positions assigned them are usually syntonic with their personalities or idiosyncracies, for instance, by having an outspokenly moral trainee take a firm stand in favor of the mores dictated by the overall society.) The supervisor gives cues, hints and directives as to what should be done: "Jack, you usually see the practical side of things, what do you think about Junior sleeping with Mom?" or (looking at a particular team member) "Does anyone on the team see another side to this?" Sometimes this can take the form of a concrete task or exercise performed in the session: "All those in favor of arguing sit on this side of the room," or "Anyone who wants to should go over with Pop and help him plan how to tell his mistress that he's still in love with his wife."

As with inexperienced team members, from the beginning the supervisor needs to nurture the therapist by emphasizing his/her natural strengths and skills. Unlike family treatment with one therapist in which the therapist normally must take an appropriate role vis a vis the family, in PDC the therapeutic system allows a broad spectrum of therapeutic "personalities" to bloom. Thus there is usually room for the parvenu therapist to fit in no matter what his or her proclivities. He/she can be given a reassuring and stable niche from which to initially operate and gain confidence. In addition, however, the therapist can proceed in exploring and expanding his or her capabilities, knowing that if he/she fails, another facet of the spectrum—another team member or group of members—will be there to compensate. Eventually, the therapist can begin to move from preprogrammed, idiosyncratic postures toward the flexibility of portraying different, even "ego-dystonic" roles, facets and positions. The therapists' range and breadth increase so that the authoritarian person can go "one down" and the dour and serious clinician can learn to tease and play.

The Otherwise Experienced Therapist as Team Member

As noted, inexperienced therapists entering the Pick-a-Dali Circus find it a safe environment—they feel protected and usually have implicit faith in the supervisor. They also have not yet (a) learned to fear that families will be lost to therapy, and (b) developed rigidity in standard linear techniques.

In contrast, experienced family therapists normally enter the PDC with set techniques or modi operandi and predetermined expectations as to what therapy should be like. Consequently, they initially become frightened and confused by the complexity and seemingly "unstructured" nature of this new, multi-faceted therapeutic modality. Naturally they don't have the same blind faith as the greenhorn, and they may also be appalled or disturbed by what they sometimes perceive as mocking or insulting behavior toward the family (whether the family sees it that way or not). They may also have difficulty with going one-down, acting crazy, etc. While such reactions are not uncommon for any fairly experienced therapist upon entering a strategic team, the experience is magnified considerably in PDC because there is no protection from the family by a one-way mirror: It is one thing to share one's primary process in private with one's colleagues and quite another to exhibit it openly and unexpurgated to a family.

After a session or two of discomfort, however, experienced therapists tend to relax and settle down more, allowing themselves to enjoy the experience, tune into their loose associations and use the method's flexibility to innovate with daring across a broad spectrum of behaviors. They can "let go" and explore the range of their therapeutic skills. Their spontaneity can often extend the interventional process beyond the limits of the supervisor's expectations and imagination, thereby enhancing the effort and extending the dimensions of the therapeutic system.

The richness eventually contributed by experienced therapists allows a change in the behavior of the supervisor. For one thing, the supervisor can afford to take an extreme position on a particular dimension and hold to it, since his/her experienced counterpart can competently handle an opposite pole without pushing too far—the team member already possesses a sensitivity to limits and a capacity to assume a myriad of roles.

In addition, the supervisor can trust an experienced therapist to enter the heat, heart and intense middle of the family, thus allowing the supervisor to withdraw at least temporarily—either for a breather or to get a meta view. (This is in contrast to working with inexperienced team members in which the supervisor must remain intensely in the middle of everything transpiring in the room.) In other words, with more advanced therapists as team members the supervisor can rely on their experience to handle the family maelstrom while moving in or gaining distance as he/she sees fit. The richness of the therapeutic system and the ranges attained in each of its dimensions become less determined by the supervisor and his or her limitations; instead they are greatly expanded by the experienced team member(s). This enables the team to treat more difficult cases and to work faster.

The Supervisor

It may be apparent that the team leader, when functioning as supervisor, is key to all that transpires in the PDC process. As Heath (1982) notes for team training in general, the supervisor is constantly faced with making moment-to-moment decisions of all kinds pertaining to the family, the other team members, the trainees, and the interaction among them all. This is especially true when the team includes trainees (versus experienced team members) and even more so in the PDC, where the safety and confidentiality of a one-way mirror may not exist.

In addition, it is incumbent upon the supervisor to be able to make sense of the therapeutic system in order both to design the interventions and to control, balance and maintain a consistent direction for change. This person must attempt to see the complete range of each of the family's various dimensions and to utilize, where indicated, the full breadth of each spectrum. He/she needs a measured knowledge of what the dimensions are, their relative importance in a given family, and how the webbing of team and family intermesh—what the interactional "grid" looks like. As with all types of family therapy supervision, then, the range and flexibility of the therapeutic system, as manifested within the Pick-a-Dali Circus, are determined as much as anything else by the limitations, creativity and leadership ability of the supervisor.

CONCLUSION

Some final thoughts on the PDC are indicated here. In many ways it is aimed at empowering families so they can make their own decisions. This point becomes particularly important with cases in which multiple systems, including both other professionals and extended family subsystems, are involved. In such situations a family often feels pulled in many different directions. The PDC, by explicating, validating and expanding the myriad of views presented by these "external" systems, reduces the likelihood that they will undercut changes that occur in sessions. These systems are acknowledged, respected and given their due. Then they will be more likely to accept positions different from their own. This releasing of "pressure" on the family thus allows it to pick its own direction—to make its own choices—within a context which is less competitive and less triangulating.

The PDC lends itself to training in a number of skills, contexts and problem areas. It is ideally suited to networking and treating extensive therapeutic systems, and, since we involve small networks of this sort regularly in our work, it is frequently used in this way. It is also helpful in making trainees competent in dealing with (a) severely disturbed families, (b) psychosomatic problems, (c) substance abuse, (d) multiproblem families, (e) the hearing impaired, (f) intra-family cross-cultural issues, and (g) inpatient cases of all sorts, both medical and psychiatric. Finally, we find the PDC to be very effective in one-shot consultations—often of the type where the main task is to put the family in charge of its own fate. In general, we feel that the PDC has great unexplored potential as a treatment and training method and see many exciting possibilities for its use in the years ahead.

REFERENCES

Andolfi, M., Menghi, P., Nicolo, A., and Saccu, C. Interaction in rigid systems: A model of intervention in families with a schizophrenic member. In M. Andolfi and I. Zwerling (Eds.), *Dimensions of family therapy*. New York: Guilford, 1980.

Bateson, G. *Mind and nature*. New York: Dutton, 1979.

Berger, M. and Dammann, C. Live supervision as context, treatment and training. *Family Process, 1982, 21,* 337-344.

deShazar, S. *Patterns of brief family therapy: An ecosystemic approach*. New York: Guilford, 1982.

Haley, J. *Problem-solving therapy*. San Francisco: Jossey-Bass, 1976.

Heath, A. Team family therapy training: Conceptual and pragmatic considerations. *Family Process, 1982, 21,* 187-194.

Hoffman, L. *Foundations of family therapy*. New York: Basic Books, 1981.

Kelley, H. H. and Thibaut, J. W. Group problem solving. In G. Lindzey and E. Aronson (Eds.), *The handbook of social psychology*, Vol. IV. Reading, MA: Addison-Wesley, 1969.

Landau, J. Therapy with families in cultural transition. In M. McGoldrick, J. Pearce and J. Giordano (Eds.), *Ethnicity and family therapy*. New York: Guilford, 1982.

Landau, J. and Stanton, M. D. The "Pick-a-Dali Circus": A model for intervening with therapeutic teams. Paper in preparation, 1985.

Landau, J. *The family in transition: Theory and practice*. New York: Guilford. In press.

Landau, J. and Stanton, M. D. (1983) Aspects of supervision with the ''Pick-a-Dali Circus'' model. *Journal of Strategic and Systemic Therapies, 2*(2), 31-39.

Landau-Stanton, J., Griffiths, J. and Mason, J. The extended family in transition: Clinical implications. In F. Kaslow (Ed.), *The international book of family therapy.* New York: Brunner/Mazel, 1982.

MacGregor, R., Ritchie, A. M., Serrano, A. C., Schuster, F. P., MacDanald, E. L. and Goolishian, H. A. *Multiple impact therapy with families.* New York: McGraw-Hill, 1964.

Minuchin, S. *Families and family therapy.* Cambridge, Mass.: Harvard University Press, 1974.

Montalvo, B. Aspects of live supervision. *Family Process,* 1973, *12,* 343-359.

Morenas, J. (1983) The third tier. *Family Therapy Networker, 7*(5), 10-11.

Olson, U. J., and Pegg, P. F. (1979). Direct open supervision: A team approach. *Family Process, 18,* 463-469.

Palazzoli-Selvini, M., Boscolo, L., Cecchin, G. and Prata, G. *Paradox and counterparadox.* New York: Jason Aronson, 1978.

Papp, P. The Greek Chorus and other techniques of paradoxical therapy, *Family Process,* 1980, *19,* 45-57.

Rohrbaugh, M., Tennan, H., Press, S. and White, L. Compliance, defiance and therapeutic paradox: Guidelines for strategic use of paradoxical interventions. *American Journal of Orthopsychiatry,* 1981, *51,* 454-467.

Speck, R. V. and Attneave, C. L. *Family networks.* New York: Pantheon, 1973.

Stanton, M. D. An integrated structural/strategic approach to family therapy. *Journal of Marital and Family Therapy,* 1981a, *7,* 427-439.

Stanton, M. D. Marital therapy from a structural/strategic viewpoint. In G. P. Sholevar (Ed.), *Handbook of marriage and marital therapy.* Jamaica, N.Y.: S. P. Medical and Scientific books, 1981b.

Stanton, M. D. Strategic approaches to family therapy. In A. S. Gurman and D. P. Kniskern (Eds.), *Handbook of family therapy.* New York: Brunner/Mazel, 1981c.

Stanton, M. D. (1984) Fusion, compression, diversion and the workings of paradox: A theory of therapeutic/systemic change. *Family Process, 23,* 135-167.

Stoner, J. A comparison of individual and group decisions involving risk. Masters' thesis, School of Industrial Management, MIT, 1961 (Reported in Brown, R. W., *Social psychology.* New York: Free Press, 1965).

Todd, T. C. Paradoxical prescriptions: Application of consistent paradox using a strategic team. *Journal of Strategic and Systemic Therapies,* 1981, *1*(1), 28-44.

12

Training and Supervision
of Behavior Therapists

Kirk Strosahl
Neil S. Jacobson

ABSTRACT. This chapter outlines our views of the training and supervision process from a behavioral perspective. One of the major issues for a behavioral training program is the unification of assessment and treatment. The importance of technology also separates behavioral training and supervision programs from others, and the very power of this technology creates dilemmas as well as opportunities for the behavior therapist. Various aspects of the technological structure are discussed, including agenda setting, self-control exercises, the use of homework assignments, and therapy techniques such as behavioral rehearsal. The importance of the therapeutic relationship is outlined and ethical issues are discussed. A behavioral model of supervision is presented, and some special training issues are discussed. The chapter ends with a caveat, reminding the reader that the data are not as yet in on these training and supervision methods, and that the value of professional training programs and clinical experience in general remain open questions.

Although recent years have witnessed a rapid growth in the popularity of behavioral treatments, less attention has been paid to the process of training and supervision. There are several factors which may contribute to the paucity of literature in this area. First, "behavior therapy" itself is an amorphous term used to describe a diverse group of therapeutic approaches, and it is difficult to identify

---

Kirk Strosahl, Ph.D., is with Group Health Cooperative of Puget Sound, University of Washington, Department of Psychology. Neil S. Jacobson, Ph.D., is with University of Washington, Department of Psychology.

183

elements common to all behavioral approaches. For example, some behavior therapies use imaginal rehearsal to achieve therapeutic objectives (Wolpe, 1958, Cautela, 1967); others may employ self-instructional strategies or attempts to modify dysfunctional self statements (Meichenbaum, 1977); still others focus on behavioral rehearsal of relevant skills (Curran, 1977). Thus, the typical behavioral training and supervision may involve a specific behavioral approach, rather than focusing on general principles applicable to a wide range of behavior therapies.

A second factor is that behavior therapies emphasize the application of specific behavior change technologies rather than the therapist-client relationship as the active ingredient of therapy. Because this behavior change technology is so operationally defined and structured, less formal training emphasis is placed on nonspecific factors in therapy such as the role of client expectancies, therapeutic rapport, treatment credibility and compliance related issues. Nevertheless, these factors play an important role in even the most behavioral of treatments, and the mark of an experienced behavior therapist (and supervisor) is the capacity to recognize and address nonspecific factors in the overall process of training and supervision.

A final factor is that, although behavioral approaches tend to focus on the development of more sophisticated behavior change techniques, corresponding theory has regrettably lagged far behind technical advances. (Strosahl & Linehan, in press). In the absence of a well developed theoretical base, the empiricism which so characterizes behavior therapies can often result in the naive therapist adopting the attitude of "what works is what I'll use." This grab bag approach can result in therapy degenerating into a series of scattered, theoretically unrelated (but highly sophisticated-looking) interventions. Clearly, knowing *whether* a procedure works (an empirical question) is not the same as knowing how it works (a theory question). The experienced behavior therapist must address the importance of both questions in the process of training and supervision.

These issues, as well as others to be discussed in this chapter, suggest that the entire process of training and supervising behavior therapists needs to be examined from a coherent theoretical framework. Our goal is to develop such a framework for training and supervision and to discuss the various procedures, pitfalls, and possible solutions to problems encountered.

THE BEHAVIORAL TRAINING MODEL:
PRELIMINARY CONSIDERATIONS

The field of behavior therapy is packed with specific behavior change strategies. Ironically, it is this diversity that is often a source of great initial confusion for the novice therapist, who tends to associate technology with theory. A useful first step in training is to ask novice therapists about their understanding of the grounding principles of behavior therapy. Answers typically convey a confusion between behavior theory and behavior therapy. Most trainees are comfortable with the concepts of stimulus/response and environmental control over behavior but are somewhat at a loss as to how to convert these principles into the practice of behavior therapy. The most common response is that behavior therapy assumes that psychological disorders result from a skills deficit. This example illustrates an important point, namely, that the atheoretical tendency of behavior therapy leads to significant confusion about its distinctive conceptual basis. Training in specific behavioral assessment and therapy techniques allows us a forum in which to continuously attack these misconceptions while deepening the therapists' understanding of assessment, treatment and relationship factors.

Training in Behavioral Assessment:
The Challenge of Uniting Assessment
and Treatment

It is safe to say that one of the hallmarks of behavior therapy, indeed a characteristic which distinguishes behavior therapy from most other therapeutic approaches, is its emphasis on the empirical assessment of target behaviors throughout therapy. The beginning therapist does not appreciate the necessity for conducting ongoing meticulous assessments of clients' progress towards therapeutic goals, or views this process as somewhat mechanical and less "romantic" than treatment. This no doubt springs from the commonly held belief that assessment precedes, and is distinct from, the act of treatment. In behavior therapy, assessment and treatment are in fact inseparable. Indeed, certain assessment strategies such as self-monitoring have been demonstrated to alter target behaviors by themselves. In training, we emphasize that ongoing assessment tends to protect the therapist from making potentially fatal therapeutic errors. For example, *research has shown that therapists tend to overestimate a client's degree of improvement in therapy.* In fact, a major source of premature termination may be the therapist's failure to realistically appraise a client's ability to function in emotionally charged situations. Hence, the therapist feels discouraged, defeated, and may blame the client, while the client feels frustrated and guilty at not living up to the therapist's expectations. Ongoing assessment in behavior therapy tends to prevent this mismatch in perceptions, even though therapists sometimes get discouraged about a client's lack of progress.

A second value of assessment is that it provides a safe operating framework for both client and therapist. The client knows that important target behaviors will not be forgotten during the course of treatment and will continue to be the focus of treatment. For the therapist, assessment tends to "anchor" the treatment process and provides clear guidelines for selecting appropriate intervention.

In general, the supervisor faces two major tasks when training new therapists about the role of assessment in the therapeutic process. First, therapists are reluctant to spend the time necessary to make assessment worthwhile. New therapists naturally want to engage in treatment and may harbor the notion that assessment interferes with treatment delivery. A second related issue is that assessments tend to focus on global rather than on behaviorally referenced criteria because global assessments of behavior are easier to conduct. However, the supervisor's task is to show how global assessments do not lead to therapeutic progress as much as specific, behaviorally referenced assessments. An ongoing aspect of behavioral supervision involves encouraging the therapist to generate specific definitions of target situations, so that ongoing assessments can be made easier.

Behavior Therapy Techniques: The Power and Dilemma of Behavior Change Technology

Arguably, the most fascinating aspect of behavior therapy is the incredible diversity of behavior change techniques which have been developed in the last 20 years. These techniques have added greatly to our therapeutic arsenal but present major challenges to the process of training and supervision. As might be expected, beginning therapists tend to become prisoners of their technology, in that they have a seemingly insatiable curiosity about how various techniques will work with a given client. While the supervisor does not wish to discourage independent initiative and creativity, the underlying philosophy to this approach is that there is always a technique available which will resolve a given difficulty. Thus, naive therapists are convinced that any impasse can be overcome if they can only identify and apply the correct piece of technology. Ultimately, this approach leads to a series of uncorrelated therapeutic maneuvers which may create more problems than they solve. Here, we see the lingering effects of the largely atheoretical base of behavior therapy, in that therapeutic methods tend to be used as substitutes for well-developed conceptualizations of maladaptive behavior. Without this underlying structure, behavior therapy itself can become top heavy with technology.

The supervisor's task in training is to encourage and guide the beginning therapist in the process of linking specific behavioral case conceptualizations with appropriate behavior change technology. New therapists have a variety of unrealistic and unjustified assumptions about the cause-effect relationship between the application of technique and subsequent behavior change. We remind inexperienced therapists that simply applying a given behavioral technique in no way insures that the client will accept it or will subsequently change any given behavior. In other words, these techniques remain barren to the extent that the therapist is not able to make a cognitive connection for the client about the relationship between a given problem and a certain technique. Even experienced therapists are prone to the idea that treatment benefits are more or less "automatic" once a behavior change tactic has been instituted (cf. Little & Curran, 1978). This is no doubt a remnant of the hard core reductionism and mechanism which so characterized early approaches to behavior therapy (cf. Strosahl & Aslough, 1981). In supervision, we encourage therapists to select a subset of techniques which will be used in therapy, to explain those techniques and their relationship to the presenting complaints of the client and to apply only a small number of techniques for a sufficient period of time so their impact can be evaluated. Here, assessment techniques clearly combine with behavior change technology.

Structuring the Session: Agenda Setting

A striking characteristic of most behavior therapy approaches is the amount of structure imposed on the therapy session. Structure should not be confused with directivity, in that behavioral approaches can vary dramatically in the degree of therapist directiveness. Establishing an agenda of items to be covered during the session is a hallmark of many behavioral approaches. Despite its apparent simplicity, agenda setting is a challenging task for even experienced therapists. In training and supervision, the importance of agenda setting is frequently discussed. It allows the therapist and client to collaborate on session content, rather than having content unilaterally dictated by either the therapist or client. Finally, we stress that the therapist who uses an agenda is more likely to remember the content of previous sessions and therefore is better able to maintain intersession continuity.

There are two major functions accomplished during agenda setting, apart from establishing major themes to be addressed. First, to review any homework assignments and assess the clients emotional status during the previous week. Second, to discuss the clients reactions to the previous week's session. This allows the therapist to elicit the client's negative and positive beliefs about what is happening in therapy. In this way the therapist can assess how new or more difficult concepts have been grasped by the client and which are likely to become sticky points in therapy.

There are two common mistakes which need to be addressed in the training and supervision. When this occurs the therapist may generate the items on the agenda with the client and then unilaterally decide which items have priority. The therapist may be acting on his or her own hidden agenda, rather than allowing the client to specify which items are important. Except in unusual circumstances, we stress that it is necessary for the client to prioritize the items both in terms of the order in which they will be discussed and the time that will be allocated for each item. This involves the client in the therapy process to a much greater extent than when the illusion of choice is presented by the therapist, who continues to dominate the flow of sessions. A second common difficulty is confusion about how to best apply the agenda. Many therapists tend to be extremely rigid in applying the agenda, once it has been agreed upon. Even though significant therapeutic issues may emerge which were not recorded on the initial agenda, inexperienced therapists insist on sticking with the original items. At the other extreme, many therapists simply refuse to enforce the agenda because of not wanting to be too "directive." Obviously, it is harmful to establish an agenda which will be quickly abandoned at the slightest provocation or too rigidly enforced. The training criterion for agenda setting involves a subtle mixture of directiveness and flexibility. For the most part, it is important to follow the items listed in the agenda. When significant variations arise during the therapy session, we encourage therapists to be flexible enough to consider altering the agenda. This is not the same as abandoning it. One plausible technique is asking the client whether this new topic should be added to the agenda and whether existing agenda items need to be reprioritized in light of the new concerns. This maintains the internal integrity of the session, while permitting clients to remain spontaneous in their identification of therapeutic issues.

Self-Control and Homework Techniques

A major achievement of behavior therapy is the sophisticated technology which has emerged for increasing inter-session continuity and teaching self-control skills. The key characteristics of these approaches are that the client becomes the agent of change and the therapist's role moves to that of advisor, instructor, and resource person. With some problems, simply teaching a client methods for noting the frequency, intensity, or duration of behavior can accelerate behavior change. In other cases, the therapist may be more interested in generating a list of problematic situations for targeting in future sessions. For example, in behavior therapy with the chronically suicidal client, daily record keeping initially is oriented toward developing a profile of daily activities, identifying problem situations where the urge to commit suicide is experienced, and assessing daily mood fluctuations. The therapist can use data from any of these arenas to serve as a jumping off point in the weekly therapy session. When activity level is the object of record keeping, it is often for the purpose of collecting "baseline" data on certain categories of behavior which the client may wish to change. Another use for homework assignments occurs when new behaviors are tested in vivo, and the client records "evidence" about their effectiveness.

Despite their utility, self-control and homework techniques constitute a potential source of failure. When done inappropriately or precipitously, these assignments can be counter-productive. They can result in increased self criticism, guilt or pessimism or an angry confrontative attitude towards the therapist. We sometimes jokingly say to new trainees that even the term "homework assignment" implies being asked to do something that you don't want to do by someone who you don't particularly like. The goal of the training process is not only to teach therapists how to present and utilize homework assignments, but more importantly to address those factors which determine their success or failure.

A common belief on the part of new therapists is that they are automatically doing "behavior therapy" when they develop homework assignments. The main issue in training is learning to differentiate effective use of homework vs. homework for homework's sake. There are numerous technical errors which the supervisor has to continually guard against. Therapists typically "give" assignments to their clients, rather than enlisting the aid of the client in putting together an assignment which will seem relevant. The label of "therapist" sometimes carries with it the improper assumption that one is empowered to tell clients what is and is not relevant in their lives. In addition, the therapist must recognize that global homework assignments are less likely to be completed, have less impact on selected targets, and may only serve to bog down therapeutic momentum. Often, therapists do not allocate enough session time for homework since the client's feedback is not regarded as a necessary ingredient in the homework formation process. Therapists may fail to insure that the client actually understands the homework assignment. On numerous occasions we have watched sessions in which only the therapist was sure what the assignment was. We urge therapists to have clients repeat the assignment and whenever possible to put it in writing prior to leaving the therapist's office. Another attitude that has to be countered in supervision is that clients must find a way to overcome obstacles to the homework assignment and that the ability to do so is in fact a test of the client's "motivation" to get better. We believe that the chief goal of any homework assignment is its successful completion. Therefore, therapists in training are encouraged to engage the client in mental rehearsal, focusing on how a particular assignment will be done. This procedure allows the client to verbalize potential obstacles to completing the assignment, so ways can be found to overcome them. Another typical error is that the therapist gives the client too difficult an assignment. Sensing that completion of the assignment is impossible, the client may simply give up. Therapists should have the client set the level of performance, clarify what the assignment will consist of and how performance will be recorded. Inexperienced therapists are often rigid when a client begins to modify a homework assignment the therapist has proposed. We again stress that the characteristic of a good homework assignment is that it is done.

New behavior therapists will often fail to debrief the clients on an assignment. By not doing so, the therapist is failing to reinforce the client for completing the assignment. When homework is completed, we instruct therapists to praise the client for success while trouble shooting failures. Further, assignments should always incorporate those elements which were difficult for the client in previous homework, so that an overlapping learning gradient can be established. This is particularly important for clients who tend to use punishment as their chief strategy for enacting behavior change. The therapist must be careful to insure an accumulation of small successes by carefully constructing homework assignments so that the potential for success is high. To summarize, self control and homework techniques are a potentially powerful tool but are also subject to many potential abuses. The supervision process should focus heavily on teaching therapists how to develop homework assignments that will elicit rather than defeat involvement in the therapy process.

Behavior Change Techniques

The diversity of behavior therapy techniques makes it difficult to adopt a uniform behavioral training model. Each technique has some unique assumptions and technical rules which may not generalize to all approaches. We cannot do justice to these here and instead will only mention them briefly in this discussion of general training principles. Most behavioral techniques have one or more of the following objectives: (a) to establish functional relationships between precipitating events and consequences ensuing from dysfunctional behavior; (b) to generate behavioral response alternatives to problematic situations; (c) to reduce the frequency of behavior which results in punishing or aversive consequences; (d) to increase the frequency of behavior which has desirable or positive consequences. Consequences involve a multitude of events, ranging from self-evaluations to more tangible environmental events. In other words, we teach therapists to focus on both self-administered and environmentally administered reinforcements for behavior. This does not mean that clients always opt for behaviors which produce maximally positive consequences (an operation learning model) or are conditioned to respond automatically to certain environmental or intrapsychic conditions (a stimulus-response model). Rather, it provides a heuristic framework that can be used by the supervisor, therapist and client.

The strongest component of the behavior therapist's arsenal is the range of strategies which exist to assist behavior change. At one pole, there are dialectically based strategies which challenge the patient to generate alternative ways of thinking to counter existing beliefs. The "devil's advocate" or "foot in the door" technique is an excellent example of this approach. Here, the therapist may advocate for a particular response style, belief, or perspective which the client has labeled as maladaptive. A similar approach is followed in some versions of cognitive restructuring. This approach utilizes a two-stage process involving the identification of maladaptive, behavior inhibiting beliefs, followed by the generation of more realistic (i.e., anxiety reducing) self-instructional dialogue. Another largely dialectical approach is the structured use of imagery in therapy, which has a longstanding tradition in behavior therapy (Wolpe, 1958). While early training models stressed that images were simply substitutes for their real life reference, it is now clear that imagery in behavior therapy is a highly spontaneous, relatively uncontrolled internal process. Research has consistently shown that patients seldom imagine the same scenes as described by their therapist but instead engage in spontaneous image elaboration (Strosahl & Ascough, 1981). This elaboration may include generation of contrasting responses, exploration of emotional responses and subtle changes in the way complex environmental and intrapsychic forces are reviewed and interpreted.

Behavior therapy training also focuses on relatively straight-forward modeling and behavioral rehearsal strategies which are derived from the social learning approach. Most skills training regimens in behavior therapy utilize a technique known as *behavioral rehearsal.* This process really involves two distinct stages. First, desired behavior is modeled by the therapist. Then, the client models the same behavior and receives performance feedback from the therapist. When conducting behavioral rehearsal, it is extremely important to identify stimulus situations which are problematic for the client. Since maladaptive behavior is heavily influenced by situational factors, accurate situational "mapping" makes it more likely that the client will actually use behaviors rehearsed during skills training. We encourage therapists to generate real life settings and situations during role play descriptions and to encourage clients to generate the same thoughts and feelings they would have if they were in the real situation. This guideline is also used when imaginal rehearsal is involved. This is an extremely important principle because there is a significant difference between a client's skill level and typical performance level (Strosahl & Linehan, 1985). Skill level refers to the client's maximum performance ability minus any cognitive or emotional distractions. Performance level is what the client is more likely to do, given the presence of cognitive and emotional distractions.

The behavior change contract is a technique which allows the therapist and client to agree on how the client will behave in certain situations and how desired behavior will be rewarded. The chief danger of any behavior change contract is that it may serve the therapist's need more than that of the client. A classic example of this dilemma is the "no suicide" contract, which is used as a short-term suicide prevention measure. Inexperienced behavior therapists tend to establish a time frame for the contract which coincidentally covers the full period before the next regularly scheduled therapy session. We like to bring up this coincidence during supervision with new therapists and to ask them how long the *client* would have agreed to remain nonsuicidal, had that question ever been asked. Hopefully, the contrast in the resulting answer will bring into focus the problem of establishing no suicide contracts which are designed primarily for the therapist's ease and convenience. Following the general approach of other behavioral procedures, it is important to let the suicidal client establish the length of the "no suicide" pact. As trainers, we are especially pleased when a therapist uses the devil's advocate position to argue that even the time specified by the client is probably too long and that an even shorter period of time may be more appropriate.

In behavior therapy, the process of terminating therapy and maintaining treatment benefits is given considerable emphasis. Like other types of therapy, behavioral clinicians must devise strategies to minimize the impact of termination and likelihood of relapse. We encourage novice behavior therapists to move away from mechanistic models of change and to focus upon reframing the client's cognitions about what to expect after therapy has ended. One commonly used set of strategies are called "relapse prevention" (Marlatt & Gordon, 1985) and originally were developed for application to clients recovering from addictive behaviors. This approach tends to emphasize the ineffectiveness of will power as a way of maintaining desired behavior in the face of extraordinary environmental pressures. It also utilizes a "predicting the obvious" approach to the whole issue of relapse. For example, it is safe to assume that at some point during the client's time out of therapy, the maladaptive target behavior will occur. This event can be interpreted by the client in a number of ways, ranging from destructive self-critical to more task oriented problem solving interpretations. We encourage therapists to "normalize" the recurrence of maladaptive behavior, by teaching clients to expect to reappear at some point. Emphasis is placed on realistically interpreting that event when it does occur.

A second popular approach to relapse prevention is the booster session, which allows the therapist and client to meet on a specified date following the formal termination of therapy. A variation on this approach is to allow the client to have a booster session as the situation may demand it. In either case, the therapist's strategy is to diffuse the stormy process of termination by providing the client with a sense of continuity. The structure of the booster session is identical to that of regular therapy sessions in that an agenda is established and various behavior change procedures are applied as deemed appropriate by the therapist. We do not know whether relapse prevention approaches for nonaddictive behaviors have a measurable impact upon the rate of recidivism. Similarly, the empirical case for booster sessions appears to be very weak at present, although the research is scant. For the supervisor, a major obstacle in training is that therapists leave school or somehow lose contact with their clients. In some cases, the trainee may no longer be working with the supervisor. Nevertheless, it is important to help the therapist carry out the booster session strategy, so that the impact of therapy maintenance procedures can be appreciated.

Behavior Therapy and the Therapeutic Relationship: A Contradiction in Terms?

Despite the public mythology about the antihumanism of behavior therapy (Kazdin & Cole, 1981), no practicing behavior therapist seriously argues that success is possible without a working therapeutic relationship. It goes without saying that if a client and therapist are not able to communicate about or collaborate on a problem, the therapist is unlikely to be viewed by the patient as a credible resource. In fact, our emphasis on relationship building skills is certainly equal to that placed on learning specific behavior change techniques. However, the relationship itself is not viewed as the "active mechanism" of therapy. The impact of the relationship in behavior therapy revolves around the willingness of the client to accept and apply the resources which the behavior change specialist has to offer.

The task of developing a credible treatment rationale is the first aspect of relationship building in therapy. Major failures in behavior therapy (and we suspect in other forms of therapy as well) occur during these initial interactions. Despite the fact that we go over the theory underpinning a therapeutic approach with trainees, we still observe therapists struggling through the initial explanation of what approach will be used or why it is the preferred treatment for a particular set of problems. New therapists often get defensive, start lecturing the client, or fail to encourage an open give and take about the treatment model. Often, clients express negativism about the mere prospect of receiving behavior therapy, equating it with mind control. These questions are very difficult for naive therapists, yet pose a serious obstacle to the client's ability to embrace the treatment model. In supervision, we emphasize that the client's concerns or skepticism about the treatment must be directly addressed, or one risks developing serious rapport problems. We may even role play these types of interactions with trainees and provide feedback about defensiveness and/or lecturing. In addition, we advise therapists to avoid use of the terms "behavior therapy," "behavioral" or "behavior modification," and to instead use "social learning" or "learning theory" to describe these behavior change strategies.

The process of "reframing" maladaptive behavior in more acceptable, less critical terms is one of the beneficial side effects of the objective approach to problem definition in behavior therapy, and is also an excellent rapport building strategy. Many clients develop elaborate explanations for their problematic behavior which typically are self-critical and trait-like. By objectifying these behaviors, the therapist undercuts self critical labeling which could conceivably dominate therapy. The essentials of the reframing process involve defining problematic behavior in an objective matter of fact way, while stressing that freedom to behave in other more adaptive ways has been compromised by complex learning related factors. In other words, the therapist helps the client externalize some of the responsibility for problem behaviors, by focusing on situational circumstances which conflict with dispositional attributions. The major obstacle to accomplishing this goal is that therapists inadvertently participate in the process of negative labeling. For example, many therapists have difficulties reframing a suicide attempt in non-pejorative terms because of moral beliefs about the act of suicide or about people who try to kill themselves. Another common error occurs when the therapist implies that slow progress in therapy is due to inadequate motivation (internal attribution) rather than to situational pressures. In supervision, we encourage trainees to take a calm, matter of fact, objective approach to even markedly dysfunctional behavior. Therapists are pressed to identify personal beliefs which might prevent them from being objective and rehearse strategies for avoiding moral-ethical impasses.

A goal of behavior therapy is to develop a "collaborative set" (Jacobson & Margolin, 1979). The collaborative set occurs when therapist and client work together rather than in an adversarial fashion. Unfortunately, when initiative and structure is with the therapist, the client becomes a bystander and is likely to develop a confrontational relationship with the therapist. We stress that the behavior therapist's goal is to be viewed as a trusted problem solving resource. The "therapist" role has both advantages and disadvantages, but being viewed as a "resource" has nearly no disadvantages at all. Many of the relationship strategies routinely employed in behavior therapy place the initiative for "movement" with the client, amidst the overall structure established by the therapist.

Another strategy used to develop the collaborative set is for the therapist to clearly specify what will be required of the client for therapeutic change to occur. This involves a description of homework assignments, problem areas to be targeted, and obstacles the client may have to overcome to complete extra session work. The client is then asked to commit to or withdraw from therapy as it has been described. We also stress with beginning therapists that the client must truly be free to withdraw at this point. The difficult aspect of this task is to be willing to accept a client's conclusion that he or she is not committed enough to pursue the therapy described. New therapists tend to take the blame for a negative decision or try to "stack the deck" by minimizing what will be required of the client. It is often useful to discuss these pitfalls in supervision prior to the therapy commitment session.

Behavior therapists do not regard "resistance" as a particularly useful concept, but frustration over the amount or rate of therapeutic progress still occurs. Behavior therapists generally assume that clients are performing to the best of their ability, given their perception of both the external and internal consequences which are likely to follow various behaviors. In training, resistances are discussed as the therapist's failure to understand the client's point of view. Our emphasis is that if blame needs to be distributed, then the therapist ought to be the one who takes it. Most clients already have a sufficient backlog of guilt experiences and do not need to be blamed for their "failures" in therapy. When the impasse created by resistance interpretations is side-tracked, clients frequently disclose that one source of paralysis is their fear of disappointing the therapist. Many new behavior therapists have prior experience with therapeutic models which rely heavily on resistance interpretations. For these individuals, it is often helpful to play the devil's advocate role in supervision, to illustrate that the client's perspective might be quite rational and reasonable. Another technique serving a similar purpose is that of role reversal, in which the supervisor takes on the role of the therapist while the new therapist advocates for the position of the client.

Many clients have been trained to believe that their dysfunctional behavior emanates from unconscious processes or deeply hidden early life experiences. Naive behavior therapists may attempt to reject this notion on the grounds that it does not adhere to behavioral theory. We encourage therapists to offer alternative but not competing explanations for the same set of events. Experienced therapists can usually take such information and show the client that while early experiences may indeed have occurred as described, a learning theory interpretation can also explain how these influences are reflected in current behavior. Many clients are in fact relieved when this strategy is followed, because what is learned can be unlearned. The amenability of unconscious issues to change is somewhat more problematic.

Another relationship issue involves the development of a confrontational interaction pattern between the patient and therapist. In supervision, we may ask the therapist to list a client's goals and motivations in taking a confrontational stance. Interestingly, aside from resistance interpretations, therapists generally tend to see their clients in fairly sympathetic terms, once the power struggle issue is bypassed. We do not attempt to link the therapist's negative feelings to unconscious conflicts or to make transference interpretations. However, we may ask a therapist to identify a similar learning situation in real life. Next, aspects of that situation which were rewarding or punishing and how that might have influenced the therapist's clinical response are discussed. Once these facets of past learning have been considered, we ask therapists to generalize principles to the current therapeutic impasse and to form a behavioral plan. This learning theory approach has been effective in reducing antagonism toward the client while avoiding many of the pitfalls associated with explanations centering on transference phenomena.

We have already described the technology devoted to the termination of the therapeutic relationship and maintenance of therapeutic gains. In any form of therapy, termination is an emotionally charged issue. In behavior therapy, termination issues are often minimized by establishing an overall, time limited structure which guides the therapy. In effect, the client is always in a position to address the issue of termination throughout the course of therapy. Even with this advantage, termination can be a delicate process, particularly when both the therapist and client agree that an effective working relationship has developed. For the therapist, the temptation is to escape from the structure of the behavior therapy regimen and to find new problems to treat. When the client knows that presence or absence of the target complaint is a chief concern for the therapist, the prospect of termination may result in increased symptomatology. Behaviorally speaking, the client senses that termination amounts to negative reinforcement for more adaptive behavior whereas increased levels of symptomatology may result in positive reinforcement in the form of therapist attention. A functional analysis of the events leading up to the increased symptomatology is a familiar yet honest way to examine client concerns about the termination. Another useful strategy is session tapering, which involves the steady expansion of time periods between therapy sessions; tapering allows the client and therapist to say their goodbyes gracefully and to slowly withdraw the mutual exchange of reinforcements that occurs during therapy. This also allows us ample time to work with therapists on the necessity of adhering to the specified therapy regimen and to address their fears about "abandoning" their clients.

Ethics and Behavior Therapy Training

An important goal of behavior therapy training is to acquaint therapists with ethical issues in the application of behavior change techniques. Because of negative publicity about the coercive use of behavior modification techniques, behavior therapists sometimes feel unnecessarily defensive about the use of behavior change technology. With trainees, this involves the fear that the therapist is overtly or covertly "manipulating" the client. This issue usually surfaces when behavior change strategies are being discussed in supervision. We point out that all therapeutic interactions are laden with reinforcements and it is better to identify a priori which reinforcement strategies will be followed rather than to accomplish this in a haphazard manner. A second and more formidable argument is that all charges of manipulation spring from the "automaticity assumption," or the notion that people are changed automatically by the application of behavior change technology (cf. Little, 1979; Strosahl & Ascough, 1981). We have focused extensively on this issue as a major myth surrounding behavior therapy. In our view, it is highly unlikely that any complex behavior can be changed without some conscious intent on the part of the client. As can be seen, behavior therapy training places a great deal of emphasis on promoting an open, direct, collaborative relationship. The notion that there is something sneaky or sinister about behavior change techniques is strictly a "straw man" argument.

THE BEHAVIORAL MODEL OF SUPERVISION

Advances in behavioral methods of supervision and training have not kept pace with the rapid growth of behavior therapy training programs. This has resulted in a rather curious situation, namely, much more is known about behavior change technology than is know about the effects of various approaches to behavior therapy training. While numerous articles have been written about behavior change techniques, few supervision models exist which integrate general behavior therapy skills, specific, non-specific, and relationship factors. The result is that behavior therapists are often ill-equipped to address clinical issues typically encountered in applied clinical settings. For example, Forehand (1985) found that practicing behavior therapists felt they were improperly trained to converse with dynamically and eclectically oriented therapists in applied mental health settings. Further, these therapists reported that they had not been trained in a variety of clinical procedures which were commonly expected of clinicians in the real world, including traditional objective and projective personality assessment. Clearly, the empirical doctrine of behavior therapy has made it a favorite approach for therapists in academic settings. The approach lends itself well to structured therapy outcome research and the subsequent publications which are necessary to insure tenure. However, the goals of the academician are often production and publication, whereas for the practicing behavior therapist they involve developing the skills required to deal with a diagnostically mixed client population. The gist of our argument is that behavior therapy training in the academic setting needs to represent not only the goals of academicians but also those of the practitioner. In essence, this is the most critical shortcoming of current training programs in behavior therapy.

The behavioral approach to training and supervision utilizes many procedures which are commonplace during ongoing behavior therapy. We have alluded to techniques such as role playing problematic situations, role reversal to address negative relationship issues, using the devil's advocate technique to develop new perspectives on client motivation, behavioral rehearsal of therapeutic responses and functional analysis of stormy or confrontational sessions. As is true with behavior therapy, application of these techniques in supervision in the absence of an overriding supervisory model simply amounts to technological overkill. In our training model, two principles act as the "glue" which hold together the process of supervision. The first principle is that of criterion referenced training. The second principle is clinical transfer of learning.

The criterion referenced training model is that specific levels of proficiency must be obtained in each of the major skill areas of behavior therapy including behavioral interviewing, session structuring skills, behavior change techniques, homework and self control monitoring skills, and various relationship skills. Figure 1 presents examples of skills in these areas as well as behaviorally referenced statements of clinical proficiency. For a therapist to "pass" behavior therapy training, a minimum level of proficiency must be obtained in each of these areas. Since each level of skill is operationally defined and quantified, it is possible to provide the therapist with ongoing feedback about his or her level of performance/proficiency in each area. As a therapist enters into behavioral training, a pretraining level of proficiency is obtained based upon analysis of audiotapes or videotapes. These ratings may be replicated periodically while the therapist is seeing the same client or may be obtained after the therapist has completed a number of cases. In either instance, the therapist has a clearly defined set of goals for the training process and an ongoing method for monitoring progress towards those goals.

FIGURE 1. Example of criterion referenced skills assessment for behavior therapy training

Assessment Skills: Score

    A) Target Problem Identification   _____

        1. No attempt to identify target problem
        2. Target problem defined but, in general terms
      * 3. Target problem defined in specific concrete terms
        4. Target problem defined in specific terms and linked
           to functional influences

Behavior Change Skills: _____

        1. No attempt made to model or role play desired
           behaviors
        2. Modeling or role playing desired behaviors not
           attempted, no feedback or repitition
      * 3. Modeling and role playing conducted with feedback;
           no repitition of behavior
        4. Modeling and role playing conducted, with specific
           feedback given, repitition of behavior

Homework Skills   Score

    A) Homework Assignment   _____
        1. No homework assigned
        2. Homework largely unrelated to clients problems
      * 3. Homework general but relevant to client problems
        4. Homework specific and individually tailored to
           clients current problems

Relationship Skills:

    A. Collaborative Set   _____

        1. Makes no attempt to enlist aid of client, confronts
           or blames client
        2. Minimal attempts to enlist aid of client, absence of
           confrontation or blaming
      * 3. Active attempts to enlist aid of client, absence of
           confrontation or blaming
        4. Active attempts to enlist aid of client, assumes
           responsibility for any difficulties

   Clinical transfer of learning is a term we use to describe the therapist's ability to extend newly learned behavior change skills to more
heterogenous populations. Whereas initial training cases may involve limited behavioral complaints (i.e., simple phobias or limited
skills deficits), later cases may involve multi-problem clients who
do not easily respond to a single behavioral intervention. In effect,
we are requiring therapists to develop progressively more and more
sophisticated behaviorally based treatment regimens with more
seriously dysfunctional clients. In doing so, we seek to accomplish a
very important objective, namely, a recognition by the therapist that
behavior therapy is not the panacea for all forms of psychological
disorder.
   A second strategy in the transfer of learning model is case conceptualization diversity. In contrast to the common training ap-

proach of simply exposing students to alternative theoretical orientations, this approach requires students to actively conceptualize their behavior change strategies in the terminology of different theoretical orientations. This better prepares the trainee for applied settings, where eclectic and dynamic approaches are still the predominant forces. We assume that the easier it is for a behavioral clinician to converse with nonbehavioral clinicians using the latter's terminology, the more effective the therapist will be in selling the behavioral approach. The advantage of this approach is that it does not restrict the behavior therapist in the nonbehavioral world. It is our experience that some behavioral training programs train their students to be dogmatic about the benefits of behavior therapy relative to other theoretical approaches (cf., Forehand, 1985). By teaching behavior therapists to coexist with other orientations, we are attempting to foster an attitude of compromise and collaboration which will only result in the increased acceptance of behavior therapy.

The relationship between the supervisor and trainee in the behavior therapy training model is not a major focus of the supervision process. When relationship issues are discussed, they generally pertain to the therapist's reaction to a particular situation which has occurred in therapy. There is nothing inherent in the supervisory relationship which is regarded as instrumental to the therapist's training. Frequently however, we may challenge a therapist's point of view or encourage the therapist to adopt alternative strategies. Behavioral techniques frequently come into play when the supervisor wishes to engage the trainee in this process. Two particularly effective strategies are the role reversal and devil's advocate techniques. The role reversal technique is especially useful when the therapist is having trouble relating effectively to the client. With the supervisor playing the role of the therapist, troublesome interactions can be imagined and role played, often with surprisingly quick results as far as the therapist's perspective on the client is concerned. The devil's advocate technique is particularly useful when the therapist is having a difficult time understanding the client's ambivalence about changing a particular problem behavior. Usually, the therapist has a finely developed appreciation for only one side of the issue (usually that side favoring behavior change) and fails to see the many powerful reinforcements which might mitigate against behavior change. By advocating for the side against behavior change, the supervisor can sometimes counteract the therapist's tendency to criticize and/or confront a client about the failure to change a problem behavior.

Structuring the supervisory session is an important step toward achieving a harmonious balance between the needs of the trainee and the needs of the supervisor. Setting a formal agenda is encouraged, because it allows both therapist and supervisor to prioritize items on the agenda and to gain a sense of what will be covered during the entire supervision session. Ordinarily, the supervisor is interested in providing feedback in each criterion referenced area and to oversee transfer of learning practice. The therapist may be most interested in receiving technical assistance. By establishing a clear agenda, each party is guaranteed time to address their particular desires.

SPECIAL ISSUES IN BEHAVIOR THERAPY TRAINING

A major challenge to behavior therapy in the upcoming decade will be to develop training models which allow it to be more effectively exported into the applied sector. In contrast to the esoteric specialized treatment programs often found in the academic setting, applied mental health settings are usually inundated with a widely diverse range of clientele. In these settings, elaborate behavioral assessment or behavior therapy treatment regimens are often regarded as too costly or time consuming to be feasible. Instead, general forms of group and individual therapy are used because they do not require specialized training and can be adapted to many different problems. The fact that such treatments are largely undocumented in terms of their outcome effectiveness has little bearing either on their popularity or usage. Behavior therapists encounter great resistance in such settings, because the ethic of numbers and ease of application usually predominates over that of empirically validated treatment. Still, it is our experience that a general behavior therapy approach is a tremendously flexible, yet effective approach and does not need to take a back seat to any form of therapy, eclectic or otherwise. This is particularly true in light of increasing pressure to develop brief treatment models which can replace more time consuming, cost prohibitive forms of treatment.

Clearly, one modality which has been neglected in most behavior therapy training programs is the group therapy modality, although many behavior therapies are routinely administered in a group format. It is incorrect to assume that a skilled individual behavior therapist will also be an effective group therapist. Group behavior therapy requires special training and supervision in many areas, including an array of group building skills and a thorough appreciation of the role of group dynamics (Rose, 1977). It is also quite likely that the mechanisms of change in group behavior therapy may differ from those of individual therapy. Behavior therapy training models must account for the fact that the treatment of choice in some applied settings is group therapy.

In the past ten years alone, there have been major advances in the development of behavior therapy techniques for such psychological disorders as depression, anxiety, and chronic pain syndrome. However, it has been difficult to export these approaches to the applied sector, because traditional forms of clinical training tend to be time consuming and costly. For example, the cost of this problem in the area of depression is enormous, in that early approaches emphasized long-term therapy, but have generally been shown to be ineffective (Hollon & Evans, 1984). The time seems ripe for the development and application of intensive behavior therapy training packages in the applied sector. Intensive, practitioner oriented-training programs could be presented to therapists *in situ*. Self-guided homework assignments using graded psycho-educational behavioral techniques might be a useful adjunct to such training programs. It appears that the traditional forum for training behavior therapists may need to be extended to the applied setting, given the speed with which innovations are occurring in contemporary behavior therapy. These training models would have to be somewhat different than those traditionally used, in that time of training would be tremendously shortened, standards of proficiency might have to be reduced accordingly, and peer group supervision might replace the traditional supervisor-therapist relationship. Despite these challenges, we believe that applied settings represent a heretofore unexplored and extremely promising forum for the application of new and innovative behavioral training models.

The Value of Clinical Training and Clinical Experience: Two "Facts" in Search of Some Data

We have devoted this chapter to the discussion of clinical training and supervision from a behavioral perspective. As behavior therapists, we are committed to basing our recommendations for training and supervision on empirically-based findings whenever possible, and to extol the virtues of tentativeness and caution when the data are not in. Therefore, it is important to note that there is no evidence to support the efficacy of these training or supervision methods at the present time. For that matter, no specific methods of clinical training and supervision from a behavioral perspective have been studied in the experimental arena. Therefore, while as clinicians we are quite invested in these methods, as researchers we are doubting, skeptical, and open to disconfirmation.

A growing body of literature on the effects of professional training and clinical experience suggests that our tentativeness is warranted. The assumption of most clinical training programs, regardless of theoretical orientation, is that there is a positive relationship between time spent in training and the therapist's clinical effectiveness. Unfortunately, the literature on this topic suggests that this assumption may be premature. For example, in studies that have directly compared the effectiveness of paraprofessional and professional therapists, results have consistently failed to demonstrate the superiority of therapists with professional training; in fact, the tendency in the literature is to support small but statistically significant superiority for paraprofessionals (Durlak, 1979; Hattie, Sharpley, & Rogers, 1984; Nietzel & Fisher, 1981)! Further, it is often assumed that experience after the completion of formal training is a major factor in determining therapist effectiveness. Experienced therapists are regarded as preferred staff members in nearly every mental health setting. Unfortunately, the literature on the relationship of experience and therapeutic outcome is also inconsistent. In some studies experience does seem to make a difference whereas in others there appears to be either no difference or a negative effect of experience. Overall, "the empirical evidence supporting the assumed relationship between therapist experience and outcome is surprisingly meager" (Stein & Lambert, 1984, p. 140).

Our rationale for bringing up this rather heretical point is simple: the enormous financial resources (federal, state, and local) which are allocated to support training programs are predicated on the assumption that extensive clinical training actually makes a significant difference in clinical effectiveness. The fact that it may not raise interesting questions for clinical training directors who are faced with increasingly severe budget restraints. Perhaps it is the application of behavior change technology, not general therapist skills, which is the dominant factor in determining therapeutic outcome, at least for behavior therapists. Lewinsohn, Antonuccio, Steinmetz, &

Teri (1984) suggest that relabeling therapists as "instructors" and therapy as "course work" does not seem to impede the process of behavior change. This would suggest that the most important skills of the behavior therapist are the capacity to develop and train others to use behavior change techniques, not the unique ability to apply them in therapy. Further research is needed to both examine the effects of various training and supervision models and to identify those skills which are necessary to produce change in behavior therapy.

REFERENCES

Cautela, J. (1968). Covert sensitization. *The Behavior Therapist, 8,* 5-8.

Curran, J. (1977). Skills training as an approach to the treatment of heterosexual-social anxiety: A review. *Psychological Bulletin, 84,* 140-157.

Durlak, J. (1979). Comparative effectiveness of paraprofessional and professional helpers. *Psychological Bulletin, 86,* 80-92.

Forehand, R. (1985). Training behavioral clinicians for a nonbehavioral world. *The Behavior Therapist, 8,* 5-8.

Hattie, J. A., Sharpley, C. F., & Rogers, H. J. (1984). Comparative effectiveness of professional and paraprofessional helpers. *Psychological Bulletin, 95,* 534-541.

Hollon, S., & Beck, A. (1979). Cognitive therapy for depression. In P. Kendall & S. Hollon (Eds.), *Cognitive-behavioral interventions: Theory, research and procedures.* New York: Academic Press.

Hollon, S., & Evans, M. (1983). Cognitive therapy for depression in groups. In A. Freeman (Ed.), *Cognitive therapy with couples and groups.* New York: Plenum Press.

Kazdin, A., & Cole, P. (1981). Attitudes and labeling biases toward behavior modification: The effects of labels, content and jargon. *Behavior Therapy, 12,* 56-68.

Lewinsohn, P., Antonuccio, D., Steinmetz, J., & Terri, L. (1984). The coping with depression course. Eugene, Ore.: Castalia Publishing Co.

Little, M., & Curran, J. (1978). Covert sensitization: A clinical procedure in need of some explanations. *Psychological Bulletin, 85,* 513-531.

Marlatt, G. A., & Gordon, J. (1985). *Relapse prevention: Maintenance strategies and the treatment of addictive behaviors.* New York: Guilford Press.

Meichenbaum, D. (1977). *Cognitive behavior modification.* New York: Plenum Press.

Nietzel, M., & Fisher, S. (1981). Effectiveness of professional and paraprofessional helpers: A comment on Durlak. *Psychological Bulletin, 89,* 555-565.

Rose, S. (1977). *Group therapy: A behavioral approach.* Englewood Cliffs, N.J.: Prentice Hall.

Stein, D. M., & Lambert, M. J. (1984). On the relationship between therapist experience and psychotherapy outcome. *Clinical Psychology Review, 4,* 127-142.

Strosahl, K. & Ascough, J. (1981). Clinical uses of mental imagery: Experimental foundations, theoretical misconceptions, & research issues. *Psychological Bulletin, 89,* 422-438.

Strosahl, K., & Linehan, M. (1985). Basic issues, old and new, in behavioral assessment. In A. Ciminero, K. Calhoun, & H. Adams (Eds.), *Handbook of behavioral assessment* (2nd Ed.). New York: John Wiley.

Wolpe, J. (1958). *Psychotherapy by reciprocal inhibition.* Stanford, CA: Stanford University Press.

13

Changing an Institution
"That Can't Be Changed"
Through a Staff Retraining Intervention

Matti K. Gershenfeld

ABSTRACT. This is the report of an organization development project which took place over four years at a large state center for the mentally retarded and handicapped. The hospital had a long history of staff difficulties, poor community image, and a series of problems both with staff and clients. The prime intervention was a consultant supervising 10 diversified staff who were selected to conduct the organizational change program. Outcomes of changes over four years are presented with positive outcomes not only in the intervention program, but even despite a serious negative incident and the planned closing of the hospital. The early intervention made possible the collaboration and success at a later time despite severe problems in layoffs and staff morale.

INTRODUCTION

This chapter is about a major intervention at Pennhurst Center, a state-owned and state-operated facility for the mentally retarded, located in Southeastern Pennsylvania, about 30 miles Northwest of Philadelphia. It will deal with the changes which occurred at the facility which would have been thought by almost everyone impossible to change.

To begin, it is important to recognize that differences exist between corporate and public-sector organizations. There is an expanding literature documenting organizational change in the

Matti K. Gershenfeld, Ed. D., is an Adjunct Professor at Temple University in the Department of Psychoeducational Processes, and is also a member of the Graduate Faculty of Pennsylvania State University-Ogontz, and President of the Couples Learning Center, an educational nonprofit corporation, which conducts innovative programs in the area of the family.

public sector (Golembiewski, 1969; Costello, 1971; Ross & Hare, 1973; Giblin, 1976; Zawacki & Warrick, 1976) and how it differs from organizational change in the corporate sector. Although public sector organizations do have many features in common with corporations, certain distinguishing features generally increase the complexity of change attempts in the public sector. There are certain variables which are frequently cited in the literature that affect the operation of public-sector organizations. This framework distinguishes those factors that frequently impact on the organization from the external environment separate from those considered internal to the organization. Both sets of factors operate interdependently and have a mutually determining influence on organizational behavior (Davis, 1979). Included among the key external sources of influence are the legislature and special-interest groups (Golembiewski, 1969), external auditors (Warrick, 1976), citizen boards and advisory committees (Wolman, 1972), the media (Bower, 1977), and the general public.

Among the key internal sources of influence typically felt in public-sector organizations are the nature of the chief operating executive's appointment (Costello, 1971) and the type of external reporting relationships; the importance of political goals (program visibility, rapid results, etc.) (Imundo, 1975); the level of diversity and contrasting ideology of the service specialists (Sikula, 1973; Wynia, 1974); the effects of vaguely defined programs and performance criteria (Gardner, 1974); the impact of the civil service personnel system (Giblin, 1976); and the effects of the regulations and procedures of the bureaucracy (Kharasch, 1973; Sharkansky, 1970).

The different forms of influence shown in Figure 1 indicate how open and vulnerable public-service organizations are to their external environments. Shifts of the external environment produce changes in public agencies far more readily than in business firms. These constant shifts of input provide the external political environment for the public-sector organization. The internal environment of the agency (Figure 2) is strongly affected by the external political context. How closely the chief operating officer's position is linked to the seat of political influence will be a critical factor affecting the leadership and direction of the organization. The appointed official close to political sources of influence is placed in the difficult position of assessing the external climate of political forces (the inputs in Figure 1) and attempting to manage the internal resources of the

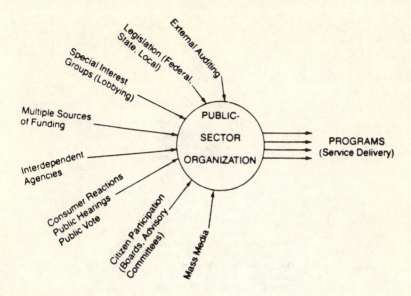

Figure 1. External Environment of a Public-Sector Organization

(Davis, 1979, p. 354) *

organization to meet these demands (Figure 2). Frequently, the organization head, who seeks to make changes, comes into conflict with the organizational staff (the career civil servants). The career civil servant has commitments to previous programs as well as to vocational and ideological ties to a particular specialty. The diversity of service specialities in many public agencies, the vagueness of goals and performance criteria, the myriad rules and procedures, and the civil service laws regulating the hiring, firing, and advancing of personnel tend to limit the chief administrator's potential for introducing purposeful or rational changes in public-sector organizations.

A second qualification concerns the notion of purposeful or rational change in public-sector organizations. Performance characteristics of public-sector organizations are frequently obscure and hard to assess, and this makes it difficult for the organization consultant to understand what is going on, let alone decide what should be going on. Generally, outputs of many public-sector agencies are

---

*The material in this section is reprinted with the permission of Sage Publishers

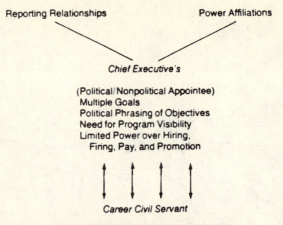

Figure 2. Internal Environment of a Public-Sector Organization

(Davis, 1979, p. 354)

vague even when performance is evaluated close to service delivery; distinguishing performance outputs become still more difficult at points inlaid in the bureaucracy. The director in many public service agencies may be pushing for action without knowing exactly what is required. Alternatively, performance may intentionally be kept obscure. The net result is that performance in the public sector can be totally subjective (individually defined) and the change processes can be completely irrational with no particular direction (Costello, 1971; Lindblom, 1959), or completely illusory, involving no real change, merely ''symbolic action'' (Edelman, 1971).

INTERVENING IN A STATE
MENTAL HOSPITAL/MENTAL RETARDATION HOSPITAL

Background

Almost since the time of its opening in 1908, Pennhurst was plagued with problems common to most large institutions, i.e., overcrowding, understaffing and inadequate financial resources. In the mid-1950s the resident population of Pennhurst passed the 3500 mark and the staff complement was in the neighborhood of 600. Many of the residents, at that time, constituted the actual work force of the institution, working the farmland and the dairy and providing most of the day-to-day custodial care for the residents who were unable to provide for themselves. By the late 1960s the resident population had been reduced somewhat to 2800 (more than 800 over its rated capacity) and the staff complement was 800.

Over the years, there were a number of investigations of Pennhurst initiated by the media dramatically recounting the overcrowded, de-humanizing conditions at the facility. However, these did little to alter the course of warehousing retarded persons and the continued provision of custodial care as inexpensively as possible. In the summer of 1968, television was used for the first time to do an exposé of the conditions at Pennhurst, bringing the plight of retarded persons to the awareness of millions of people on the evening news.

In the wake of this series of news reports, some things began to change at Pennhurst. Community living arrangements were developed for many of the more capable residents, and the census began to drop. With this depletion of the "residential work force" came, by necessity, an increase in the staff complement. By 1970 the resident population stood at a little over 2000 with a staff complement of nearly 1100.

Another change had a significant effect on the facility through the 1970s. The old "custodial care, medical model" philosophy was replaced with an "educational, developmental" approach to the care and treatment of Pennhurst residents. No longer was it sufficient to see to it that the residents were fed, cleaned and kept free from harm. The new orientation required that individualized programs be developed. These programs were to be designed with the long-range goal of helping each person achieve his or her maximum developmental potential.

Although Pennhurst was improving, the tangible results were not keeping pace with the changing theoretical and philosophical ideas regarding the treatment of retarded persons (e.g., "normalization" and "deinstitutionalization"). In 1974 a lawsuit was filed against Pennhurst by the parent of a Pennhurst resident. Through the addition of a number of co-plaintiffs (including eventually, the United States of America) and the filing of amended complaints, the focus of the suit was switched from an attempt to force improvements at Pennhurst, to closing the institution. By the time the case actually came to trial in 1977, there were 1400 residents living at Pennhurst and the staff complement was over 1750 (which included 200 federally funded CETA workers).

The closure of Pennhurst was ordered in March 1978. This was to be accomplished over a period of years, in an orderly and structured manner, which would be monitored by the court. Individual habilitation plans would be developed for all residents and transfers would be accomplished to community living arrangements in the resident's home county. These plans were to be developed as a joint effort by Pennhurst staff members and the County Mental Retardation Offices.

Not only was the case of Pennhurst tried in courts, but also in the magazines and newspapers of the Philadelphia area. The following appeared in The Philadelphia Inquirer (Epstein, 1980):

> Life at Pennhurst, the lawyers told the Supreme Court, has been characterized by "deterioration, regression, physical injuries, sexual assaults, deaths, misuse of dangerous drugs, solitary confinement, inadequate and unavailable programs, outbreaks of infectious diseases, urine and excrement in living areas and just general disregard of minimal personal standards".

In another part of the article: "Some judges have written that the understaffing, filth, violence, and enforced inactivity and other horrors make Pennhurst, in the opinion of one well travelled expert 'one of the worst institutions of its kind in the world'."

In the wake of the court ruling, another change occurred at Pennhurst. George A. Kopchick, Jr., was appointed as the new Director of the facility in May 1978. Kopchick was a new kind of Director, trained in Special Education. He came to Pennhurst committed to a developmental approach to the treatment of retarded persons and, incredibly, to the idea of making Pennhurst the best facility of its kind for the remaining years of its existence. He instituted a number of administrative and organizational changes within the facility to improve the quantity and quality of services provided to the residents. He also expressed a concern about the de-humanizing conditions inherent in a traditional institutional setting and set a goal to introduce a staff training program which would attempt to improve the "quality of life" at Pennhurst for both the residents and staff members.

Toward the end of 1979 an effort was begun to bring into being a training program which would overcome many of the daily indignities of institutional life; things like yelling and shouting, treating people like objects and herding them around in large groups. Goffman (1961) in his book, *Asylums* described this procedure for the effective and efficient control of an institution; control which is accomplished through a process of depersonalizing the individual.

While there were attempts at Pennhurst to overcome the depersonalization of a large institutional physical environment, it was recognized that this process also occurs in interpersonal behavior among staff members and between staff and clients.[1] A major intervention was thus sought to alter the attitudes and behavior of staff members as they dealt with one another and with the residents; an approach which would improve the quality of life for all concerned.

Organization Entry

As Rubin, et al. (1974), indicated, the most effective way to introduce an organization change is "to be asked in." When a consultant is in a position of "asking to be let in" it is less likely that he/she will be able to diagnose and define the problems that will be confronted. In this particular case the consultant was invited in. Kopchick had decided what was necessary was to make a widespread organizational change in the institution. He recognized the need for an outside consultant to diagnose, create, and implement the strategy for an organizational change. A number of consultants were asked to present their plans for creating change at Pennhurst. At the meeting this potential consultant attended, with the Director and two other administrators, the situation was presented as follows:

There is a staff of 1500. Their median age is 40. The average staff

---

[1]One form of change in cognitive structure occurred with changing the name of the population served from "patients" to "clients." Patients are sick and are attended in a directive even abusive manner since the staff "know best." The word "client," has the inference of someone to be served and as someone to be treated with respect—as a realtor serves clients and takes them around to houses and tries to be helpful and knowledgeable. Just using the word client, infers a different relationship of the staff to the person being served.

member has been at Pennhurst 10 years. Pennhurst is currently the largest employer in Spring City.

The staff is burned out and discouraged. Hospital procedures are carried out not according to the treatment plan for the clients, but rather for the convenience of the staff. The staff is the system. The staff treats clients like devalued objects. There is not overt obuse, but a small example is that the staff takes the good chairs in the lounges and the clients huddle at the walls on benches.

The caregiver, the staff, looks at the recipients of care as a child or as an object. Why is de-humanization taking place? Why is there objectification? Clients are seen as things who will never change.

The staff see the work as routine and boring and with the adverse publicity they feel negative about being at Pennhurst; devalued by the external environment. In the internal environment, they believe the media and devalue each other. Pennhurst is a badge of shame and perhaps one way of coping is to relate as little as possible to other staff. It is as if there is a self-fulfilling prophesy: unfolding as they feel themselves devalued. Displaced anger is projected on to the clients.

It was noted that there was extensive functional specialization. There was an administrative staff made up of unit directors and program coordinators. The core unit staff consisted of a unit director, an assistant unit director, a program coordinator, program specialist, nurses, and secretaries. In each living area there were aides, program coordinators and specialists on all three shifts.

Although Kopchick wanted an organization development program, there were formidable resistances to such an intervention which included:

1. Staff members said that they didn't want to know each other—they were paid to do their jobs; they didn't want to be "friends."
2. People did not speak to each other and said frankly, "no way do we want to talk to other members of the staff."
3. "It has been done before. Here we go again, another training program where those outside experts will come in and tell us what to do."
4. The legitimacy of the consultants. That is, outside consultants may have fancy ideas, but they do not know what our jobs are like, and who are they to give us advice. They don't know the realities with which we live.

5. We do not need it. We have our own way of doing things that works for us. They cannot possibly understand what happens here. All they will do is intrude.
6. The major resistance of nursing was that they only accepted a medical model. They would only do what doctors told them to.
7. Unit directors were opposed because they saw their leadership style threatened.
8. MRA III's (first level supervisors) supervised the aides and had a history of doing things their way. Training in the past has tried to change them, but to no avail.
9. By and large, the senior administrative staff felt that with constant newspaper reports of current court cases there was such continuous, ongoing demoralization almost anything was doomed to failure. And, even if it were attempted, how could change be evaluated? Could this intervention be objectified and quantified?

The odds of success didn't sound good. Kopchick listened to a number of consultants and decided to hire this consultant after hearing her organization development plan and intervention strategy. (A part of his decision to hire me seemed to be based on three years of training programs I had conducted for the Department of Public Welfare which had been evaluated positively.)

The Organization Development Plan

The situation as described and the resistances expressed were considered carefully in developing a design for the organization intervention. It was based on an understanding of the system and the creation of a training design. [For analysis of the essential components of training design, see Napier and Gershenfeld (1983) Chapter 4.] The training design was to develop in three stages over the next three to five years. The intervention would involve the entire staff, cognitively restructuring their feelings about themselves and the Center. It would involve major attitude changes, and motivation for environmental change (Schein, 1980). The first step would be training the top administrative staff, and the "trainers" to be in a 40-hour organization development Transactional Analysis program. The organization development aspect would have participants work in a variety of small groups, in dyads, triads, clusters, and as a total community of thirty. The Transactional Analysis aspect was to build a common language and some new interesting concepts which would be the content for looking at their behavior as individuals, as staff members, in relation to clients, and as part of the hospital. This initial one-week training program was to have "top management" involved and knowledgeable about what would be taking place. The Director, in consultation, would select ten staff members, representing all levels of the staff and different specialties to become the training staff. This training staff, who would be released from their work 20% of their time, would conduct the 40-hour training program with the entire staff of the hospital; in two-person teams, every other week, in maximum groups of thirty, for all three shifts. Fifteen hundred (1500) staff would be trained over two years.

The consultant would conduct the initial program and this would be video taped for reference by the TA trainers. The consultant in the next week would work with the trainers to teach them, not only how to teach this 40-hour program but, also, how to publicize it, inagurate it, find space for it, make administrative decisions about it, and do the short-term evaluations. The Center's Research Director would do an extensive evaluation of the program. The consultant would continue to meet with the trainers one day a month for the next years to supervise them and the program.

— By having trainers who were members of the Pennhurst staff, it was assumed there would be much less resistance then to outside experts.
— By having a heterogenous group of thirty (30) in each training class it was hoped that the norms of the organization could be changed as staff members would get to know and work with staff members they had only seen briefly in a hall or cafeteria. In the program, staff would work together cooperatively in many exercises. The week's experience would be intensive, fun, and a good learning experience.
— It was hoped that participants would return "different." They would have separated from their routine duties for a week, have experienced themselves differently, and worked with other staff where the focus was on learning, communication, and building confidence. Each group, it was hoped, would leave the week's experience enthusiastic and reinvigorated, and return to their unit with an infusion of excitement and energy. In addition to an "infusion" into the unit, it was hoped

that this excitement would lead to more volunteers signing up to be in the program.

While Kopchick agreed that the program would be mandatory for every staff member, it was hoped that the mandatory aspect might be delayed as long as possible.

It was a bold program which involved a tremendous commitment from the Center and the Director. The second step of the program, after this two-year initial phase, was to be a team development program for each unit—again, with the trainers being taught to become internal consultants, and the consultant training and supervising the trainers. Concurrent with the second phase, there was to be a special program in leadership for the top administrative staff. In the spring of 1980, the program began.

The Launch—The First Week

The first day of the training program everyone was apprehensive, frightened, and at the beginning of an "invasion" which it was hoped would go successfully—but, which might be a disaster. Some staff were furious at being required to be there. Some sat impassive waiting for another failure. Some were grumbling, "here we go wasting more State money with another dumb idea."

The ten (10) trainers selected also felt the full range of emotions. Some had volunteered and were excited at the growth potential of their having been selected. Some were frightened of what loomed ahead. Some were downright angry at being assigned to become a trainer; they didn't know what it meant and didn't want to do it,— but, it was supposed to be an "honor" and they were going along. The stage was set. There were expectations at every level; the Audio-Visual director was poised behind the video machine, his assistant was walking around with hand mikes for audibility; the program began.

Each day the mood of the group changed to become more positive, more involved, more energetic. People laughed, they shared experiences related to concepts being taught, they reported how they used what they learned in class. On the last day, various sub-groups voted to each bring food and share lunch together. They even brought in a photographer to take a group picture, and each person contributed for their print. The evaluations of the helpfulness of the program, rated on a scale of 1 to 7, had the vast majority of the respondents evaluate the program as 7—extremely helpful. No one scored less than 6—very helpful. While the training staff was somewhat terrified at the expectation that they would run such a program, they were regenerated at seeing the changes which occurred in that one week. Not only were all of them now eager to be part of the program, but five other participants volunteered to become trainers, in the event any of those selected had to drop out.

Training the Trainers

In working with the training staff, the first objectives were to create positive, supportive, group norms. They would be working together during possibly quite difficult times. It was important, above all, that they know each other, value each other as individuals, and become committed to the goal of being instrumental in changing the atmosphere at Pennhurst. Much of the first day was spent in variety of "getting to know each other" experiences. Some of the exercises follow:

Six minutes: critical incidents. "If we are going to spend a lot of time together, we need to know each other more than superficially! If you were given *six* minutes to tell some critical experiences in your life so that we would really understand you—what would they be?"

The group agreed, each one would take a turn. The consultant went first. Then, each person talked about him/herself for six minutes; then the group could ask questions of that person for another five minutes; and then they moved on to the next person.

Every day another group building personal experience was used.

A microlab. In a microlab (a series of short experiences where time is used as a dynamic variable) "trainers" were in dyads and answered these questions:

1. "What was your first experience with a retarded person?"
2. "What did it mean to you?" (Shift, new partner.)
3. "When you were a teenager, what did you think of retarded or retarded and handicapped? Tell an incident." (Shift, new partner.)
4. "Have you ever known anyone well prior to coming to Pennhurst who was retarded? What was that experience?" (Shift, new partner.)

5. "How did you decide to come to Pennhurst? What will you always remember about your first day?"
6. As a total group, each person comment: "How do you feel about retarded and handicapped now? What still gets to you?" (Continue discussion.)

Pennhurst fairy tales. Another group building experience attempted to foster a developmental understanding of Pennhurst and also to encourage creativity. Trainers were divided into groups of two to four—depending on how long they had been at Pennhurst. One group consisted of people who had been there fifteen years or more; another of those who had been there between five and fifteen years, and a third group consisted of those who had been at Pennhurst less than five years. Each group was asked to create a fairy tale with kings and princesses and villains based on their first experience—those first years at Pennhurst. Each group created and read their imaginative "fairy tale" of life at Pennhurst. In listening to each story there developed an understanding of sequence of what had happened to the "kingdom" over time. This was the basis for discussion of an understanding of Pennhurst as it existed in the present.

The "Best" and The "Worse." Another day, trainers were grouped in dyads telling their worst personal experience at Pennhurst to one partner, and with another partner their best; sharing the worst thing they had seen happen to a client and the best. Expressing what they were angriest with at Pennhurst and with what they were most frustrated.

Fantasy, Pure Fantasy. Another unit was built on fantasy. "Given the current budget and the current staff, describe what would be for you a fantasy/ideal/perfect day at Pennhurst." Each person shared theirs, amidst gales of laughter. Common elements were recorded, leading to a discussion of how any of this might come to be.

At other times the trainers, in small groups, dealt with content issues of the training design. The consultant went through the design, teaching the concepts again, and clarifying what they meant. There were role plays and critique practice units; and an endless series of "what ifs." Examples were:

— What if someone calls out hostile remarks; how are they to be handled?

— What if someone arrives and refuses to participate; what happens?

— What if the trainer's mind goes blank, or he/she explains a concept wrong; what happens?

And then there were the organizational issues.

— How could the program be initiated successfully?

— What were to be the procedures for signing up?

— Where would the program take place?

There were myriad problems to be dealt with. It had to be in a room which was not client space. If possible, it was to be light and attractive and be able to comfortably seat thirty (30) people at tables for five or six. There should be a less institutional environment and a place where there could be coffee.

There was much negotiating—to find a room; to get permission to use it every other week; to get attractive furnishings for it (to be acquired from all over the Center). It took weeks of negotiating for teams from the training group to eventually get a beautiful, bright staff conference room.

— How would the program be initiated?

It was decided with a letter, from the Director, indicating that it was for improved communication and better client care. The training staff formulated the letter so that it would sound warm and caring. They wrote many drafts, until they arrived at one that suited them.

— How would people check out the program?

The training staff decided on an "open house" and created a training design for the open house so that people would feel involved. They baked refreshments and brought flowers so that the room would be inviting. They created provocative posters to grab people's attention and put them every place. They discussed and created the forms for people applying to the program.

They decided on a coordinator who would make up application forms, and developed a structure so that applicants would request admission through their supervisors. Each supervisor was to allow up to two people to attend a training class.

They developed a schedule of when classes would begin, and established teams who would be teaching together. They developed a system of back-up; what would happen if a person were sick or for some reason could not teach the week he was assigned.

During that second training week, each of the problems, when named, was listed on the board as an agenda item. Each day the group would decide which agenda items needed to be dealt with and in what order. Typically two or three sub-groups in different combinations handled each question. They would discuss it in their sub-group, report it out, and the entire group would analyze the suggestions. From that discussion, the group made decisions about how next to proceed. The prime role of the consultant was to raise questions, to divide the training group into sub-groups, and to help them analyze the implications of their decisions (Schein, 1969). It was an on-going process of knowing each other and learning to work together.

The most difficult problem which emerged involved each person listing with whom they would like to work. (The training was to be done by teams of two.) In the first "secret ballot" each person listed their first three choices. Difficulty arose when one person was not selected by anyone; no one wanted to team with her. One of the reasons was that she was having a series of personal, emotional problems relating to her husband; she frequently was depressed and crying. After a second ballot, when again no one selected her, this information was shared. Sheepish, but concerned, the group discussed what would happen in the program. What evolved were five teams. Three teams with 2 people; one with 3 people; and one person teaching alone. The "one person" was hurt, maybe devastated, but, she vowed she would be the best trainer ever. She was an excellent teacher and she continued to teach as a one-person team with a back-up for an emergency.

At the end of the week, everyone was exhausted. They had worked incessantly. For most, there were longer hours and harder work than they had anticipated. But, they were excited about spear-heading a program which they now believed would make a difference at Pennhurst. They were frightened about teaching the content and the openness of some of the design, but were convinced they could do it. They were willing (and did) spend hundreds of hours reading, listening to tapes of the consultant, practicing and practicing.

As part of the training, the consultant met privately for one hour with each of the trainers to discuss any specific questions they had. Also, on the second or third day, when the trainers conducted their first program, the consultant observed for half a day and fed back her observations. (Overall, each trainer was well-prepared and was proficient. Especially obvious was the good interaction and support between the team members.)

THE TA PROGRAM

The trainers learned a training design for a team development cooperative, collaborative mode of conducting their classes. The following is an outline of the content aspect of what they taught.

I. *Transactional Analysis (TA)*
   overview
   origins
   use in therapy, education, communication skills
   use with various populations
   effectiveness

II. *Psychological Hunger and Strokes*
   importance of research
   four types of strokes (unconditional positive, conditional positive, conditional negative, unconditional negative)
   discounting
   four behaviors with strokes (give, receive, reject, ask)
   implications

III. *Personality Development*
   Ego States (child, parent, adult)
   development
   use of each

IV. *Communication Patterns*
   three rules of communication
   examples of each

V. *Life Positions*
   four positions defined
   behaviors expressed
   feelings about self
   ways of resolving conflict using four life positions

VI. *Integration of Concepts*
case studies
practice units
skill building activities
personal action plan

The closing segments were directed toward transferability of learning from the classroom to work in their unit. This involved participants in groups creating and discussing case studies and then developing recommendations for action. They realized that as a group and as individual staff members they could in fact make a difference. Finally, there was an action plan that each person created with two others as a support team to demonstrate how they would be different as a result of the program. The case studies and the action plan encouraged participants in the class to try out their new skills after the program. Some of the case studies were created from a client perspective; it was an effort to personalize or "subjectify" clients rather than to continue to see them as objects. Two examples follow:

Case Study #1: The Case of the Non-aid Aide

The setting is Pennhurst Center in the Hatfield unit on the fourth floor. I am a client who lives there, and my problem is that my primary aide either ignores me or else yells at me all the time. Yesterday, I walked up to her so she would notice me; she said, "Go sit down, you 'tard'" (for retard).

I cannot do anything myself about this problem since I am non-verbal, cannot write, and don't know sign language. I suppose the only person who can solve this problem is my primary aide's supervisor; I overheard her telling my primary aide the other day not to call clients nasty names.

I try to adjust this aide's behavior by behaving better when she calls me by name and doing what she asks me to do—and by misbehaving and not obeying, when she calls me "tard."

I hope the aide becomes more sensitive to my feelings soon.

Case Study #2: Client's Position

Staff is frequently inattentive to clients and often spend their time talking with each other or watching television. Specifically, on the evening "Jesus Christ Superstar" was being shown, clients were bathed and put to bed at 6:30 p.m. for the convenience of staff so staff could watch television. What are my rights? Usual bedtime is 8:30 p.m.

The following are two examples of case studies focusing on staff problems: (Groups were encouraged to write case studies in the following format.)

Case Study #1: Who Supervises the Nursing Supervisors on the 2nd and 3rd Shifts?

Situation

On day shift the nursing supervisors have a Directress of Nursing and her assistant to provide direct supervision. However, on the other two shifts, there is no one directly responsible for supervision of the supervisors.

Specifics

All supervisors are equal in job responsibility and have no authority over another supervisor. Therefore, when decision-making must occur, there is great room for conflict and confusion with lack of communication.

Question

How can I respond to the problem without causing conflict and confusion?

Case Study #2: The Case of Doing High Level Tasks by Severely Handicapped People

Statement of the Problem (question)

How do we maintain quality control for our sub-contract standards while programming the multi-handicapped?

Situation

The types of jobs contracted to us are sometimes more difficult than our workers can handle. Program coordinators also need to make sure the clients go to useful activities.

Specifics

Quality control is necessary if we are to continue getting job contracts. But, many of our handicapped people are unable to perform the job in a satisfactory manner, whether because of behavior or inability to comprehend how to do the tasks.

Question

Are there suggestions for how we can solve this problem?

Evaluations

Although the training team was rightly apprehensive as they conducted their first programs, from the beginning the classes were a success. At the conclusion of the program participants filled in an extensive evaluation. It was not unusual for their checks to be at the extreme righthand side. They found the program beneficial, they felt the course exceeded their expectations; that the teachers were well-trained, transmitted information well, and answered their questions. They felt they could apply what they had learned to working with their clients and at the Center.

The trainers found by the end of the week that so much change had emerged in the group that they were ''high.'' The consultant received many letters, from both the training team and whole classes who could not believe what was happening to them. Two excerpts follow:

> Our first 4 days are over and are we high!! We had People so involved that each day was difficult to break at 4:30—But the big day was Thursday—People were like babies and we were the umbilical cord, and again they didn't want the class to be over—We are so high and truly feeling good—What an experience—People were hugging each other—tears were flowing about. It's hard for us to believe we could get People to respond to each other but we did it. We didn't have one Person who didn't share the enthusiasm—After everyone left all we could do was hug each other again and again.
>
> We would like to thank you Matti for making this all possible for us.
>
> Love Ya
> E and J''

The following letter is a letter from the entire class. Each member signed it. The letter, while addressed to the consultant, was sent to the Pennhurst Center Director.

> The third T.A. class at Pennhurst would like to commend you on the wonderful program that you initiated at our center. Not only is the program both enlightening and invigorating, but the instructors are very inspiring to the class.
>
> As a whole, the class has noticed the difference in themselves after being active participants in the course. We now look for the positive in ourselves as well as in others. We are sure that this will serve us well in the future.
>
> "The Warm Woolies"
> T. A. Class #3"

After each class, participants returned to their units with enthusiasm and a motivation to act differently. As these people were behaving in a different style there was an influence on the others in the unit. And, to ensure that one person would not feel overwhelmed, they had been placed in a support team of three at the end of the class. They then could continue to use them as a support even after the class had ended.

1980-1983

In the first two and a half years of the TA program, through the training team and meetings as a group with the consultant, many changes occurred to improve the quality of the program and its transferability to working with clients. Some examples are:

— The program was changed from a five-day program to a program which ran Monday through Thursday the first week, and then Friday the second week. This developed so that class participants could practice some of their skills and return to the group to discuss problems or difficulties they had encountered. It also encouraged participants to act on their action plans with the impetus of having to report back the next Friday.
— Class participants got involved in wanting to make changes in the Institution; often evolving from their case studies. They created recommendations for change which they would initiate

and implement. Each class would develop their recommendations; they would present them at a meeting with the Director, and then plan to institute their recommended changes.

— Each class developed a strong personal identity. They had a name (like TA Class 3). There were large window shades in the room where the group met. Each group left their "mark" by decorating a shade. There developed slogans, songs, art work, posters. Each class was proud of their originality and their "legacy" to future classes. When the twelve shades were filled, they were moved in to the walls of the staff cafeteria for everyone to see and admire, and a new set of shades were put in the training room.

— To make sure that the warmth and collaboration was not extinguished over time, there developed a two-month follow up. A class would come together for half a day led by their original trainers; and in a training design share their experiences since the class. To continue the growing process, they also learned a new TA concept.

— To hold on to the feeling of cohesiveness and pleasure, the training team held an "Open House" prior to Christmas to "celebrate" and had a picnic during the summer for TA class participants. Each of these events was special with games, skits, singing—not perfunctory or institutional.

— They created a library of TA books available to participants who might want to read further and created their own Transactional Analysis Handbook, applying TA concepts to Pennhurst (Berne, 1967; Berne, 1976; Dusay, 1977; James & Jongeward, 1971; Jongeward & James, 1973). They created a manuscript for the book, illustrated it, had it printed and it became the textbook for the course.

In the course of the two and a half years, members of the training team were promoted. Some were promoted to Unit Directors. Unit Directors were not permitted to continue on the TA training. (It was felt that position required continuous presence on their unit.) Trainers left to return to graduate school, to have babies, to take on new positions; not at Pennhurst. One trainer, in her first class, found that she could not cope with hostility from participants at any time; she withdrew from the program.

The trainers knew they were successful and they understood working collaboratively. They needed new trainers and developed a fair, creative method for interviewing and adding to the training team. The original purposes of a diversified training staff and working in teams were continued; these continued to be strengths of the program. There was no dirth of applicants. The TA trainers had a reputation for being talented, charismatic, and each week creating "the miracle at Pennhurst." They took the responsibility for training the new trainers. Between 1980 and 1983, there were "three generations" of trainers. There continued to be a complement of ten trainers, but by 1983, only three of the original training group remained. In that time there were sixty-four classes completed and over 1200 people trained. Evaluations were received from 96% of the participants. Sixty-seven percent rated the program excellent; 30% rated the program very good. In summary, 97% evaluated the program as very good or excellent. The training produced outstanding results with each team, consistently over time.

Not only did those at Pennhurst know of the changes that were occurring, but the word spread. Two other hospitals astounded by what had happened in the "impossible situation" at Pennhurst contacted the consultant and initiated their own organization development/Transactional Analysis programs for institutional change.

1982 TO PRESENT: FROM DISASTER TO "STRESSBUSTERS"

There are cynics who would say change is only a happy interlude between disasters. They would say Pennhurst could not really be changed. In the Spring of 1982, disaster struck in two forms.

One involved claims of continued client abuse. An undercover policewoman came in pretending she was an aide and uncovered eight staff members on the second shift who had in fact been abusive. Exposés of Pennhurst were not only expected, but as a recurrent theme continued to make news. Despite all that had occurred, Pennhurst was again in the news, on television, radio, and on the front page of the papers for having a "staff that was abusive of clients." Eight out of 1500 were indicted, but the external environment created an image to the world that nothing at Pennhurst had changed.

In addition, the Director was furious that some staff had been fearful of reporting what had happened and some had even falsified records of client checks that were not made. He called a meeting of the staff and vented his fury by raging he was ashamed of them and they were a disgrace. He said all of the terrible things that an infuriated father might say.

The internal effect on the system was that morale plummeted and there was a feeling of "what's the use." This was coupled with a Commonwealth emphasis to reduce the Pennhurst budget so that funds could be shifted to community programs. It meant that clients would be transferred from the Center as soon as possible. The State fiscal year begins on July 1st; the new budget at Pennhurst was substantially smaller. Rumors of closing abounded, panic set in. Six weeks prior to July 1st over 200 "furlough notices" were sent. The furloughs were not based on seniority, as might be expected, but on vast changes in functions in departments. For example, "dietary" went from 60 to 12 employees. Henceforth, meals would no longer be prepared at the Center, but would be contracted out and prepared meals would be brought into the Center. One employee, for example, an A.V. specialist with 28 years service at Pennhurst was terminated with six weeks notice. In November 1983 the Commonwealth revealed its plan to close the facility.

The outrage, despair, frustration, and futility were overwhelming. Staff at Pennhurst felt that they had been duped. There was a new level of despair. They thought the Director cared about them, and really was committed to having the Institution b· a humane place to work and care for clients; now they felt they had been "conned" and that the Director and the State Welfare system couldn't care less.

ROLE OF THE TA TEAM

The impact of the Director's blow-up at the staff and then the State termination letters on such short notice was overwhelming. The first phase of the TA program had been completed and now the creation of change through influencing thirty (30) people each week was over. With the hospital being phased out, there would never be a second team development phase. In preparation for this second phase, there had been considerable TA team training on process consultation and organizational psychology (Schein, 1969; Schein, 1980). The training staff had learned about planned theory of change, the use of survey instruments for diagnosis, and intervention strategies within units. All this might be academically interesting, but would never be utilized. Further, the trainers felt an over-whelming despair and that in their enthusiasm and optimism about change that they had been harmful to people, getting their hopes up that things could be changed. Two difficult sessions were spent with the consultant as the training staff dealt with their anger, frustration, and grief.

By the third session, there was a re-emergence of what they were about, and what they now needed to do. An analysis of the current situation developed from focusing on Kurt Lewin's force field anal-ysis and action research theory (Lewin, 1951; Marrow, 1969). There had to be motivation and a driving force to create change at Pennhurst, and they were hopeful that it could be done and that they would do it.

The training staff re-emerged, now in crisis to really be internal process consultants to the Center. The norms of working together, of brainstorming and being creative, of being collaborative, of all of those classes where individuals came in angry and hostile and left as a group enthusiastic and caring—re-emerged in full force. As before, in small groups, they sat down and decided on strategies to make Pennhurst work. The present state of morale was to be a chal-lenge.

Two initial plans emerged. One was to have the director meet with key staff and rebuild his credibility at the Institution. The staff was reluctant to deal with him and had a tremendous lack of confi-dence in him, after his venting his fury at them and the names he called them. A series of training designs for conducting the supervi-sory meetings were created. This training staff would be consultants to the Director, to help him implement and to serve as support staff at the monthly Director's meetings. At the first meeting, the Direc-tor began by apologizing and vowing to learn the group skills and to work successfully with them. Given the crisis conditions and the layoffs, the supervisory staff was encouraged to work in groups, create task forces, and resolve difficulties emerging as a result of the termination letters.

The Director had built a great deal of trust in the consultant, and recognizing the horrendous position he was in, was open to creating these meetings and this new method of involving supervisory staff in management of the Center. While initially all the supervisory staff wanted to do was vent their anger and their frustration, after two meetings they too were willing to work cooperatively with the Di-rector.

The second major strategy, developed by the training team, was the creation of a newspaper called, *Straight Talk*. With rumors abounding, with confusion about how to transfer to another State institution, and with great credibility gaps everywhere, it was decided that the training team would write, illustrate, type, run off, and distribute "straight talk" on what was happening at the Center. The paper included interviews, statistics, resources, cartoons, slogans, even a cryptogram. It was four pages of hard information told in simple straightforward language from TA (the Adult Ego State—the facts), it included humor in what was a painful situation; (the Child Ego State—feelings and humor), there was the spunky child being creative and insightful; and there were proverbs and short inspirational messages (the Parent Ego State—parent messages), for example, a quote from James Baldwin: "Not everything that is faced can be changed, but nothing can be changed until it is faced."

Straight Talk came out biweekly. People rushed to read it, to get information, and to laugh. It could be depended upon for accurate, up-to-date current information.

In the subsequent year there arose a question about the legitimacy of these "TA trainers" becoming internal consultants in the Center. Who were they to take on this role? The training team seriously heard what was said and responded in what was now their normative fashion. They brainstormed on names to convey their function; they changed their name to "The Stressbusters." Maybe a little like in the movie, "The Ghostbusters," they were to evoke an image of rushing in to cure the impossible. If not in this instance ghosts, the impossible was to ferret out and crush the stresses at Pennhurst. The change in name created not only a humorous title but an acceptance by the staff, as those "crazy" people committed to making Pennhurst a better place. Since then the "Stressbusters" have created twelve (12) programs at Pennhurst to build a staff morale, continue client programs and care, increase participative management, and help the Director to be supportive and feel supported. Some of the programs are:

REAP Workshops 2 (Re-employment, Education at Pennhurst)

A five-session training program was developed to give staff the "know how" to apply for new jobs. It included guerrilla tactics on searching for employers, sophisticated methods for writing resumés, networking, and transferability of skills from Pennhurst to the private sector. It even included all the information anybody needed and more on unemployment benefits and the idiosyncracies of local unemployment offices.

After initial training, The Stressbusters conducted the workshops in teams on an ongoing basis. This is the pattern of each of the workshops.

Stress workshop. Stress workshops were created with didactic and experiential units, teaching staff to recognize their stresses and the eight strategies for coping with stress.

Coping with depression. One-day workshop for staff utilizing information from cognitive therapy to deal with situational depression. Participants learned about "automatic thoughts" and "underlying assumptions;" not only a theory presentation with examples, but also practice units and handouts for monitoring their own depression.

Motivating employees in a closing institution. A two-day workshop for supervisors focusing on understanding individual value systems and what motivates each individual. Special work on strategies for rewarding/stroking staff under conditions of constant consolidation, reduction of staff, and continuous "catastrophe." This is not only a skills workshop, but the building of a sense of a team and a support system among supervisors caught between State guidelines of minimal standards of coverage and often insufficient staff.

"George's fifty minutes." A team development program created to involve on a rotating basis staff members of each unit with the Director. Bimonthly meetings in which the Director reports on the most current information about the Center, deals with rumors, and answers hard-hitting questions. Also, the Director praises individuals and units for actions "over and above the call of duty." A representative from each unit and each shift attends the meeting and then reports back on what they learned and briefs the person to attend the next session with the Director. The Stressbusters take turns providing an agenda and serving as staff to the Director at these meetings.

Touring: stroking. Twice each week the Director makes an announced visit to different areas of the facility. He meets staff members, chats about what has been happening, especially strokes and commends staff members who have worked in difficult situations. (For example: accepting mandatory double shifts, taking a client who has no visitors home with a staff member over a weekend.) The Stressbusters again act as consultants, setting up the time for the visitations, having a preliminary meeting with that unit to learn the names of staff, learning about what they would like to discuss with the Director. They accompany the Director at the visit, take notes on what he promises to follow-up on and give him a one page summary of what happened, with their feedback based on observations of how the tour went.

There are other strategies that the Stressbusters developed. Each evolved from their looking at the Institution, based on their experiences in their own units and at all levels of the organization, and deciding what kind of an intervention could be made. The outcomes, given the situation in the Center, are unbelievable. Staff members would like to be able to stay at Pennhurst. There is real sadness when they have to leave. There is a cohesiveness among the staff as they deal with existing problems.

The Stressbusters have evolved from a group of ten staff members chosen by some vague criteria to lead a TA/organization development program, and have emerged as a highly competent team of internal consultants. They have created new programs, have dealt with recurrent crises, and have emerged at even a higher level of being process consultants to help the organization meet its goals of continued client care and helping the organization be effective. Pennhurst, the organization "that could not be changed," has not only been changed despite major adversity, but in fact has become a model. At the 1985 Annual Conference of the professional organization (AAMD) there will be presented the *Pennhurst Model* for an organization change strategy and methods for involving the staff in the closing of a hospital. Who would believe that Pennhurst is the model for how to do things well.

SUMMARY

At the conclusion of his book Schein (1980) discusses those internal organizational conditions which appear to be necessary for effective organization coping to occur. The organizational conditions he identified will resemble what he calls, "the ultimate criteria of health." He lists the following five conditions required for successful coping:

1. The ability to take in and communicate information reliably and validly.

2. Internal flexibility and creativity to make the changes which are demanded by the information obtained.
3. Integration of and commitment to the multiple goals of the organization, from which comes the willingness to change when necessary.
4. An internal climate of support and freedom from threat.
5. The ability to continuously redesign the organization's structure to be congruent with its goal and tasks.

In a bold four year organization development program a major change was created in an organization which now meets the above stated criteria of health. Through the efforts of a Director motivated to create change, through an external consultant trained in process consultation, and primarily through the development and supervision of a heterogeneous staff team—creative, far reaching, ongoing changes in the organization were implemented. These internal consultants, currently The Stressbusters, have created changes so that Pennhurst has emerged from being an institution of ridicule to one which has become a model of how an organization can successfully cope with change, the most drastic change being the closing of the Institution.

REFERENCES

Berne, E. (1967). *Games people play.* New York: Grove Press.
Berne, E. (1976). *Beyond games and scripts.* New York: Grove Press.
Costello, T. W. (1971). Change in municipal government: A view from the inside. *Journal of Applied Behavioral Science.* Vol. 7 (pp. 131-145).
Davis, T.R.V. (1979). OD in the public sector: Intervening in ambiguous performance environments. In J. E. Jones & J. W. Pfeiffer (Eds.) *Group and organization studies* Vol. 4, 3, (pp. 352-365). San Diego, CA: University Associates.
Dusay, J. M. (1977). *Egograms: How I see you and you see me.* New York: Harper & Row.
Edelman, M. (1971). *Politics as symbolic action.* Chicago: Markham.
Epstein, A. (1980). Hearing set for retarded. In *The Philadelphia Inquirer,* (June 13).
Gardner, N. (1974). Power diffusion in the public sector: Collaboration for democracy. *Journal of Applied Behavioral Science,* Vol. 10 (pp. 367-372).
Giblin, E. J. (1976). Organization development: Public sector theory and practice. *Public Personnel Management* Vol. 5, (pp. 108-119).
Goffman, E. (1961) *Asylums: Essays on the social situation of mental patients and other inmates.* New York: Doubleday & Co., Inc.
Golembiewski, R. T. (1969). Organizational development in public agencies. *Public Administration Review,* Vol. 29, (pp. 367-378).
Imundo, L. V. (1976). Ineffectiveness and inefficiency in government management. *Public Personnel Management,* Vol. 4, (pp. 90-95).
James, M. & Jongeward, D. (1971). *Born to win: Transactional analysis with Gestalt experiments.* Reading, Mass.: Addison-Wesley.

Jones, J. E. & Pfeiffer, J. Wm. (Eds.) (1979). Group & organization studies [S. i.]. The International Journal for Group Facilitators, Vol. 4, 3 (pp. 353-365). San Diego: CA: University Associates.

Jongeward, D. & James, M. (1973). *Winning with people: Group exercises in transactional analysis.* Reading, Mass.: Addison-Wesley.

Kharash, R. N. (1973). *The institutional imperative.* New York: Charterhouse.

Lewin, K. (1951) In Cartwright, D. (Ed.). *Field theory in social science: Selected theoretical papers.* New York: Harper & Row.

Lindblom, C. E. (1959). The science of muddling through. *Public Administration Review,* Vol. 19, (pp. 79-88).

Marrow, A. J. (1969). *The practical theorist: The life and work of Kurt Lewin.* New York: Basic Books.

Napier, R. & Gershenfeld, M. (1983). *Making groups work: A guide for group leaders.* Chap 4. Boston: Houghton Mifflin.

Permann, G. Short History of Pennhurst Center.

Ross, J. D. & Hare, G. (Eds.). (1973). *Organizational development in local government: Results of an IPA grant. First tango in Boston.* Washington, DC: NTL Institute.

Rubin, I., Plovnick, M., & Fry, R. (1974). Initiating planned change in health care systems. *Journal of Applied Behavioral Science,* Vol. 10, (pp. 107-124).

Schein, E. H. (1969). *Process consultation: Its role in organization development.* Reading, Mass.: Addison-Wesley.

Schein, E. H. (1980). *Organizational psychology* (3rd ed.). (pp. 239-248) Englewood Cliffs, N.J.: Prentice Hall, Inc.

Sharkansky, I. (1970). *The routines of politics.* New York: Van Nostrand.

Sikula, A. F. (1973). The values and value systems of government executives. *Public Personnel Management.* Vol. 2, (pp. 16-22).

Wynia, R. L. (1974). Federal bureaucrats' attitudes toward a democratic ideology. *Public Administration Review.* Vol. 34. (pp. 156-162).

Zawacki, R. A. & Warrick, D. D. (Eds.) (1976). *Organizational development: Managing change in the public sector.* Chicago: IPMA.

14

Themes and Patterns

Florence W. Kaslow

ABSTRACT. In this concluding chapter an endeavor is made to highlight the major themes and common threads that emerge from the complex tapestry of ideas and models presented in the foregoing articles. Some comparisons, contrasts and divergent approaches will also be alluded to in this effort at synthesizing the contributions of the numerous authors.

A MULTIPLICITY OF VIABLE MODELS

What becomes apparent in reading this volume is that the authors are espousing the principle that there is definitely not "one right way only" in either supervision or training. These reports on a spectrum of paradigms being utilized, each creatively evolved, tested and refined clinically, provide the reader with many models to choose from, replicate and evaluate. These chapters represent the authors' mutually shared view that models of supervision, consultation and staff training should be dynamic rather than static, creatively evolving rather than rigidly repetitive, clinically relevant and tested through applied research studies for their reliabiity and validity, and revised or discarded if they prove to be less effective than other approaches.

SUPERVISEE/SUPERVISOR AND OTHER DYADIC "MATCHES"

What isn't stated in many chapters but that seems implicit in several is that individual supervisors and trainers and their trainee counterparts are likely to gravitate toward that methodology(ies) which is(are) most compatible with their own philosophy, personality and style. If pressured into utilizing or submitting to an approach that is ego dystonic, it is likely to not prove viable for a specific supervisor or supervisee; conceivably he or she will in some

237

way sabotage its effectiveness in order to demonstrate its unworkability so as to be free to utilize a process, model, (or supervisor) more congruent with his/her own theoretical base and personal modus operandi. In the case of a trainee in a rigid training setting, he/she may have little choice but to appear to accommodate if the program assigns one supervisee to one supervisor and assesses progress mainly in terms of ability to work through relationship and theoretical differences—with the burden for resolution of the incompatibility placed primarily on the trainee. This dilemma points out the theme of the importance of supervisee/supervisor and consultant/consultee match on several salient variables. This theme is most clearly delineated in Chapter 9 *"Seeking and Providing Supervision in Private Practice."*

Just as I have stressed therein the critical import of a wise selection of a supervisor or consultant when such choice is permissible, no doubt based on similar attitudes, values and professional experiences, Rice in his discussion of supervision of co-therapists points out the importance of *choosing* a co-therapist carefully. He emphasizes that comparable levels of status and experience are desirable if the pair are to achieve and model an egalitarian relationship for patients. Further he recommends that they have compatible theoretical preferences and complimentary styles. Because patients often attempt to "split" the team, and because therapists may have their own competitive strivings which come out in relation to the patients and the supervisor, they must be able to manage their competitive feelings. In addition, Rice advises that one is wise to select a co-therapist with whom they have a high level of trust and where there is a mutual recognition and understanding of differences in personality.

STAGE OF DEVELOPMENT:
A CRITICAL FACTOR TO THE SUPERVISORY PROCESS

Friedman and N. Kaslow set the tone for a dominant theme—that the supervisee's stage of development in their own learning process and in the formation of a sense of professional identity is an important contributory factor to what they need from supervision in terms of content and relationship and how it should be conducted to be maximally productive. They articulate the following six stages—indicating that these are not discrete: (The progression may involve periodic regression and therefore some overlap).

1. Excitement and anticipatory anxiety
2. Dependency and identification (on and with the supervisor)
3. Activity and continued dependency
4. Exuberance and taking charge
5. Identity (as a professional) and independence
6. Calm and collegiality

It is important to remember that they are describing the developmental stages of the graduate student, intern or resident. Perhaps what has occurred too often is that a supervisor beginning with a junior but moderately experienced clinician errs by assuming that they are in stage 2 or 3 and therefore expects and fosters too much dependency and squelches initiative and autonomy. This is likely to be met with hostility and resistance as the therapist seeks not to be infantalized, that is, forced to regress to an earlier level of development so that the supervisor is comfortable and not intimidated. This is particularly apt to occur when the supervisee is truly more knowledgeable and/or skilled in a particular area than the supervisor, or if the supervisor is accustomed to working with fledgling but not advanced therapists. The old adage "start where the patient is" is equally applicable here in the form of assess where the trainee is and then start there. If the supervisor does not possess the flexibility to tailor his/her methodology from beginning, to intermediate to advanced supervisees, then they should either expand their horizons and repertoire or limit their supervisory practice to working with beginning level trainees (Stages 1 & 2).

In the event of content mismatch, that is, a student needing supervision in an area like group supervision or hypnotherapy, in which the supervisor is barely knowledgeable, a transfer should be arranged without any accompanying emotional interpretations or fall out. No one needs to be omniscient; it is as unethical to supervise with inadequate knowledge of and competency in a content area as it is to practice in an area that falls outside of one's competency. This stance is in keeping with the APA Code of Ethics (APA, 1981) Principle 2—Competence—that

> The maintenance of high standards of competence is a responsibility shared by all psychologists in the interest of the public and the profession as a whole. Psychologists recognize the boundaries of their competence and the limitations of their

techniques. They only provide services and only use techniques for which they are qualified by training and experience.

Without extending the analogy too far, Friedman & N. Kaslow point out the similarities in the dependency, growth, separation and individuation process in parent-child and supervisor/supervisee relationships. Just as it is difficult for some parents to acknowledge their adult children's autonomy and ability to assume responsibility for their own thoughts and actions; so too for some supervisors, particularly if one has become a devoted (and perhaps somewhat enmeshed) mentor. To let go can mean a profound sense of loss and confronting an "empty nest" in both situations. Although rationally we know that continued symbiosis is unhealthy for both members of the dyad, breaking away and letting go are sometimes accompanied by much ambivalence. Watching one's supervisee move toward collegial status, begin to publish and present and ultimately toward becoming a supervisor and teacher in their own right may evoke feelings of pride—tinged with competition, n'est ce pas?

Although Hess, drawing on a substantial body of prior literature, comes up with 4 major stages instead of the 6 cited above elucidated by Friedman & N. Kaslow, clearly he moves in a similar direction and his work on the stages the supervisee passes through are complimentary to and compatible with theirs. He goes with the terms:

1. Inception—characterized by insecurity, dependency, and inadequacy
2. Skill development—moving from dependency toward autonomy and adequacy
3. Consolidation—the development of self confidence and the shift from conditional dependence to individuation, and
4. Mutuality—a time of creativity and independent practice.

His stage 1 approximates their stages 1 & 2; his stage 2 parallels their 3 & 4, his 3rd phase is comparable to their 5th and their final stages are equivalents.

In addition, Hess considers a relatively untouched aspect—that of a developmental process in becoming and being a supervisor. Here he highlights three rather clear phases:

1. Beginning—characterized by structuring sessions and learning supervisory techniques

2. Exploration—a period when the student's learning needs take priority over the supervisor's and when interest in the student's process and progress is greater than interest in one's own, and
3. Confirmation of the supervisor's identity—a time of feeling confident about one's knowledge and supervisory skill.

In line with two themes developed earlier, probably only supervisors who have arrived at stage 3 are a "proper" match for supervisees at stages 5 & 6.

Rice, in his chapter on *Supervision of Co-Therapy* further illuminates and broadens the developmental stage formulation, positing that different types of supervisory input are required as the therapeutic pair gain experience in working together. The co-therapy developmental stages that he formulates are:

1. Formation—a preparation and encounter time when each one's *intrapsychic* issues need to be resolved
2. Development—power and control needs may surface more at this time as the interpersonal relationship of the pair becomes more focal. Polarization may (should) be superseded by complimentarity and the ability to draw upon each other's strengths
3. Stabilization—a time of integration of the co-therapy teams' functioning when they feel safe and close enough in the relationship that their energy and attention can focus on the patients and on theoretical and clinical concerns inherent in the case, and
4. Refreshment—when their relationship is sufficiently stabilized that they can flourish as an effective, efficient co-therapy team.

When the cycle is complete, and their working together has become smooth and gratifying, often in the case of trainees their joint cases are ready to be terminated and or their internship/residency is completed. They too, like parent and child, supervisor and supervisee, consultant and consultee must handle the mixed emotions which accompany—

5. Separation—from each other and their patients and perhaps from exciting and provocative conjoint supervisory sessions.

THE IMPORTANCE OF THE THERAPIST AS A PERSON

The theme of concern about the therapist as a person emerges most clearly in Charny's chapter. He suggests that supervisors be attuned to what their supervisees worry about. One's primary anxieties are likely to vary not only in accordance to one's personality but also in relation to their own level of professional development. Thus, in terms of Friedman & N. Kaslow's or Hess' models elucidated earlier, in the first stage trainees are apt to be "worried about" such critical and existential questions as:

1. Should I be a therapist? Is it what I really want?
2. Will I be a good enough therapist?
3. Will I be able to become a technical and tactical "genius"— and will it happen quickly enough?
4. Will I please my supervisor?

Later in the developmental sequence and as more rapport and trust are established in the supervisory relationship, concerns may shift to a deeper level of subjective reality and revolve around such central issues as:

1. What is happening inside the self as one tunes into patients?
2. Is the neophyte sensitive enough to respond to the nuances— for his/her primary process thoughts and feelings to tune into the patients' unconscious and meta messages?
3. What is going on in the heart, mind and body of the trainee therapist that will impede or facilitate the therapy? What of this should or should not be shared with the patient? When it should, in what manner?
4. How much self disclosure is relevant to the learning goals of the supervisory process? How much is safe?
5. Which apprehensions and misgivings should be dealt with in supervision? Which belong in therapy?

In Charny's style of experiential supervision, predicated on psychoanalytic, humanistic and existential approaches to the understanding of behavior dynamics and personal and professional growth—tuning into the inner life of the supervisee as it impacts on their therapeutic tasks is an important and essential aspect of the supervisory process. Just dealing with the facts of a case would be inadequate. One must help the person know and accept the parts of self they perceive as "childish" and "not nice" while providing a safe harbor in supervision so they can do this; in essence modelling how they will transform this experience into a process they can utilize with their own patients.

Charny also suggests, as does F. Kaslow, that self supervision is often in order and that here the critical point of entry is the query— what about this case worries me?

At the opposite end of the spectrum on the theme of the "Therapist as Person" is the chapter by Strosahl & Jacobson on *Supervision & Training of Behavior Therapists*. They state that supervision involves conceptualizing the case under consideration from alternative viewpoints and the teaching of trainees, especially in group supervision, about particular techniques such as behavioral rehearsal, behavioral contracting, restructuring or relapse prevention. It is a case centered and goal oriented supervisory approach—where frequently encountered problems are targeted and progress toward therapist/client agreed upon goals is appraised. The supervisor may point out certain characteristics of the therapist's style, such as being "too mechanical", or not ascertaining whether the client understands an assignment or not helping the client identify potential obstacles to assignment completion. Thus, as they indicate clearly, the behavioral approach does not place much emphasis on the supervisor/trainee relationship as a vehicle of training.

Since Sharon's ABCX model is task and not feeling oriented, client outcomes and not the therapist as person are the salient concern. Supervision based on this model, like that of the behavioral model, focuses on the selection of the most "functional resources" to bring about change, i.e., determining the most appropriate intervention techniques for the therapist to use to foster the best coping skills in the client. Supervision also should entail accurate anticipation of outcomes based on sound prognostic skill of the therapist and facilitating a heightened sense of mastery and control in the client. Another central element of the ABCX model is its emphasis on evaluation, testing and retesting effectiveness against changing realities, and intervening in a fashion scientifically established to be efficacious.

In describing the *In Vivo Rotation Model* they utilize with psychology graduate students, Brodsky & Myers also address the issue of the therapist as a person. Since the entire team is in the treatment room with the clients for the 13 weeks of the therapy sessions, everyone's actions are on display. The risk taking aspect is dealt with carefully, as it must be. The supervisor serves as therapist for the first 4 to 6 weeks and again for the last wind up sessions. In between, the student trainees each conduct several sessions. Thus they have the advantage throughout of learning from a variety of perspectives—in addition to observer and therapist; they participate in group feedback plus in patient and therapist debriefings. The format is conducive to rapid learning and generates high enthusiasm, both of which reinforce the trainee's professional self image. Brodsky and Myers have found that this training approach not only enhances the use of oneself in the treatment situation, but also leads to increased public and private personal self awareness. It contributes to creating the capacity for close self scrutiny. These two authors point out that one of the crucial questions beginning therapists learn to raise with themselves is: What am I doing wrong? Since the ability to do this is best acquired in the kind of atmosphere of trust, risk taking, consideration and commitment to self improvement this model advocates, it is probable that trainees exposed to such a model early in their careers will emerge as therapists with a built in self evaluative focus who can also ask others, without fear of derogation, to observe and critique their work.

Brodsky and Myers indicate that trainees who rotate through their supervisory program seem to become "desensitized to scrutiny"—probably a valuable asset for clinicians whose work is increasingly viewed—either by videotape, one way mirrors, live in sessions or when they present at conferences. Further, they report that from seeing several others treat the same clients they do, they can glean the comparative reactions of clients to different personality styles and therapeutic interventions. And an intellectual gain to the trainee as a person and as a professional is that tutelage in this model leads to expansion of the number of one's personal constructs and perceptual and cognitive categories for understanding behavioral dynamics.

Using the catchy title of the *Pick-a-Dali Circus Model* for their approach, Landau and Stanton, like Brodsky and Myers, have the whole team in the room during therapy. In addition, they incorporate aspects of network family therapy (Speck & Attneave, 1972) into their supervisory methodology and invite family, friends and the referring person to participate. In terms of the impact of this model on the person of the therapist of inexperienced trainees, clinicians inexperienced in family therapy, and experienced family therapists new to their model, all can learn from the experienced lead therapists who are present conducting and modelling the active, flowing process of this surrealistic happening. They are not thrust into going it alone before ever seeing how one skilled in the methodology utilizes it. This serves to alleviate apprehension and enhance confidence about one's own interventions as each new trainee gradually takes a more active part. No one's input is stifled; instead everyone's opinions, (extended) family members and therapists alike, are explicated and validated and then integrated into a composite whole from which the family can make its own choices without being triangulated or being in danger of sabotage. What a different experience from the not uncommon one in individual or group supervision of having one's ideas and strategies challenged derogatorily.

This sounds like a tremendously supportive and expansive model that trainees would find stimulating and exciting—like a smorgasbord—or in Landau and Stanton's words—a "theatre of the absurd". In its ever changing, kaleidoscopic nature, utilizing metaphors and enactments, it is bound to provide rich learning and be conducive to unfreezing (getting unstuck) and change for both patients and trainees. In observing and experiencing patient couples/families being placed clearly in charge of their own decisions and fate, the supervisees should surely realize the eloquence of the message and that the same applies to them.

Another approach to *Working in Teams, the Pros and Cons,* is presented by Cade, Speed and Seligman of the Cardiff (Wales) Family Institute. They are heavily influenced by the Milan approach and utilized the supportive and informative consultation of Cecchin and Boscolo of Milan (see Chapter for citations). That the format they describe for working in teams has been adapted by and adapted for use in the two countries mentioned above as well as in the United States, Canada, Belgium, South Africa and numerous other lands underscores two other basic premises of this volume (1) the universal applicability of sound supervisory methodologies, and (2) the internationalization of the knowledge and skills base of the mental health professions.

Cade, Speed and Seligman's team model differs greatly from those of Brodsky and Myers, and of Landau and Stanton. Not all of the team members are in the therapy session—usually two are in the room and two are observing behind the one way mirror. Therapists and observers do not switch roles during the course of therapy, observers are not trainees but are usually of equal rank and stature with the therapists and have a supervisory/consultative function. Since the methodology is described elsewhere, the purpose of reviewing this much briefly here is for comparison and contrast to other supervisory models discussed herein regarding their impact on the person of the therapist.

Because the team is a constantly evolving phenomenon, it follows that its members must also be dynamically evolving and not statically fixed. During the early experimental phase of the team's function, all involved experienced their work as exciting, creative, and effective. Nonetheless, there were some angry struggles—interesting because it stimulates and engages these feelings rather than the more usual practice of nullifying them and causing them to be repressed. During the middle phase, when procedures and ideas become formalized and the approach is more clearly articulated, the work becomes less innovative and adventuresome. There is increased concern for one's own internal processes and less for the evolution of the external approach. Some team members may feel constrained and bored, missing the heady excitement which accompanies experimentation. As the method becomes crystallized and rules are established, more rebellious team members may feel terribly constricted by the structure.

Their experience, after seeking assistance from Boscolo and Cecchin as consultants external to their team system, was that they shifted into a third phase in which they were able to loosen up the team's structure and allow the rules to become more flexible and the boundaries to be more permeable. This atmosphere suited the team members personalities well and the sense of excitement and creativity were heightened again and they realized that differences could be tolerated and need not always be resolved.

The personal benefits Cade, Speed and Seligman report having derived include: continual challenge and feedback, support and mutual learning from direct exposure to each others' work, immediacy of consultation, shared laughter, and joint winding down—in their case, in a local pub. These benefits should also accrue to those participating in In Vivo Rotation Supervision and the Pick-a-Dali Circus Model. Hopefully, well matched co-therapy pairs supervised conjointly derive similar positive experiences.

This team from Cardiff posits that ''any team has a limited creative life span'' and that it is important (for the team's viability and effective functioning—editor's interpretation) that new members be added periodically and/or that they interact with other teams. This changing of personnel is built into the other team models previously discussed—a point on which they differ significantly in the original conceptualization.

Other factors which characterize this model and make it appealing to many therapists are that it generates a sense of optimism that change can occur which augments the likelihood that it will, and, it is fun. Are these not two essential ingredients for any supervisory/consultative approach?

In his pithy chapter which presents an analysis and critique of *Peer Supervision in a Community Mental Health Center,* Roth, perhaps inadvertently, juxtaposes two sometimes contradictory sets of needs many therapists have (1) the commitment to equality, and (2) the quest for excellence. To the extent that "peer supervision in the extreme," his critical phrase for the arrangement when there are no vestiges of a vertical hierarchy, falsely reassures the neophyte practitioner and the incompetent senior persons as well of their professional equality with highly qualified experienced personnel, it may bolster their self esteem and make them more comfortable and secure. But, and this is a serious limitation, it stymies motivation for the pursuit of competence and special expertise since these are, in essence, denigrated. There is a settling for mediocrity as generalists who can supervise and be supervised by anybody and everybody on the clinical staff becomes more the norm and specialization is downgraded. To the curious, the ambitious, the seeker of top quality such a model is ego dystonic, and to survive in such a system would probably require a compromise of one's integrity and a serious blow to one's desire to achieve one's fullest potential (Maslow, 1968). Thus, the spirit and professional drive of some clinicians would be dealt a severe blow in such a model. This approach certainly represents the antithesis of Charny's model, of those by Friedman & N. Kaslow, and Hess, and the other authors who see therapist growth, clear individuation and acquiring a stronger sense of uniqueness as goals and byproducts of supervision.

Further, as Roth points out, the approach embodied in "peer supervision in the extreme" is predicated on the belief that supervision does not require any special skill. Rather every one has it and no one needs training in it. Not only does our combined clinical experience and much of the literature indicate that this assumption is false, but we believe such a downgrading of the role and process as a skilled one to be detrimental to the self image of supervisee and supervisor alike and to the best interests of the client.

OVERCOMING RESISTANCE:
A PHENOMENON WITH MANY VISAGES

Most of the chapters deal with this theme implicitly or explicitly. Here we will only highlight the thrust of a few articles to illustrate the range of commentaries and strategies.

In F. Kaslow's discussion of supervision sought from a private practitioner, the amount of resistance encountered is likely to be attributable to whether supervision is sought voluntarily and a clear contract specifying goals and responsibilities is negotiated and adhered to or whether it is sought because it is required (but not desired) for organizational membership, state licensure or other credentialing procedures. In the latter instance, or when one has had prior negative supervisory encounters, resistance is apt to be strong and will need to be worked through for effective supervision to occur.

Strosahl and Jacobson discuss a quite different kind of resistance: that which trainees are likely to encounter when they enter the real workaday world and find hostility toward behavior therapy and its proponents in interdisciplinary settings. Other staff may try to sabotage the treatment endeavors of behavior therapists. To prevent this Strosahl and Jacobson stress the need for eclecticism and flexibility and for understanding that behavior therapy is not a panacea for all symptomatology and dysfunction; further they convey to their trainees the belief that other training modalities are also acceptable and that behavior therapy has limitations. Since it is partially the empirical basis of this model that causes consternation, they recommend that in applied settings the clinical utility of a methodology be deemed of more importance than its empirical effectiveness.

Gershenfeld, in discussing "Changing an Institution that Can't Be Changed Through a Staff Intervention" described massive resistance at the microsystems level of (1) a large institution for the mentally retarded, and of (2) the state's political and legislative bodies. Following Schein's guidelines on organizational conditions conducive to creating a healthy climate, she selected ten diverse staff members to bring about organizational change. In her training design, these individuals were to be retrained and supervised by the consultant (herself). The project continued for four years and focused on establishing:

1. A reliable and valid communication flow,
2. Internal flexibility and creativity to make the changes demanded by information obtained,
3. Integration and commitment to multiple goals of the organization,
4. Internal climate of support and freedom from threat, and
5. The ability to redesign the organizational structure to be congruent with its tasks and goals.

In order to make it possible for this to happen in a milieu characterized by staff and patient demoralization and by the omnipresent threat that the institution would be closed, she undertook the herculean task of gaining acceptance and did this by making connections with key staff. Next she involved the potential trainees in the planning, slowly building a trusting relationship amongst the trainees and between them and herself. Throughout she encouraged them to think and act creatively.

Like other contributing authors to this volume, Gershenfeld worked from a developmental stage perspective—keeping attuned to the pace and rhythm at which the trainees could progress toward increasing autonomy and responsibility. Here too the concept of the trainees as a change agent team incorporated the assumption that having fun together is an element in building esprit de corp. Coming up with labels such as "The Stressbusters" connotes the light touch applied to achieving some very serious objectives. The trainee group coalesced as a team and made some major improvements in patient care and morale and staff attitudes.

A SUPERVISORY CORNUCOPIA

A plethora of models have been described, compared and contrasted. It is our hope that from this overflowing horn of plenty each reader will find thought provoking ideas, paradigms and encouragement to be creative, to follow his or her own drum beat in experimenting and modifying while also rigorously evaluating the impact of his/her endeavors.

REFERENCES

American Psychological Association. (1981 revision). *Ethical principles of psychologists.* Washington, D.C.: American Psychological Association.

Maslow, A. (1968). *Toward a psychology of being.* New York: Van Nostrand.

Speck, R. & Attneave, C. (1972). Network therapy. In A. Ferber, M. Mendelsohn, & A. Napier, *The book of family therapy.* New York: Science House.

Index

ABCX supervisory model, 69-94,243
  adaptation to therapy, 70-83
  components, 70
  continuity, 80-83
  discrepancies, 78-80
  events, 72-73,84
  implications for supervision, 83-94
  interacting variables, 80-83
  intervention outcome, 75-78,87-89,
    90-93
  perception of event, 74-75,84
  problem-solving tasks, 72-78
  resources to meet events, 73-74,84-86,
    89-90
accountability
  of supervisor, 2,148-149
  of therapist, 25
agencies. *See also* organization
  development
  consultation in, 149
  team therapy and, 110-111,114-115
agenda setting
  in behavioral therapy, 187-189,203
  for supervisees, 64-65
American Association for Marriage and
  Family Therapists, 150
American Board of Forensic Psychology,
  144
American Board of Professional
  Psychology, 144
American Psychiatric Association, 150
American Psychological Association
  code of ethics, 146-147,239-240
  directory, 150
  fellowship requirements, 144
  psychotherapy education standards, 59
anxiety
  behavior therapy for, 204
  of supervisee, 38,41,55
    countertransference and, 41
    in professional identity development,
      33-34

assessment, behavioral, 185-186
authority, of supervisor, 2,4

behavior change contract, 193
behavior change techniques, 184,
  186-187,191-194
  behavioral rehearsal, 192-193
  booster session, 194
  contracts, 193
  relapse prevention, 193-194
  supervisory applications, 200
behavior therapists
  resistance towards, 195,196-197,203,
    248
  supervision/training, 183-199,243
    agenda setting, 187-189,203
    behavior change techniques,
      186-187,191-194
    behavioral assessment, 185-186
    in clinical procedures, 199-200
    clinical transfer of learning, 200,
      201-202,203
    criterion referenced model, 200-201
    devil's advocate approach, 192,197,
      202
    ethics, 198-199
    homework techniques, 189-191,204
    model, 185-199
    self-control skills, 189
    special issues, 203-206
    supervisor/supervisee relationship,
      202-203
    therapeutic relationship, 194-198
    value of clinical training, 204-206
behavior therapy
  a theoretical basis, 185, 187
  behavioral approaches, 183-184
  marital, 120
  termination, 193-194,198
  theoretical basis, 184
behavioral assessment, 185-186
behavioral rehearsal, 192-193